About Island Press

Since 1984, the nonprofit organization Island Press has been stimulating, shaping, and communicating ideas that are essential for solving environmental problems worldwide. With more than 1,000 titles in print and some 30 new releases each year, we are the nation's leading publisher on environmental issues. We identify innovative thinkers and emerging trends in the environmental field. We work with world-renowned experts and authors to develop cross-disciplinary solutions to environmental challenges.

Island Press designs and executes educational campaigns in conjunction with our authors to communicate their critical messages in print, in person, and online using the latest technologies, innovative programs, and the media. Our goal is to reach targeted audiences—scientists, policymakers, environmental advocates, urban planners, the media, and concerned citizens—with information that can be used to create the framework for long-term ecological health and human well-being.

Island Press gratefully acknowledges major support of our work by The Agua Fund, The Andrew W. Mellon Foundation, The Bobolink Foundation, The Curtis and Edith Munson Foundation, Forrest C. and Frances H. Lattner Foundation, The JPB Foundation, The Kresge Foundation, The Oram Foundation, Inc., The Overbrook Foundation, The S.D. Bechtel, Jr. Foundation, The Summit Charitable Foundation, Inc., and many other generous supporters.

The opinions expressed in this book are those of the author(s) and do not necessarily reflect the views of our supporters.

Marine Ecosystem-Based Management in Practice

Marine Ecosystem-Based Management in Practice

Different Pathways, Common Lessons

Julia M. Wondolleck and Steven L. Yaffee

ISLANDPRESS

Washington | Covelo | London

Library of Congress Control Number: 2016961569

Printed on recycled, acid-free paper ✺

Manufactured in the United States of America

10 9 8 7 6 5 4 3 2 1

Keywords: Island Press, Albemarle–Pamlico, biodiversity, Channel Islands, coastal community resilience, coastal management, coastal protection, collaboration, collaborative planning, collaborative problem solving, community-based resource management, conflict management, conservation partnerships, dispute resolution, ecological restoration, ecosystem-based management, ecosystem management, ecosystems, environmental conflict resolution, fisheries management, Florida Keys, Gulf of Maine, Gulf of Mexico, human dimensions of wildlife, integrated resource management, interagency cooperation, marine conservation, marine governance, marine protected areas, marine reserves, marine stewardship, Narragansett Bay, national estuary programs, national marine sanctuaries, natural resource management, natural resource planning, nearshore resource management, network organizations, ocean management, ocean policy, Port Orford, POORT, Puget Sound, regional planning, San Juan Marine Resources Committee, science-based management, transnational collaboration, Wadden Sea Trilateral Cooperation.

CONTENTS

LIST OF ILLUSTRATIONS

Figures

Table

Boxes

We have been studying and writing about ecosystem-based management (EBM) for a long time. Having spent the first decade of our careers examining environmental conflict and the impasses between groups like environmentalists and loggers (Wondolleck)[1] and the ineffective decision making of public agencies like the Forest Service and the Fish and Wildlife Service (Yaffee),[2] we were sorely in need of a more proactive and hopeful model. And in the early 1990s, *ecosystem management* and *ecosystem-based management* were the terms of art.

On one hand, the principles the terms embodied seemed obvious. Of course, natural resources are parts of large, interconnected systems, and to manage them in a fragmented, parochial way made no sense. Analysis and decision making at larger, landscape scales were necessary. It seemed clear that the escalating sets of demands and claims by lots of different people and groups had to be managed in a different way to avoid impasse and conflict; the answer lay in some way to find an informed balance, while also ensuring that the health of the underlying systems was sustained. In a world where it is clear that unpredictable change occurs and we know only so much, taking more explicit account of uncertainty and acting with more humility and less hubris seemed a no-brainer.

But it was so very hard. Indeed, in studying hundreds of cases of attempts to shift toward an ecosystem-based approach, it was clear that well-intentioned people faced a range of daunting challenges: ineffective incentives for encouraging people to rise above their parochial, short-term perspectives; limited information and bias in the way science is prioritized; decision making that is dominated by power and turf; and limited capacity, even in very affluent countries. These and other factors constrain adoption of a larger-scale, more holistic, and more satisfying style of management.

Fortunately, we discovered innovative people in a variety of places who were shifting the management style in small but significant ways. Fifteen years of case studies made us advisedly hopeful that some level of EBM was possible, and that it enabled improvements in the level of social capital in communities; that is, it reduced conflict, strengthened relationships, and improved the quality of resource management choices. In some places, it was clear that their work produced higher levels of natural capital by both improving the condition of and reducing the threats to natural systems while also yielding the values that people seek from those systems. Indeed, improvements in social conditions and governance were necessary precursors of improvements in natural systems, and these social improvements were an important facet of EBM.

We published compendiums of ecosystem management cases and books and websites identifying lessons from places that were employing more collaborative styles of public decision making.[3] Our work has been decidedly nontheoretic. We have looked closely at the experience in real-world places and drawn lessons about similarities and differences, challenges and facilitating factors. Our interest has been in shifting the practice of resource management, and we hope that we have been helpful to practitioners in land-based agencies.

It was encouraging when marine scientists, managers, and policy makers embraced EBM around 2000, a decade after their terrestrial peers. The two national oceans commissions adopted the concept, as did the International Union for the Conservation of Nature and other international institutions. Foundations, including the David and Lucile Packard Foundation and the Gordon and Betty Moore Foundation, began funding research and place-based efforts to shift management toward an EBM approach.

And so, ten years ago, when Kristen Sherwood from the Packard Foundation called to ask whether we were interested in developing case studies of marine EBM, we initially said, "No." While our research had drawn largely from case studies in terrestrial and freshwater systems, we had spent a *lot* of time developing case studies and cross-case lessons. So our gut-level response to Kristen was, "Been there, done that; time to move on with our lives." But then we became intrigued: How did the context of ocean and coastal management relate to that of the cases we had been evaluating in land-based systems? Were the challenges of implementing an EBM approach in the ocean similar or different? Did the fact that marine scientists took so much longer to recognize the need reflect more challenging circumstances, or simply the split between disciplines and resources that often fragments thinking and understanding?

Many marine scientists and managers were also arguing that new legal mandates and top-down structures were needed to advance an EBM approach, yet our earlier work suggested that intangible factors, like respected and motivated people who champion change, seemed to be as important to success. Many also focused on the need to extend the amount of no-take protected areas in the ocean, yet our land-based work suggested that there was only so much property one could put into reserves (that is, wilderness on land). Progress required management of a much more complicated set of stressors, and walling off natural resources from human demands had only limited political viability.

So after two years of incremental engagement in dialogue about marine EBM, we said, "Yes, we'll do it." Not only would it enable us to learn about these questions, it would engage us with an entirely new community of scientists and policy makers who, unfortunately, had limited interaction with their land-based peers. It would also enable us to support and work with a great group of graduate students who could assist with case development, and as it turns out, would develop an understanding of marine systems and policy that would propel them into careers working for the National Oceanic and Atmospheric Administration, coastal state agencies, and foundations.

Our Packard-funded project began in 2008. We developed an evaluation framework, identified a broad population of EBM sites around the world, and developed a research team that could profile a subset of those sites; develop rich case studies of an even smaller set; and draw out cross-case lessons that could help practitioners, stakeholders, and researchers better understand EBM in practice, and how to navigate its challenges. Many of these lessons are profiled on our website (www.snre.umich.edu/emi/mebm).

We examined over sixty marine EBM initiatives worldwide and quickly determined that no single model captures the full range of their experiences. While there are important characteristics shared in common across all cases, which we describe in detail in chapters 7 and 8, there are also notable differences that affect how an initiative functions and what it is able to accomplish. The initiatives we examined varied along several critical dimensions:

Scale—The cases ranged from relatively small-scale, community-based initiatives to very large-scale transnational processes. As scale increases so too does the complexity of natural and social systems, and the number of governmental jurisdictions, agencies, experts, and stakeholders that must be engaged to ensure an informed and credible process.

Authorities—The initiatives we examined were officially sanctioned in different ways. Some were established by law, policy, or executive directive; bottom-up initiatives sometimes created themselves as nonprofit organizations. All find ways to exert "authority," though only those with regulatory authority are in a position to directly restrict access and limit use of marine resources and employ zoning strategies.

Purpose and scope—Like scale, the specific purpose and scope of the initiative and the number and types of issues it addresses affect its functioning and dynamics. Some initiatives are comprehensive, encompassing fisheries issues or upstream terrestrial ecosystems, while others more narrowly address single issues and adopt single strategies, such as education or restoration.

Genesis—Who establishes an initiative, how and why, directly affects the dynamics of the process. While top-down initiatives tend to have greater formality and stature, bottom-up initiatives tend to exhibit greater ownership and commitment.

Age—Some of the cases were long-standing classic cases of regional action; others were much younger and were dealing with issues associated with startup. Older initiatives provide valuable insights about how efforts sustain themselves over time, in part by navigating transitions. Older initiatives were also better able to demonstrate accomplishments and effective measures for evaluation.

While it is easy to get lost in variation and differences, we spent considerable effort after the end of the Packard-funded research trying to find similarities and categories that could help people better understand the suite of EBM efforts. We developed the taxonomy of five types of projects detailed in chapter 1 and used it as a framework to organize chapters 2 through 6. From our compendium of cases, we drew out two situations to illustrate each of the EBM categories. While all of our profiled cases are drawn from North American examples, many of the same lessons held in cases from other places. Our research was conducted between 2009 and 2012, and each case has continued to evolve given new challenges and opportunities. While we have tried to provide updates about the present-day state of the cases, we do not claim to fully represent their current situation, including staff and structure, which can be found in the website references provided in the endnotes. Despite their inevitable evolution, the case experiences shared at the time of our interviews provide enduring lessons about creating momentum, adapting to change, and sustaining progress, and that is the focus of the book.

In an effort to describe some clear rules of thumb from within complicated and contextually rich situations, it became clear to us that a simple categorization of "bricks" and "mortar" was very helpful to organize the tangible and intangible factors that promoted the effectiveness of these marine cases. The structural "bricks" of an MEBM process can be distinguished from the human motivations and behaviors constituting its "mortar." Combined, however, these tangible and intangible factors were evident in some form in all the cases we examined and were central to their ability to make progress. The problem with nonstructural and intangible factors, however, is that they seem hard to do anything about. And indeed, some view the mortar factors as soft and touchy-feely, or even as common sense. Twenty years ago, we might have felt the same way. But, in fact, these are essential place-based factors that can be enhanced without major policy or institutional change; we believe that highlighting them is empowering to people on the front lines, struggling to make progress. And as far as these factors being common sense, when one looks closely at the frenzied efforts of scientists, managers, and policy makers in many places, it appears that common sense isn't so common.

Over time, we came to believe that the worlds of marine EBM and those of terrestrial and freshwater resource management were not so different.[4] They faced many of the same challenges and were helped by many of the same strategies. Perceptions were different: It is harder to "see" the problems of the ocean; hence it is more challenging to engage people in action that improves ecosystems hidden below the surface of the water. Property rights issues are different; on-land management had to deal with firmer private property rights than is usually the case on the water. However, overlapping and fragmented jurisdictions including governmental (federal/state/county), administrative (agencies dealing with fisheries management versus energy development versus marine transportation), and historical use (tribal versus commercial versus recreational) all create an equally challenging "rights" situation in the marine setting. The good news is that people concerned with marine, terrestrial, and freshwater situations can learn from each other, and that there are enough case studies of practice that provide a solid foundation for adaptive learning.

This book would not have happened had Barry Gold, Kai Lee, and Kristen Sherwood, Packard Foundation program officers at the time of our research, not recruited us into the world of marine conservation. Some of the marine scientists that this work connected us to were Heather Leslie and Leila Sievanen at Brown University and Lisa Campbell at Duke University, whose work on case studies in California, the Baja, and the Western Pacific was carried out using an evaluation framework that we developed in close collaboration. Interactions with Karen McLeod and others at COMPASS helped advanced our understanding of EBM in the marine context. We also benefited from the many insights shared by colleagues immersed in the world of marine conservation, including Ellen Brody (NOAA National Marine Sanctuary Program), Chris Feurt and Alison Krepp (NOAA National Estuarine Research Reserve System), Lauren Wenzel (NOAA

Marine Protected Areas Center), Sara Adlerstein-Gonzalez and Sheila Schueller (University of Michigan). We have enjoyed the expansion of our worldview into the research and management challenges associated with coastal and marine ecosystems.

The case studies described in this book were first researched and drafted by our graduate students at the UM School of Natural Resources & Environment, including Clayton Elliott, Dave Gershman, Jason Good, Matt Griffis, Colin Hume, Jennifer Lee Johnson, Amy Samples and Sarah Tomsky. We also benefited from a close partnership with former student and postgraduate researcher Sarah McKearnan, whose work on the initial evaluation framework and Gulf of Mexico case was exceptionally thorough and insightful. Our broader understanding of the many nuances of marine EBM has also been informed by complementary research conducted with other graduate students, including Ricky Ackerman, Amanda Barker, Anna Bengtson, Todd Bryan, Christina Carlson, Sara Cawley, Kathy Chen, Kate Crosman, Alyssa Cudmore, Katie Davis, Jennifer Day, Julia Elkin, Michael Fainter, Matt Ferris-Smith, Kristina Geiger, Elizabeth Harris, Troy Hartley, Kirsten Howard, Elise Hunter, Chase Huntley, Camille Kustin, Josh Kweller, Kate Lambert, Margaret Lee, Nat Lichten, Sue Lurie, Bill Mangle, Stacy Mates, Samantha Miller, Rachel Neuenfeldt, Joe Otts, Naureen Rana, Eric Roberts, Carolyn Segalini, Cybelle Shattuck, Mariana Velez, Maggie Wenger and Michelle Zilinskas. We greatly appreciated the work of all of these former students and continue to admire their accomplishments in the "real world."

We want to thank numerous interviewees who generously shared their time and perspectives on their EBM initiatives. We hope that we have successfully captured their stories in a manner that will enable others to follow in their footsteps. We also want to thank Island Press editors Barbara Dean, Erin Johnson and Sharis Simonian for their guidance and support through the publishing process. Last, but not least, we want to express love and gratitude to our daughters, Anna and Katie, for their tolerance in the face of a skeptical outlook on yet another book project. While it is easy to be discouraged by climate change forecasts and divisiveness in public discourse, we remain optimistic about the world they will inherit. Many people, both ordinary and extraordinary, are obviously committed to finding a pathway to a better future and are working hard in the face of many challenges. That alone is a cause for hope.

Chapter 1

Drawing Lessons from Experience in Marine Ecosystem-Based Management

In December 2011, managers from three states and two Canadian provinces celebrated twenty years of working hand in hand to advance marine conservation in the Gulf of Maine. Together, they have leveraged millions of dollars to enable restoration projects, advance scientific understanding, and coordinate monitoring and management on both sides of the border. When they began meeting twenty years earlier, federal officials suggested they were "incredibly naive" to think they could make a difference in what had become a highly contentious environment. The U.S. State Department discouraged their efforts. Recalling this skepticism, one of the group's co-founders laughs and says, "For some of us who are still around, we kind of smile and say, 'Here we are twenty years later!'"[1] From its humble beginnings with the simple objective "to learn and network and share information so that we can all do our respective jobs better," the Gulf of Maine Council on the Marine Environment has become a model for transboundary marine conservation worldwide.

When the federal government established the Florida Keys National Marine Sanctuary in 1990, outrage ensued. A coalition of fishermen, residents, treasure hunters, real estate interests, and others who despised federal regulation hung signs and banners denouncing the U.S. National Oceanic and Atmospheric Administration. The sanctuary's first superintendent, Billy Causey, was hung in effigy, twice in a single day. While all shared concern for the region's declining fisheries and frequent vessel groundings in sensitive coral reefs, many people feared a loss of control that would destroy the Keys' unique culture and way of life. Today, residents and fish-

1

ermen work side by side with state and federal sanctuary managers to protect this iconic resource and the communities that depend on it. They are proud of their accomplishments. Populations of heavily exploited species are rebounding, and vessel groundings have dropped dramatically. As one fisherman recalled, "When we first heard about marine reserves, there was a lot of fear. But once people got involved . . . the fear started to fade away."[2]

Oregon's Port Orford Ocean Resource Team (POORT) received the National Oceanic and Atmospheric Administration's 2010 Award for Excellence in recognition of its innovative community-based approach to sustainable fisheries. In 2012, POORT received the Governor's Gold Award for Outstanding Contribution to the Greatest of Oregon, recognizing that the state's first marine reserve had been established at the behest of Port Orford's fishermen. Ten years earlier, fishermen in this community were in a very different place. They felt isolated and unable to influence management decisions that were profoundly affecting their livelihood. Leesa Cobb, a local fisherman's wife, understood the pain and challenges confronting local fishermen and began working tirelessly on their behalf, eventually helping them to establish POORT. "When we started the organization," she recalls, "fishermen were facing a lot of changes. There had been a salmon disaster coast-wide, collapse of our urchin fishery locally, and we were headed into a groundfish disaster. Nothing that was passing as fisheries management was working for us, that's for sure. People were ready for change." The process by which change emerged in Port Orford provides a model of effective community-based stewardship of marine resources.

Throughout the world, at scales large and small and through formal and informal processes, people are working together to advance ecosystem-scale considerations in marine conservation and management. Their task is not easy: marine ecosystems are complex, science is incomplete, stakes are high, and conflict is inevitable. Nonetheless, people in places as disparate as the Gulf of Maine, the Florida Keys, and Port Orford are persevering and making a difference. They are advancing scientific understanding, leveraging resources with which to restore habitats and ecosystems, raising awareness and concern, and demonstrating that progress is possible on seemingly intractable marine conservation issues. Although their stories unfold in unique ways, their experiences reveal remarkably similar lessons with broad relevance to the practice of marine ecosystem-based management (MEBM). What enables distinct places like these to make progress? What challenges do they encounter, and how are these challenges addressed? What advice do those involved offer to others hoping to follow in their footsteps?

Ecosystem-Based Management in Practice

To answer these questions, this book draws from the experiences of places that have been experimenting with MEBM. Few of the people in these places set out to practice MEBM. Rather, they wanted to solve problems like fisheries declines, coral collapse, or poor water quality, and traditional single-species, single-resource, or single-agency approaches had not succeeded. Most realized that they had to expand their focus to a regional scale in order to connect those people and organizations needed to make progress. They built relationships across boundaries to access scientific knowledge, resources, and authorities. Ultimately, most sought integration and balance between users and objectives so that management activity could produce more sustainable outcomes. At bottom, their desire to solve problems where other strategies had not been successful led participants to embrace ecosystem-based management principles.

While definitions of MEBM vary, most include the following five elements:[3]

- **Scale:** An MEBM perspective encourages use of ecologically relevant boundaries rather than political or administrative boundaries, and often involves management at larger geographic scales and over longer time frames.
- **Complexity:** An MEBM perspective recognizes marine resources as elements of complex systems and seeks to employ strategies that acknowledge and use complexity in management.
- **Balance:** An MEBM approach seeks to balance and integrate the needs of multiple human user groups while maintaining the health of the underlying system that supports those needs.
- **Collaboration:** Since managing across boundaries involves the interests of more people and organizations, and managing complexity involves more areas of knowledge, an MEBM approach engages a diverse set of organizations and individuals.
- **Adaptive management:** Given the existence of uncertainty in what we know and the inevitability of change in the future, an MEBM perspective encourages adaptive approaches that involve monitoring and evaluation linked to changes in future management.

A number of scientific and policy factors have accelerated a push toward MEBM. Drawing from earlier efforts to shift from multiple-use to ecosystem-based management of public lands,[4] marine resource policy began to promote ecosystem-scale management in the early 2000s.[5] The U.S. Commission on Ocean Policy and the Pew Oceans Commission developed ocean policy guidance and recommended that MEBM should be a primary focus of future marine resource management.[6] Many of the commissions' recommendations were later incorporated in an executive order signed by President Obama in 2010. It mandates ecosystem-based management as the first of nine priority objectives for U.S. ocean, coastal, and Great Lakes management.[7] The National Ocean Plan, released in 2013, is grounded in an ecosystem-based management process. Coastal states have similarly adjusted ocean policy toward an ecosystem-based management approach. Both California and Massachusetts, for example, have enacted ocean protection laws that mandate an ecosystem-based management approach.[8] Similarly, Canada's Oceans Act requires an integrated oceans management approach.[9]

As federal and state agencies began to grapple with the implications of an ecosystem-based management perspective and approach, and philanthropic organizations with interests in ocean conservation began to fund science and regional processes, some policy makers, managers, and affected groups pushed back. They argued that there was too little scientific understanding and too much uncertainty to manage at an ecosystem scale. Some noted that different people mean different things when they argue for an ecosystem-based management approach.[10] In response, the Communication Partnership for Science and the Sea (COMPASS) facilitated development in 2005 of a "consensus statement" on MEBM in which over two hundred scientists and policy experts agreed that "ecosystem-based management is an integrated approach to management that considers the entire ecosystem, including humans. The goal of ecosystem-based management is to maintain an ecosystem in a healthy, productive and resilient condition so that it can provide the services humans want and need. Ecosystem-based management differs from current approaches that usually focus on a single species, sector, activity or concern; it considers the cumulative impacts of different sectors."[11]

Translating this general statement into action may seem challenging, and some proponents of ecosystem-based management have argued that specific steps are necessary. Some view legal mandates as essential. Others argue that an ecosystem-based approach must consider all issues simultaneously. Still others advocate for new regional institutions to cope with overlapping governmental jurisdictions. Many view comprehensive marine spatial planning—the application of land use planning and zoning approaches to the oceans—as the way forward.[12]

Our observations of dozens of processes worldwide suggest that there is no single template for practicing MEBM. Instead, myriad pathways are being followed to advance ecosystem considerations in marine conservation; each is a function of its context, genesis, composition, and objectives. If no legal mandate exists, those involved find other ways to incentivize action. Smaller-scale initiatives find ways to connect with larger-scale activities, and vice versa. Comprehensive marine spatial planning is but one strategy among many.

Different Paths but Common Lessons

We have spent the last eight years listening to people tell their stories, share their struggles and accomplishments, and offer advice for others hoping to advance MEBM principles in places that matter to them. With support from the David and Lucile Packard Foundation, we identified dozens of cases worldwide that exhibited MEBM principles in action, regardless of whether those involved had explicitly adopted the MEBM label.[13] We initially sought emblematic examples of ecosystem-based management as defined in the literature but quickly unearthed a tremendous variation in practice. There was no single model; instead there were many paths being followed.

We examined two dozen cases in detail, comparing and contrasting the key attributes that they shared in common and the notable ways in which they differed. They all adopted an ecosystem perspective and were collaborative and adaptive. They all functioned within existing laws and policies and found synergies that enabled them to work across scales. They all fostered coordination and enhanced communication that was previously weak or nonexistent. But they pursued different strategies, encountered unique challenges, and carefully tailored their governance structures to fit their particular context and objectives.

Most of the cases we examined are best described as experiments. Those involved were iteratively molding their efforts to fit their place, organizations, and objectives; they tailored their process and strategies to the issues, institutions, and capabilities that were within their grasp. Many of those we interviewed would laugh or challenge our judgment when we said we were studying their work because their stories seemed promising and could provide a model for others to emulate. "We're still trying to figure it out," was a common refrain. But in their sustained experiments at "figuring it out," they have unveiled some notably similar and valuable lessons that transcend scale, scope, or sociopolitical context.

Five Types of Marine Ecosystem-Based Management Initiatives

While the many initiatives we examined shared important characteristics, they nonetheless varied in notable ways, depending on their context and objectives, as well as the manner in which the process was initiated. Some were top down; others were bottom up. Policy makers initiated some; others arose through the efforts of managers, community members, or nongovernmental organizations. Some have complex, highly formalized governance structures; others have simpler organizational forms. They also varied depending on the nature of the authorities they possessed. While some can manage resources and regulate uses, most are limited to planning, coordinating, or advisory roles. This book describes five different types of MEBM initiatives and the unique challenges associated with each.

Large-Scale, Transnational Initiatives

Formalized by high-level cooperative agreements, this type of MEBM initiative links nations across political boundaries. These initiatives recognize common interests and concerns for a shared marine ecosystem but also honor national sovereignty and institutions. Like many international agreements, these initiatives have no authority to require a nation to undertake specific actions; all engagement and activity is voluntary. These large-scale, transnational initiatives are challenged by the need to navigate different cultural, political, and legal systems.

Examples of transnational initiatives include the Gulf of Maine Council on the Marine Environment and the Puget Sound Georgia Basin International Task Force, which independently arose to foster MEBM between the United States and Canada and the states and provinces bordering the two marine systems. Similarly, the Trilateral Cooperation on the Protection of the Wadden Sea encourages collaboration between the Netherlands, Germany, and Denmark to conserve their shared United Nations Educational, Scientific and Cultural Organization World Heritage Site in the North Sea. The Benguela Current Commission, established in 2007 by Angola, Namibia, and South Africa, advances integrated management of the Benguela Current Large Marine Ecosystem.

Multistate, Regional Initiatives

Somewhat smaller in political and institutional scale, but not necessarily in size, are multistate, regional initiatives in a single country. Established by cooperative agreements or national policy, these efforts link individual states and/or the federal government in joint endeavors to advance marine conservation. Largely voluntary arrangements with no authority to require action, they are established to acknowledge shared objectives, coordinate activities, find synergies or efficiencies within their independent programs, pool science and expertise, and attract funding that otherwise would be difficult to acquire individually. Often initiated by elected officials, they must find ways to move beyond initial political directives to develop on-the-ground traction to weather transitions in political administrations that can undercut commitment.

Examples of multistate voluntary initiatives include the federal Gulf of Mexico Program and the state-initiated Gulf of Mexico Alliance. The West Coast Governors Alliance on Ocean Health, and the Northeast and Mid-Atlantic Regional Ocean Councils, are similar regional initiatives designed to encourage multistate collaboration. They seek to ensure that broad ecosystem perspectives are considered when states take individual action.

Top-Down, Regulatory and Management Initiatives

Some MEBM initiatives have teeth. Established by law and possessing explicit authority to manage marine resources, these efforts are often under the control of a single federal or state agency with the power to establish enforceable marine protected areas or regulate use in management zones. Examples in North America include the U.S. National Marine Sanctuary Program, marine protected areas created by the California Fish and Game Commission under authority of the California Marine Life Protection Act, the Eastern Scotian Shelf Integrated Management Initiative under Canada's Oceans Act, and regional Fisheries Management Councils established by the Magnuson-Stevens Act. The Great Barrier Reef Marine Park Authority in Australia, the Galapagos Marine Reserve in Ecuador, and the Mafia Island Marine Park in Tanzania are all initiatives that embodied the same objectives and faced similar challenges despite their widely dispersed locations and diverse institutional contexts.

While these formal government initiatives have the force of law, they nonetheless all reside in a sociopolitical context that affects what they are able to do. Cooperation and coordination are often critical because stakeholder-based conflict can be intense. Additionally, in order to deal with overlapping state–federal jurisdictions, these initiatives often must establish formal agreements delimiting the reach of their authority.

Top-Down, Nonregulatory Initiatives

Not all top-down initiatives have teeth. A number of programs have been established by states or the federal government and serve as a mechanism for advancing MEBM, but they do so without management or regulatory authorities. These initiatives do not directly manage resources, nor do they direct or restrict the activities of others. Often medium or large scale in size, these initiatives are authorized to plan, coordinate, educate, and enable others to take action. Not surprisingly, their lack of explicit authority can be challenging; they must devise ways to encourage or enable voluntary action, such as by convening groups, raising issues for consideration, providing seed funding for others to act, or instilling ownership in management plans that others implement. When done well, this "enabling" role can change agency behavior, which ultimately translates into improvements in ocean health.

The implementation plan for the U.S. National Ocean Policy calls for an expansion of initiatives that elevate awareness of ecosystem-scale issues and encourage greater coordination and attention to these issues at state and regional levels. One example is the Great Lakes Restoration Initiative, a voluntary effort that links eleven federal agencies and their state counterparts in advancing an adaptive, science-based framework for restoration of the Great Lakes. Washington State's Puget Sound Partnership and Northwest Straits Commission similarly encourage an ecosystem perspective among communities, agencies, and stakeholders. The Environmental Protection Agency's National Estuary Program has set up numerous ecosystem-based efforts of this sort, including the Albemarle–Pamlico National Estuary Partnership and the Narragansett Bay Estuary Program. These initiatives are successful by coordinating conservation activity despite their lack of regulatory authority.

Bottom-Up, Community-Based Initiatives

Not all initiatives were created by government. Some emerge organically from citizens who take action and give voice to community-level objectives and issues. Relatively small in geographic scope, these bottom-up initiatives can be organized informally as voluntary groups or formally as nonprofit organizations or local government advisory committees. While the smaller scale of community-based efforts can diminish cross-jurisdictional complexity and other challenges, their lack of authority means that these initiatives must find ways to influence the actions of those who have authority in order to have a meaningful impact.

Community-based initiatives are prevalent throughout the world.

The Port Orford Ocean Resource Team in Oregon is a good example of a bottom-up effort in which fishermen established an initiative that tapped into the energies and concerns of the local community; POORT has accomplished a number of MEBM outcomes despite lacking regulatory or management authority. Nearly a decade's work by the fishermen in Puerto Peñasco, Mexico, to manage the dive fishery through an informal community-based structure resulted in creation of no-take marine protected areas in 2002; concessions in 2006 gave the dive fishermen exclusive access and management authority over portions of the rock scallop fishery.

Bricks and Mortar

Although MEBM initiatives differ in a variety of ways, there are general principles that help promote progress regardless of initiative type. These efforts are kept afloat and productive by a combination of what we refer to as *bricks* and *mortar*, an admittedly unusual metaphor for flotation devices. Each initiative has a carefully constructed governance structure that outlines its reach, roles, and responsibilities. This structure often explicitly embeds science in discussions and ensures that diverse interests are recognized. Intergovernmental agreements, laws, mission statements, and resources define the scope and possibilities of a process. These tangible, replicable features—the bricks—provide an essential infrastructure; some form of them was evident in all of the initiatives we examined.

Bricks are necessary but not sufficient to make progress on MEBM. A coral reef that is just a skeletal structure is a sad, lifeless place; it requires organisms, trophic dynamics, nutrient flow, and interconnections to make it an integral, functioning system. In the MEBM initiatives we examined, the behaviors and motivations of the people involved gave them life. Relationships, commitment, a sense of place, and a shared sense of ownership were the mortar that held the initiatives together and sustained them. This mortar was readily apparent in the respectful ways in which individuals with divergent perspectives worked together to address shared issues. Thus mortar gave strength and energy to all of the initiatives we examined.

Navigating the Book

We have organized this book to accomplish three objectives. First, we seek to describe the unique characteristics, challenges, and strategies that distinguish each type of MEBM initiative. Second, we spotlight the factors shared in common across MEBM initiatives. Our final objective is to discuss the policy and management implications of these varied real-world experiments and offer advice for practitioners, policy makers, communities, charitable foundations, nongovernmental organizations, and others seeking to advance the state of marine conservation and management.

Chapters 2 through 6 present case studies of MEBM through the experiences and voices of those directly involved (fig. 1-1). Each chapter compares and contrasts two cases, and highlights the nuances evident within one of the five different types of MEBM processes. Each chapter describes the unique challenges encountered in the cases and the factors that enabled progress or constrained them from making progress. All of the featured cases in these five chapters are located in North America, though the lessons learned are strongly mirrored in places across the globe.[13]

- Chapter 2 highlights MEBM initiatives that cross national borders and contrasts the experience with the Gulf of Maine Council on the Marine

FIGURE I-I. Location of case studies.

Environment and the Puget Sound Georgia Basin International Task Force. Both of these initiatives were designed to bridge the U.S.–Canadian border, a highly visible line in a geopolitical sense, but one that has limited meaning within the highly dynamic marine ecosystem.

- Chapter 3 tells the story of two processes in the Gulf of Mexico, where MEBM efforts moved from a federally initiated Environmental Protection Agency Gulf of Mexico Program into the Gulf of Mexico Alliance. The Alliance was initiated and sustained by strong gubernatorial support from the five Gulf States. The chapter explains how those involved managed the challenges inherent in bridging state–federal and state–state jurisdictions.

- Chapter 4 describes MEBM led by a federal agency with authority for designating reserves, managing resources, and regulating uses. The National Marine Sanctuary Program's management of sanctuaries in the Florida Keys and California's Channel Islands highlights the ways in which both sanctuaries carefully exercise their authorities while navigating contentious issues.

- Chapter 5 explains how a government program that lacks management or regulatory authority, the Environmental Protection Agency's National Estuary Program in New England's Narragansett Bay and North Carolina's Albemarle and Pamlico Sounds, can still enable MEBM. Both cases illustrate innovative approaches for instilling shared concern and voluntary activity by agencies and communities bordering the estuaries. Each seeks "authority" through nonregulatory means.

- Chapter 6 presents the bottom-up experience and unique challenges associated with two community-based MEBM initiatives, the Port Orford Ocean Resource Team in Oregon and the San Juan Marine Resources Committee in Washington. It describes the challenges encountered by citizens in these two places and how they were able to influence marine management in their backyards despite their seemingly limited power and authority.

- Chapters 7 and 8 examine elements of the cases that cross-cut different types of initiatives and highlight the importance of "bricks and mortar" in successful MEBM. Besides our featured case studies, these two chapters draw from our research on MEBM initiatives throughout the world.[15]

- Chapter 7 reviews the tangible brick-like elements, such as governance structure, laws, formal agreements, and resources, that are often the most visible components of an initiative. They provide a foundation and infrastructure within which managers and stakeholders can pursue marine conservation objectives.

- Chapter 8 describes the less tangible mortar-like factors, including participant motivation, commitment, relationships, understanding, and trust. These often invisible factors are what enliven an initiative, enabling the bricks to hold together and have on-the-ground impacts.
- Chapter 9 discusses our overall conclusions and the policy implications of the lessons embodied in the MEBM experiments described in the book. If both bricks and mortar are essential, how can policies and policy makers create conditions that foster "brickmaking" and the "mixing and application of mortar?" How can managers and practitioners design and manage future processes that will help them realize the potential of an EBM approach?

We hope that the stories, observations, and analysis contained in this book will prove useful for *policy makers* seeking to advance policy and programmatic priorities; for *foundations* that want to structure their marine conservation investments to maximize impact; and for *students* who are preparing for careers in marine conservation and need to understand the varied roles they might play and the skills and expertise they should acquire while in school. Moreover, we hope that *practitioners* who aspire to advance MEBM principles can apply the lessons contained in this book to begin developing an initiative, to understand how to support one that is under way, or to diagnose factors that might be undermining an initiative's progress and how those shortcomings could be rectified.

Our goal is to describe past practice, reflect on its meaning, and offer help to practitioners, managers, decision makers, communities, and nongovernmental groups. While there is no single right way to advance MEBM, there are rules of thumb and strategies that can help initiatives get under way and sustain their progress. Regional-scale and inclusive processes will be part of resource management decision making in the future. Indeed, forces such as climate change, globalization, and the spread of invasive species and loss of biodiversity are challenging the scale and character of past management. We should learn from the many real-world ecosystem-based management experiments already under way. We can apply what works and avoid what does not, and, in so doing, build better bridges to advance the sustainability of marine ecosystems.

Chapter 2

Navigating International Boundaries in the Gulf of Maine and Puget Sound Georgia Basin

Since many marine ecosystems cross international borders, effective management requires transboundary interaction between agencies and policy makers. National borders may not stop marine organisms, but they definitely constrain the amount and character of interaction between scientists, managers, and decision makers. At minimum, an international border can complicate communication, travel, funding, and project implementation. More significantly, differences in law, political systems, and culture need to be navigated.

Two innovative marine ecosystem-based management (MEBM) processes bridging international boundaries were established more than twenty-five years ago to encourage communication and coordination between U.S. and Canadian agencies, ministries, states, and provinces responsible for managing marine resources. Located on opposite coasts, these two initiatives—the Gulf of Maine Council on the Marine Environment, and the Puget Sound Georgia Basin International Task Force—were formalized by high-level agreements between their respective state governors and provincial premiers, and were later embraced by both national governments. Both were established in a context of conflict, and neither possessed regulatory or management authority.

When viewed at a distance, these two initiatives look remarkably similar in structure and purpose. However, while the Gulf of Maine Council still plays an important role in its region today, the Puget Sound Georgia Basin International Task Force has been disbanded. Their parallel stories reveal valuable insights about the unique challenges encountered in transnational marine conservation as well as the critical factors that sustain these initiatives.

13

The Gulf of Maine and the Puget Sound Georgia Basin

While located on opposite sides of the continent, the Gulf of Maine and the Puget Sound Georgia Basin are fairly similar targets for MEBM. Both are very large geographically and provide homes and livelihoods for millions of people. These people and their livelihoods contribute contaminants and nutrients, which, in turn, stress fisheries and iconic marine mammals. Both locations present the unique management challenge of spanning the U.S.–Canadian border. Both provide an important sense of identity and essential ecosystem services to their surrounding states and provinces.

The Gulf of Maine

The Gulf of Maine is an international semi-enclosed sea bordered by Massachusetts, New Hampshire, Maine, New Brunswick, and Nova Scotia. It covers 36,000 square miles (93,200 sq. km) of ocean from Cape Cod in Massachusetts in the south to the upper Bay of Fundy in the Canadian provinces to the north. Winding inlets and roughly five thousand islands make up the coastline, which covers an impressive 7,500 miles (12,000 sq. km). The watershed extends almost 200 miles inland and covers a total drainage area of 69,000 square miles (178,700 sq. km).[1]

The Gulf provides habitat for hundreds of species of fish and shellfish and more than eighteen species of marine mammals, including the endangered North Atlantic right whale. A remarkable 70 percent of the region's commercial fishery species depend on the Gulf's estuaries for some portion of their life cycle. Coastal habitat areas in the Gulf of Maine are recognized as "the most important southward staging areas for shorebirds in eastern North America."[2] Tens of thousands of shorebirds migrate between breeding grounds in the Arctic and wintering sites to the south.

The Gulf of Maine watershed is home to more than six million people who use the Gulf for recreation, fishing, aquaculture, transportation, tourism, and development opportunities. However, extensive discharge of partially treated sewage to the Gulf has damaged productive shellfish habitat.[3] Additional contaminants from industrial discharges, urban runoff, and agricultural practices combine to alter the dissolved oxygen and nutrient balances in the Gulf.

To better address these issues, the Gulf of Maine Council on the Marine Environment (GOMC) was formalized in 1989 by an agreement among the governors and premiers of the three states and two provinces surrounding the Gulf. The agreement recognized that "natural resources of the Gulf of Maine are interconnected and form part of an overall ecosystem that transcends political boundaries."[4] According to the agreement, "the most effective means of protecting, conserving, and managing the region's resources is through the cooperative pursuit of consistent policies, initiatives, and programs." The Council was established to provide a vehicle for transboundary collaboration.

The Puget Sound Georgia Basin

The marine ecosystem consisting of the Puget Sound, Strait of Georgia, and Strait of Juan de Fuca is known collectively as the Salish Sea and is one of the largest inland seas in the world, with a surface area of nearly 6,000-square-miles (17,000 sq. km) and a 4,700-mile (7,500 km) coastline.[5] The 42,000-square-mile (110,000 sq. km) watershed includes the major cities and surrounding metropolitan areas of Seattle, Vancouver, Tacoma, Everett, Victoria, Nanaimo, Bellingham, and Olympia.[6] It is home to a population of more than seven million people, which is projected to increase to 9.4 million by the year 2025.[7] The marine ecosystem is critical to the economy of the region, with its large population relying on the waters for food, shipping, transportation, recreation, and aesthetic enjoyment.

The Puget Sound Georgia Basin marine ecosystem is one of the most ecologically diverse in North America.[8] It comprises a variety of coastal and open-water habitats, including sea grass, kelp, rocky intertidal, salt and brackish marshes, and sand, mud, and salt flats. These habitats provide for more than 200 species of fish, more than 120 species of birds, 20 species of marine mammals, and more than 3,000 species of invertebrates.[9] Culturally iconic species include orca whales, giant Pacific octopus, bald eagles, great blue herons, and Pacific salmon.[10]

Despite its richness and diversity, the ecosystem faces numerous pressures, most notably resulting from rapid population growth. Pollution from shipping and urban and agricultural inputs, sewage dumping, and the threat of oil spills from tankers traveling in and out of the Salish Sea make marine water quality one of the largest concerns. Other stressors include toxic contamination in sediments and biota, including salmon and orca whales; overfishing; nearshore habitat loss from dredging; development resulting in the loss of coastal wetlands; freshwater diversions upstream; and introduction of nonnative species, notably through ships' ballast water.[11]

Efforts at managing the ecosystem across the border officially began in 1992 with the signing of an Environmental Cooperation Agreement between the State of Washington and the Province of British Columbia, which led to the creation of the Environmental Cooperation Council (ECC), under which the Puget Sound Georgia Basin International Task Force was created in 1994. The Task Force included representatives of federal, state, and provincial agencies and First Nations; its mission was to focus on environmental issues in the shared marine ecosystem of the Strait of Georgia and Puget Sound. The Task Force operated until 2007, when it was disbanded.

Getting Started: Bottom-Up versus Top-Down Origins

MEBM initiatives that bridge an international boundary and that hope to substantively impact management and policy need to be formally sanctioned. While little precludes managers on two sides of an international border from talking to each another, a meaningful and ongoing collaboration with substantive goals and activities requires some form of official sanction. The Gulf of Maine and Puget Sound Georgia Basin (PSGB) processes differed in their early genesis and pathways to formalization.

Both the Gulf of Maine and PSGB initiatives were motivated by concerns about declining water quality and conflict among user groups. Both had champions pressing for mechanisms to achieve a coordinated response. Both look similar in that they involved deliberations among agency managers and secured endorsements by high-level officials. However, the Gulf of Maine Council was largely a product of middle-level agency managers who recognized a need for transboundary communication and who created mechanisms to enable it, while the PSGB Task Force emerged from the directives of high-level elected and appointed officials. These subtle differences in origin appear to have influenced a differing level of ownership of the process by middle-level bureaucrats in the former case (GOMC) versus a waning interest when high-level officials moved on in the latter (PSGB Task Force). They help to explain the durability of the GOMC and the transiency of the PSGB Task Force.

Gulf of Maine Council: A Bottom-Up Process Rooted in the Initiative of Midlevel Agency Managers

The idea for a regional group discussing common interests within the Gulf of Maine ecosystem is attributed by most to David Keeley. Keeley was director of the Maine Office of Coastal Programs and was troubled that no forum existed within which he and his counterparts in the region could meet to discuss issues of shared concern in the Gulf. Coastal and marine managers in Massachusetts, New Hampshire, Maine, New Brunswick, and Nova Scotia all border the Gulf of Maine and have management responsibility for resources within this ecosystem but had few opportunities to easily share information and coordinate management. According to Keeley: "That realization caused me to go to then-governor McKernan and say, 'Why don't we think about forming an international council that would involve both the three states and the two Canadian provinces?' So I organized a meeting of folks from Nova Scotia, New Brunswick, and the three states."[12]

Keeley remembers the initial resistance his international council concept encountered at the national level. "When I first suggested it," Keeley comments, "we got a lot of critiquing memos from members of the U.S. State Department who suggested we were trying to create an international treaty and only the State Department could propose such things. We got letters from colleagues in NOAA [National Oceanic and Atmospheric Administration] who suggested this is incredibly naive that the states would be proposing such a thing because clearly there had been a long and rocky road between the New England states and the Canadian provinces about trade, blueberries, potatoes, lumber, labor, and the World Court's Hague Line decision about the boundary between the U.S. and Canada." Recalling the skepticism, Keeley laughs and says, "For some of us who are still around, we kind of smile and say, 'Here we are, twenty years later!'"

From this inauspicious beginning, the Gulf of Maine Council on the Marine Environment was soon a formally sanctioned organization. In 1989, the governors and premiers of Massachusetts, New Hampshire, Maine, New Brunswick, and Nova Scotia announced their Agreement on Conservation of the Marine Environment of the Gulf of Maine between the Governments of the Bordering States and Provinces. The provisions of the agreement called for establishment of the Gulf of Maine Council on the Marine Environment to discuss and act upon environmental issues of common concern. This groundwork led to the following mission statement: "To maintain and enhance environmental quality in the Gulf of Maine to allow for sustainable resource use by existing and future generations."[13]

The Council was initially composed of three representatives from each state and province, with these fifteen individuals appointed by their respective governor or premier. The Council decided in 1995 to formally add representatives of U.S. and Canadian federal agencies to its membership, acknowledging the relevant national-level policies and programs in the region. "In the beginning," Keeley notes, "we called them observers in part because of the State Department's concern over engaging federal agencies" in nontreaty international discussions. Today, many partners from nongovernmental organizations, industry, and tribal and First Nations are actively involved in the Council's many committees and working groups.

Puget Sound Georgia Basin: A Top-Down Process Initiated by a Governor and Premier

In Puget Sound Georgia Basin, U.S. and Canadian pressure for an expanded response to marine ecosystem issues came partly from mounting concerns about each other's contributions to the problem. In the early 1990s, these concerns escalated. Officials in the United States were particularly worried about Canada's "apparent lack of progress" in sewage treatment and the destructive impact that continued discharges from large, waterfront cities like Victoria and Vancouver would have on the quality of the marine environment.[14] Canadians were concerned about U.S. activities in shared waters, including supertanker shipments of Alaskan crude oil to the Lower 48 states via Puget Sound and their potential for catastrophic oil spills.

As Jamie Alley of the British Columbia Ministry of Environment wrote, tension characterized relationships in the region:

> By the early 1990s, politicians, the media, and community leaders on both sides of the border were outdoing each other in pointing fingers of blame for a perceived decline in marine water quality. Secondary sewage treatment had been installed in Washington under threat of lawsuit by the EPA, and the lack of similar action in Canada was much resented. Business leaders in Seattle and Puget Sound began to organize a tourism boycott of Victoria to protest the slow pace of change in the Capital Region and Greater Vancouver. Some American yachtsmen were lobbied to stay away from the prestigious annual Swiftsure Classic yacht race. . . . On the Canadian side, officials and politicians pointed to the liquid-waste management planning processes under way in British Columbia and, despite the slow pace of deliberations, warned the other side not to interfere in legitimate democratic processes in a sovereign country.[15]

With tensions rising, executives in the B.C. Ministry of Environment and the Washington Department of Ecology met informally in May 1991 to discuss ways to promote more effective cooperation.[16] Soon, Washington governor Booth Gardner and B.C. premier Mike Harcourt took on the issue. They had become friends and felt that the time was ripe to address shared issues in the region head-on in a collaborative and coordinated manner. They signed an Environmental Cooperation Agreement in May 1992. Their agreement established the British Columbia/Washington Environmental Initiative, which soon after became the Environmental Cooperation Council (ECC).[17] Most thought this agreement signaled a new era for a region better positioned than most to care for its natural resources. The ECC consists of the director of the Washington Department of Ecology and the deputy minister of the B.C. Ministry of Environment (formerly Environment, Land and Parks), as well as formal observers from regional offices of the U.S. Environmental Protection Agency (EPA), Environment Canada, and Fisheries and Oceans Canada.[18]

One of the ECC's first major tasks was to create an independent Marine Science Panel in 1993, consisting of six university and government scientists from both British Columbia and Washington. The Panel was to assess the state of the marine environment in the shared waters and to provide recommendations for action. As Jamie Alley recalls, "No issue facing the council [ECC] was as politically charged or aroused as much public acrimony as that of marine water quality, and probably no issue has seen as much apparent progress. This also arguably was the single most important issue in the establishment of the council."[19]

In August 1994, the Marine Science Panel delivered twelve recommendations to the ECC. The ECC, in turn, established the Puget Sound Georgia Basin International Task Force to act on these recommendations. The International Task Force was cochaired by the B.C. Ministry of Environment and the Puget Sound Water Quality Authority, and its membership included representatives from the U.S. EPA, NOAA's Northwest Fisheries Science Center, Environment Canada, Fisheries and Oceans Canada, the Washington Department of Ecology, the Washington Department of Natural Resources, the Washington Department of Fish and Wildlife, the Northwest Indian Fisheries Commission, the Northwest Straits Commission, and the Coast Salish First Nations in British Columbia.

Bridging a Single Ecosystem but Two Distinct Institutional Contexts

For the GOMC and the PSGB Task Force to have an impact, they had to find ways to deal with the institutional realities of transboundary action. Different nations have different laws, competing interests, varying political systems, and diverse cultures. As a result, relations between levels of government, elected and appointed officials, and government and nongovernmental parties may differ greatly, even in the ways that information is collected and organized. As Lee Sochasky, of New Brunswick's St. Croix International Waterway Commission, noted, "With the two countries, about all they share is the English language. But politics and management and perceptions are very different on either side of the border. . . . That's what makes a transboundary project so much more difficult because you're dealing with barriers that most people don't even perceive."

What were the challenges encountered by these two initiatives as they tried to build a bridge across their international border? How did they frame a reasonable agenda to begin their work together? How did they ensure that individual national policies and programs were respected? Answers needed to be found for even the seemingly simple questions of where to meet and how to manage those meetings.

The Impact of Political and Institutional Context

In commenting on challenges facing the GOMC, Councilor Sochasky noted the lack of common laws between Canada and the United States for protecting environmental quality or managing the marine environment: "In many respects the Canadian system is not as far advanced in both management tools and legislation and policy as the American system is. Part of that is based on need. The [US Clean Water Act] came about in 1972, and Canada just got around to passing one fairly recently. We don't have shoreline zoning. Don't have surface water classifications. Things that have been around forever in the U.S. are still evolving on the Canadian side."

To challenge matters further, adjacent nations may well be competitors in the effort to harvest natural resources, and those competitive relationships may be hard to overcome when trying to foster cooperation. For example, Canadian and U.S. fishing fleets compete for a limited fishery and use their governments to try to secure an advantage. In the late 1970s, both the United States and Canada declared exclusive economic zones (EEZs) of 200 nautical miles offshore. This resulted in overlapping claims to the productive Georges Bank fishing ground. In 1979, the two nations first attempted to negotiate a fisheries conservation agreement, but a strong fishing lobby blocked the bill in Congress. By the end of the year, tensions surrounding the maritime boundary in the Gulf of Maine grew so fierce that the International Joint Commission was called upon to settle the matter, which ultimately awarded most of Georges Bank to the United States.[20]

Participants in the Puget Sound Georgia Basin process encountered more fundamental issues. As International Task Force cochair John Dohrmann of the Washington Department of Ecology explained,

> [The Canadian] parliamentary system is just a fundamentally different beast: the balance of laws between what's federal and what's provincial. We have all of this "federal law delegated to the state delegated to the local" kind of structures. How you would implement an idea—people shouldn't build docks over eelgrass—the way you would make that happen in Washington is so radically different than in B.C. At some point in the work groups when you get down to the nuts and bolts of how you make this stuff happen, you don't have much to share because they're talking about completely different structures.

The difference between agency responsibilities arises not only between the state and the province but also between the respective national governments. In Washington, state government regulates water quality under the federal Clean Water Act, and the state has a good relationship with the EPA. In British Columbia the relationship is more complicated, and the province's water quality laws are overshadowed in some respects by federal laws under Fisheries and Oceans Canada. In general, the federal–province relationship in Canada is more complicated than the parallel relationship in the United States. According to Jamie Alley,

> [B.C. Oceans and Marine Fisheries] is a branch within the Ministry of Environment. It's an area where the province has no constitutional jurisdiction, but has a very deep and abiding interest, and it's an area where they are working to influence the federal government in how they exercise their duties and responsibilities under the constitution for those matters. [However] the Supreme Court of Canada ruled that the seabed of the Strait of Georgia belongs to the province not the federal government. It's a lot more complex than in the U.S., where you have your three-mile limit and jurisdiction is more clear cut. In Canada, it's a really entangled web.

The United States and Canada also have fundamentally different rules when it comes to public involvement in government decisions. In the United States, agencies are required to hold public meetings or hearings and solicit public comment before major decisions are made. In Canada, information is often not released to the public until a final decision has been made. This difference has caused challenges in day-to-day transboundary work as well as in higher-profile issues. As John Dohrmann described,

> We would claim that we were forming a transboundary work group on toxics or something, and you would go to appoint the people and the Canadians would say, "We can only have people from these ministries there, and they can't talk about their work until it's been completed and approved by their ministries. No members of the public or representatives of First Nations are invited and our meetings are not public." We'd say, on our side, "We're inviting three tribes and the Washington Toxics Coalition and the Sierra Club, and the pulp and paper mills want to send somebody. We're going to publish notice and all of our meetings will be open to the public."

Even simply compiling and analyzing scientific information runs head-on into the institutional differences inherent in a binational effort. "It's more than just changing degrees Celsius to degrees Fahrenheit," commented Tom Laurie, Washington coordinator for the ECC. Michael Rylko, of the EPA, provided additional examples:

> We have water quality data that is organized by a hierarchical organization of watersheds. They're nested; one watershed reliably flows into a larger watershed as it works its way down to marine waters. On the Canadian side, they monitor their watersheds by watershed groups—compatible watersheds by elevation, vegetation, soils—so that they're comparing similar things. That makes sense in one respect, but they don't flow into one another, so they would have watershed groups that flow both into the eastern basin and into Georgia Basin. . . . We also don't interpret satellite data for land cover in a compatible way.

Shared Data Sets and Indicators

To overcome these institutional hurdles, both GOMC and PSGB started with strategies that were not very controversial but could provide a clearer image of the watersheds and their problems. For example, both initiatives worked at developing new information and coordinating existing data sets. As Tom Laurie explained, "Better sharing of scientific information is easier because you're not intruding in anyone's jurisdiction." There was logic in advancing this scientific dialogue as a means for building collaboration in PSGB. Jamie Alley concurred, commenting: "At a technical level, it's really easy. There's lots of good exchange between the scientists and there's lots of good information for one another and that stuff goes relatively smoothly. When you get further up the hierarchical chain, that's where some of the differences in the institutional structure of government begin to have more of an impact."

As they, too, sought to enhance their ability to take action, organizers of the Gulf of Maine Council realized that an important first step was to develop a shared understanding of the science of the Gulf of Maine ecosystem. If nothing else, Sochasky commented, shared data sets would "level the management playing ground" among agencies with varying levels of ability in creating information for their own operations. One key need was to develop Gulf of Maine maps, which did not exist at the time, so they developed the Gulf of Maine Mapping Initiative (GOMMI), which conducts comprehensive seafloor imaging, mapping, and biological and geological surveys. As Ted Diers, director of the New Hampshire coastal management program, explains: "GOMMI serves as a place to do mapping and keep track of what's been mapped. If we ever get toward broader ecosystem-based management or marine spatial planning, we're going to need very basic information to do that. We can't do marine spatial planning until we have extraordinarily good benthic mapping of the entire Gulf of Maine."

GOMC also helped establish the Gulf of Maine Ocean Observing System (GoMOOS), which hourly delivers open-source oceanographic data that is used by commercial mariners, coastal resource managers, scientists, educators, search-and-rescue teams, and public health officials.[21] Diers explains the value created by GoMOOS:

> You can point to a lot of interesting things that have happened because of the buoy data coming out of GoMOOS and because of the tools that they have created. I've certainly used it, especially during storms. We're understanding a little bit about what's going on and being able to explain that to people, to make a case for different kinds of activity, maybe climate change adaptation, stuff like that. Because of that data you can see what's going on out there. That data has been used for search and rescues; it has saved people's lives.

The Puget Sound Georgia Basin International Task Force also invested in development of shared scientific information. As one review of the Task Force's history concluded, "The Task Force has placed a great deal of emphasis on creating a shared, cross border understanding of issues and approaches through workshops and joint research."[22] EPA Puget Sound estuary manager Michael Rylko explains that the task force recognized fairly early that there were no common data sets across the border; hence the task force could not produce the required reports: "We came back with a recommendation that, if we had more time, we could at least make these half dozen data sets work. We would really have to rework them—it wasn't just like sewing them together."

Another key mechanism for transboundary data sharing has come through a focus on indicators and monitoring. For example, the Ecosystem Indicator Partnership, a GOMC committee formed in 2006, provides regional-scale indicators and a reporting system to reflect the overall "health" of the Gulf. Over one hundred volunteers representing interests and organizations from around the Gulf of Maine assist the Ecosystem Indicator Partnership in selecting and compiling information on specific indicators of ecosystem health. A GOMC committee also developed Gulfwatch, a chemical-contaminants monitoring program funded by GOMC and the U.S. EPA.[23] Since 1993, Gulfwatch has measured contaminants in blue mussels to assess the types and concentrations of contaminants in coastal waters of the Gulf of Maine. It is one of the few monitoring programs to be coordinated across international borders.

Developing a set of transboundary ecosystem indicators to indicate status and trends of key aspects of the environment was also an important focus of the Puget Sound Georgia Basin initiative. Indicators were developed by the Statement of Cooperation Working Group with representatives from the federal, state, and provincial agencies.[24] The indicators do not focus solely on the marine ecosystem; taken together they give an indication of overall ecosystem health in the Salish Sea and the surrounding basin.

The group initially chose six indicators: population, air quality from inhalable particulates, solid waste, persistent organic pollutants in harbor seals, species at risk, and terrestrial protected areas.[25] The list was later expanded to include air quality, freshwater and marine water quality, marine species at risk, shellfish harvesting, stream flow, and toxics in the food web.[26] Each indicator is monitored by the appropriate agency on each side of the border, and data are compiled and analyzed to determine the overall status of the indicator.

Michael Rylko, who cochaired the indicators working group, noted that looking at the data from both sides of the border can paint a better picture of ecosystem trends:

When we were going to our independent data sets, we interpreted the data on the Puget Sound side in terms of "Are we holding our own? Are we losing ground? Are we improving conditions?" To some extent it's a subjective call interpreting the data. It's pretty sparse, and it's over a big geography. When we looked at how we interpreted it when we just looked at half the border, we were more optimistic.

When we put the two data sets together in the development of the 2006 indicators, we ended up seeing patterns that, when you step back, you say, "You know, that's not so good." We realized we were giving our respective interpretations too much benefit of the doubt. . . . It sounds like a little step, but we ended up doing that through all nine data sets. . . . Every indicator was negative or neutral at best. There were no positive indicators. There had not been a time on either side of the border where we had made that kind of interpretation, let alone broadly publicized it. Probably our boldest statement of the ecosystem's condition was when we worked together on it.

Forums and Networks for Interaction and Communication

Both initiatives also created new structures that enabled leaders and staff to interact across the international border. They created mechanisms within which middle-level managers and staff could communicate and collaborate, while also providing linkages to high-level officials who had sanctioned the processes. For example, the GOMC comprises representatives appointed by the governors, premiers, and federal agencies, but a working group and numerous committees and subcommittees do the bulk of the GOMC's work. These committees enable staff to interact on topics such as habitat, contaminants, and maritime activities. Other forums have spun off, including the Regional Association for Research on the Gulf of Maine, an association of institutions involved in research, management, and stewardship activities. As Mel Cote of the U.S. EPA explains, "It provides a forum not just for policy people and managers but for scientists as well. It just leads to more efficiencies among them and just more effective management ultimately."

These forums and networks provided a place to convene in a way that honored the national sovereignty and jurisdiction of the two nations and the individual states and provinces. These structures were *enabling* but *not mandating* because neither initiative possessed independent authority. Instead, they fostered shared understanding and coordination; translation to action happened via independent member activity. In essence, they created a cascade of information, priorities, and relationships, which take root by ultimately changing individual agency behavior. John Dohrmann, who served as cochair of the PSGB Task Force, explained this dynamic:

> We would do these joint studies on coastal shoreline management issues; develop long lists of recommendations that were applicable on both sides of the border. Then we had this implementation structure on the Washington side and we would just pump that right in. The next update of our management plan or biennial budget would reflect that stuff. When Washington State updated its shoreline management rules that govern all shoreline management in the state, a whole bunch of these issues and ideas that were developed through the Task Force got glued in there.
>
> It's not magical because it's the same people. To do the Task Force we'd form a technical group, we'd get the agencies to send their people who were experts to the meeting, and they would spend months hassling these issues and all reach some common ground on it. And they'd go back to their day jobs and that's what they would advise their agency directors should be done.

While their efforts are informal, by all accounts, they are powerful. Part of the effect comes from learning about others' approaches. Knowledge gained through interaction provides an ability to coordinate activities and leverage scarce resources. As Mel Cote commented: "I think that the ability to try to align our respective agencies' and organizations' missions and priorities makes a lot of sense because we can help leverage our often limited resources to a great effect if we're able to find common ground, especially across the border with our Canadian partners."

Creative solutions can result from sustained interaction. As GOMC councilor Lee Sochasky commented:

> One of the great successes of the Council is bringing people from these different jurisdictions and different backgrounds and different perspectives together, and they now understand how each other work. They can find the common ways to make things happen.
>
> The more time they spend together, the more they get to know how the other person's side works, and then they can come up with ways to solve things together. That has been a real valuable function of the Gulf of Maine Council, especially to the working groups. Now that they understand the other person's toolbox, they can go wrestling through their joint tools and find a way to do something.

GOMC coordinator Michelle Tremblay believes that transboundary communication would be minimal without the existence of the forum for interaction provided by the Council: "The federal jurisdictions, like DFO [Department of Fisheries and Oceans Canada] and NOAA, probably wouldn't talk to each other as much. They might not collaborate as much. The state and the provincial agencies would be much less aware, if aware at all, of each other's work. There wouldn't be any collaboration on joint projects because I don't think that the vehicle would exist to do it."

Similarly, a 2001 report on the PSGB International Task Force described the difference that forum had made in fostering dialogue across the international boundary:

> Short of eliminating the international border, the Puget Sound Georgia Basin International Task Force is probably working better than any other thing you could do to effect transboundary ecosystem management. Genuine effort has been made by parties on both sides of the border to be inclusive in all efforts that are relevant to the work of the Task Force. . . . In the last 10 to 15 years, practitioners have gone from barely talking to their counterparts on the other side of the border to actively participating in each other's activities.[27]

These new forums for dialogue fostered establishment of working relationships and networks between agencies and individuals with significant effects beyond the interactions in formal meetings and gatherings. As GOMC councilor alternate Mel Cote noted, "When we are developing plans and implementing programs, we probably think a little more broadly about who we will choose to engage in planning and implementation because we have a network; we have this network you can rely on to help expand your effectiveness under various authorities . . . you can be more effective if you're working with others that have resources to contribute to making your programs more effective." GOMC councilor Lee Sochasky concurs, "Political systems and legislatures are focused on their own jurisdiction. It is only by building these bridges that you're able to work within the other person's system, and come to the table, and have many sides agree to make a small change in their normal way of doing business to better the ecosystem as a whole."

Surviving the Transition from Initiation to Institutionalization

Despite these similar efforts to overcome the challenges associated with advancing marine ecosystem-based management principles across a national border, the experiences in the Gulf of Maine and Puget Sound Georgia Basin differ from one another. Whereas the GOMC continues to make progress and is seen as a valued component of the regional marine conservation landscape, the PSGB Task Force has been disbanded, replaced by new structures that also appear to be languishing. What explains the varying long-term experiences of these two initiatives? Why does the GOMC endure, having survived the transition from initiation to institutionalization, while the PSGB Task Force has faded away?

Several factors help explain the divergent pathways. The initiatives showed different levels of identity with a shared ecosystem. The GOMC was propelled by a sense of common problems and issues that never seemed to adequately develop in the PSGB Task Force. Both were buffeted by a shifting political landscape, one that the GOMC alone was able to weather. Finally, while seemingly insurmountable administrative barriers confronted both, the GOMC was more often able to find ways around these barriers. These varied experiences shed some light on what sustains MEBM across an international boundary.

A Shared Ecosystem Focus

Shared identity with a specific, well-defined watershed or region is important, since it enables a common focus and helps create bonds among those involved. In these cases, perception of the Gulf of Maine as a single, geographic space appears to have been stronger than that evident in the Puget Sound Georgia Basin initiative. GOMC councilor Priscilla Brooks identified "passion for the Gulf of Maine among the members of the Council" as a notable sustaining force for that initiative. She added, "All the agencies, NGOs, business members share a passion for this resource, and an understanding of just how important it is on a global scale and how magnificent it is."

This strong sense of regional identity associated with the Gulf was constantly being reinforced by the GOMC. For example, it published the *Gulf of Maine Times,* a quarterly newspaper for the region. Besides reminding interested people in the region of the Council's work, the *Gulf of Maine Times* helped foster a sense of shared connection and identity with the Gulf ecosystem. The GOMC website includes tools, such as the NGO Directory and People Finder, which identify institutions and agencies active in the Gulf. Their Action Plan Grants Program recognizes and offers financial support to regional nonprofit organizations whose work helps to advance GOMC's goals. All of these activities help embed a strong shared identity with the Gulf and its issues.

GOMC leaders recognize the importance of keeping people motivated, and they recognize and reward contributions. Each year, the Council presents awards to individuals and organizations in recognition of their service to the Gulf. The Gulf of Maine Visionary Awards are bestowed annually to two individuals, businesses, or organizations within each state and province bordering the Gulf in recognition of innovation, creativity, and commitment to protecting the marine environment. The Gulf of Maine Industry Award similarly recognizes businesses demonstrating innovation and leadership in improving the Gulf of Maine ecosystem. The Longard Volunteer Award is named for one of the GOMC founders and is given annually to an outstanding volunteer. The Susan Snow-Cotter Leadership Award honors coastal management professionals who exemplify outstanding leadership or mentoring.[28]

In contrast, a compelling shared identity for those involved in the Puget Sound Georgia Basin International Task Force proved elusive. There are undoubtedly many reasons why a stronger ecosystem focus was never instilled. One reason may be subtly evidenced in the initiative's name. British Columbia's priority was the Georgia Basin and the State of Washington's was Puget Sound. Some tried to create a stronger sense of a single marine ecosystem by adopting the name Salish Sea for the waters encompassing the Strait of Georgia, Puget Sound, and the Strait of Juan de Fuca, but this unifying vision never took hold during PSGB's tenure. The initiative was never able to develop deep roots as a regional ecosystem effort; instead their activities largely occurred in a parallel fashion on opposite sides of the border, focused on their respective half of the ecosystem rather than in an integrated manner.

Sustained Attention to a Common Agenda and Shared Issues

Closely connected to the idea of a strong, shared identity with the place is sustained attention to a common agenda and shared issues. The degree of concurrence on a common agenda and shared issues, and the degree of collaborative attention to those issues, varied between the two initiatives. One possible explanation for this distinction is found in their varying levels of willingness and ability to engage in joint planning.

A COMMON ACTION PLAN

The focus of the GOMC was on problems and issues in the Gulf that member organizations agreed needed attention. This focus and concurrence was instilled and reinforced by a sequence of action plans developed collaboratively. In the Gulf of Maine, the region's governors and premiers explicitly directed the GOMC to develop joint action plans. As David Keeley explained, "The initial agreement between the governors and premiers basically did two things: it created the Council and it called for the Council to create five-year plans."

This task and deliverable helped provide an immediate focus for the group. In Keeley's view, the planning process provided an opportunity to "create a common agenda for agencies to work on." Action plan goals were largely drawn from the jurisdictions' existing management plans and synthesized to create opportunities for synergies. While members describe the Council's role as "leading from behind," and its action plans provide a compass for individual member agency activities, nevertheless, they are captured in Gulf-scale plans. Five action plans have been produced since the GOMC was founded.

The experience in Puget Sound Georgia Basin differed considerably. As John Dohrmann described, "One of the early initiatives of the Task Force was to talk about joint strategic planning. We had a white paper and a meeting and the conclusion was there's no energy and no structure to implement a joint plan. The thing that's implementable is if each of us does a plan and says, 'Look, we're doing one in Puget Sound. Hey Canada, we will aggressively ask for your advice and expertise in our plan, and we're more than willing to provide the same if you choose to do a plan.'"

At bottom, divergent motivations resulted in uneven capacity for sustained effort. Some participants were motivated by a sense of concern for the ecosystem and a belief that the processes provided a unique opportunity to effect change. Others were motivated by high-level mandates that required their participation. Once these mandates weakened, their motivation to continue participating waned. From John Dohrmann's perspective, the end of the International Task Force is attributable to varying levels of commitment to a common agenda for the ecosystem: "If you look at the demise of the Puget Sound Georgia Basin International Task Force, to me it's been the mismatch between the level of interest and effort in Washington State on really taking a comprehensive approach to the ecosystem issues, and the fact that, in B.C., they really don't see it as that big of a problem and haven't launched a similar effort."

CONTINUITY AMONG PARTICIPANTS

Another factor that likely strained any sense of a common transboundary agenda was a lack of continuity among those involved. Agencies in both

British Columbia and Washington were reorganized several times during the Task Force's tenure, affecting continuity among participants. In Washington, the Puget Sound Water Quality Authority became the Puget Sound Action Team, and then the Puget Sound Partnership. Similar changes occurred on the B.C. side of the border.

These reorganizations resulted in shifting personnel assignments to the ECC and PSGB Task Force. Tom Laurie noted that he has had at least five different counterparts from British Columbia over the course of the many years he served as the Washington coordinator for the ECC. Discussing the International Task Force, John Dohrmann noted the following:

> The ebb and flow of what the province is interested in from time to time has really changed a lot over the years. From 1992 to 2007, on the Washington side we had two different cochairs of the task force. I had been a member the whole time and cochair for half the time, and maybe a third of the Washington task force members had been there the whole time. [In contrast,] eight or nine different people on the B.C. side had this put on their desk or on the corner of their desk at one time or another.

An issues orientation

Clarity about purpose also seemed to differ between the two cases. The GOMC was focused on priority issues in the Gulf ecosystem, whereas the PSGB Task Force at times seemed stymied by a procedural focus on how best to work together. It is possible that this subtle difference between the two initiatives was rooted in their early genesis. The Gulf of Maine Council was constructed in a bottom-up manner, and it was largely the managers who framed and pursued its priority objectives. They possessed a level of clarity, consistency, and commitment to addressing shared issues in the Gulf. This level of concerted focus on shared problems and issues was fleeting in the PSGB Task Force.

The PSGB Task Force's genesis as a top-down initiative of political officials who directed agencies on their respective sides of the border to work together seemed to have created a focus on *transboundary work* in contrast to *shared problems and issues*. As one observer commented, "It is noteworthy . . . that few government officials on either side of the Georgia Basin Puget Sound ecosystem have 'transboundary partnership-building' written into their job descriptions, and few, therefore, have support within their systems to undertake the continuous learning required of them." Framing the purpose of their interaction around "transboundary work" and "cross-border interaction," rather than around broader ecosystem issues begging joint attention, may have challenged the potential of the Puget Sound Georgia Basin process from the outset.

The final few years of the PSGB Task Force's history illustrate this wavering focus. As PSGB Task Force cochairs noted at both the 2003 and 2004 ECC meetings, "Commitment and participation by members on the Task Force and work group varies," and "Implementation of recommendation actions is a challenge."[29] The ECC directed the Task Force in April 2003 to "review its mandate and return with a recommendation as to the future of the group."[30] At the time, the Task Force was already in the process of developing an action plan "in response to the relative dormancy of several of the work groups." It was hoped that this action plan would "serve as a two-year work plan for revitalizing the Task Force."

Minutes of the next ECC meeting in 2004 indicate that the future of the PSGB Task Force was again discussed, including whether it should be "permanently disbanded" or "placed in abeyance until such time as an issue arises that warrants its reactivation."[31] At the time, the Task Force consisted primarily of "separate U.S. and Canadian working groups for each priority issue." Collaboration appeared to be lapsing. The Task Force report at this meeting concluded, "While communication and relationship-building facilitated by the Task Force are valuable, they do little to contribute directly to achieving the specific goals of the member agencies."[32]

Discussion of the future of the Task Force occurred again at the 2005 ECC meeting, with Task Force cochairs directed by the ECC to "look at governance options and bring back recommendations."[33] At the next meeting, John Dohrmann presented four options for "renewed collaboration," each of which acknowledged the new national emphasis on ocean and coastal issues that posed a challenge for maintaining Task Force focus on the Salish Sea.[34] Following this meeting, the PSGB Task Force was disbanded.

An effort to resuscitate transboundary collaboration occurred when the British Columbia–Washington Coastal and Ocean Task Force (COTF) was established to replace the PSGB Task Force in June 2007 by agreement of the premier and governor. As the name implies, the scope of the COTF was broadened beyond the Salish Sea to include the outer coasts of British Columbia and Washington. Its goals, however, mirrored those of its predecessor in emphasizing increased communication and collaboration on ocean and coastal issues.[35]

A draft three-year plan for COTF was presented at the 2008 ECC meeting. Ironically, the following was the first item in the draft plan: "Examine regional oceans governance models drawing from lessons learned from the Gulf of Maine Council and other transboundary or regional oceans management arrangements."[36] Since the 2008 ECC meeting, however, the COTF has faded from view. "I have to admit that I think it might be a virtual task force as opposed to a real task force," noted cochair Kathleen Drew in 2009. Chris Townsend of the Puget Sound Partnership echoed Drew's perception: "The COTF is pretty informal and it's frankly not extremely active at the moment."

The tenuous state of the COTF does not mean that communication and collaboration on marine issues no longer occurs across the British Columbia and Washington border. In particular, the biennial Salish Sea Ecosystem Conference has grown in prominence over time, with attendance of over 1,100 scientists, managers, and policy makers. This conference has elevated the visibility of and concern for the shared Salish Sea ecosystem on both sides of the border, and its role in identifying issues, advancing knowledge, and fostering communication has expanded since the inaugural conference in 2003. Nonetheless, what has been lost is the forum for structured and sustained collaboration to advance action on issues of shared concern that originally prompted establishment of the Puget Sound Georgia Basin International Task Force.

Accomplishments That Sustain Engagement

Once involvement in an initiative begins to lag, a vicious cycle is set in motion. If people stop showing up, little can be accomplished, and it becomes less useful for others to keep participating. Although a handful may remain committed, they seldom can make needed progress alone.

Participation was sustained in the GOMC because participating agencies and individuals found its activities valuable to achieving their own interests as well as those of the overall Gulf. Few of the participants have active engagement in a transboundary initiative as a major item of their job description. As Ted Diers, who assumed the GOMC secretariat position in June 2009, noted, "It's all side-of-the-desk kind of work." As such, it has to reward those who participate with a sense of accomplishment; without accomplishment, attention will turn to other priorities.

The GOMC is best described as an *enabling* organization. That is, it enables the actions of those organizations with authority and jurisdiction over resources in the Gulf of Maine to undertake priority projects that fulfill their own responsibilities but also benefit the Gulf of Maine ecosystem. Seed money for restoration and other projects generates accomplishments that in turn motivate continued engagement. As Ted Diers explained, "We fund core activities which . . . catalyze other things to happen around them." For example, the GOMC–NOAA Habitat Restoration Grants Program provides grants to support marine, coastal, and riverine habitat restoration in Maine, Massachusetts, and New Hampshire. Grants are strategically directed to groups with interest and capacity to implement projects that further GOMC objectives. Grants typically range between $40,000 and $70,000, with a cap of $100,000, and may be used to support feasibility, planning, engineering and design, implementation, monitoring, or any combination of these activities. These grants require a 1:1 nonfederal match. As David Keeley explained:

> We put out something like two hundred and fifty to three hundred thousand dollars a year in grants to local groups, and the match on that is really truly phenomenal. The leveraging that's going on really excites NOAA and, as a result, when we go to re-up, they're like, "Wow, compared to other regions around the country, you guys are doing really well." The reviews that they have done of our program have been really strong.

It is estimated that the program has leveraged $3 to $5 on average for every NOAA dollar invested. Additionally, in 2009, the GOMC developed the Gulf of Maine Restoration and Protection Initiative to develop a unified restoration strategy for the Gulf. The Initiative involves public and private groups on both sides of the border and is intended to strategically position the organization to receive restoration funds as they become available. As noted on the GOMC website, "The 2010 Federal Budget line item of $475,000,000 for Great Lakes restoration provides a powerful example of the importance of having a comprehensive plan in place."[37]

An Organizational Structure That Maintains Focus and Propels Progress

The GOMC evolved a structure and set of roles and responsibilities that build a shared sense of ownership in the Council and its activities while avoiding the "side-of-the-desk problem" that both the GOMC and the PSGB Task Force confronted. A GOMC secretariat was established that gave leadership responsibility to each state and province on a rotating two-year cycle. As such, the states and provinces share the administrative burden of the process. Most important, the rotating leadership helps to avoid a perception that the initiative is really just window dressing for one jurisdiction's interests. The secretariat is responsible for convening Council and working group meetings and developing meeting agendas and materials. It provides leadership in developing GOMC two-year work plans and five-year action plans, and assigns chairs for GOMC committees and working groups. Its rotating cycle and central role in initiative management instills ownership and responsibility for the process across all member states and provinces; in so doing, it keeps them engaged.

In the PSGB Task Force, multiple organizational layers had been established to encourage communication about transboundary issues. However, the existence of multiple, overlapping transboundary structures, including the ECC, task forces, and Statement of Cooperation Working Group, while all well intended, may have been "too much of a good thing." They appear to have created confusion about roles and responsibilities and seemed duplicative to participating staff. Since these transboundary organizations typically involve the same individuals, they placed a significant burden on agency staff that had to attend multiple meetings. Achieving substantive accomplishments is difficult when time is consumed by meetings with different agendas, focus points, and priorities. As Chris Townsend pointed out:

> It's confusing having all these different levels of coordination and different agreements. Often people from the Statement of Cooperation group do attend the Coastal and Ocean Task Force meetings, especially if they're on a particular topic, and Coastal and Ocean Task Force people attend Statement of Cooperation things. It seems to be redundant. I can't say that it's helped or hurt, but I think it could be done better if it were coordinated and really only one group that's dealing with these issues.

Rather than creating synergies, the many collaborative initiatives appeared to be taking the wind out of each other's sails. "It does not make any sense when you have limited resources and a fairly general mandate," Townsend explains. Rylko concurs: "It's really inefficient having a bunch of bilateral processes, especially when each bilateral process goes through a broad multilateral invitation list. Everyone is being invited to everyone else's bilateral. It's diluting them in a way. We're really not getting behind one process that we can stand behind and support in a multilateral fashion."

In recent years, there has been a new focus on ocean policy. Driven by the Canadian Oceans Act, the President's Commission on Ocean Policy, and the Pew Oceans Commission, this focus on the outer coast in addition to the inland Salish Sea has taken some of the energy out of the transboundary initiatives that focus only on the Puget Sound Georgia Basin ecosystem. Speaking about the end of the PGSB International Task Force, Jamie Alley noted that both sides were running out of steam:

> On the Canadian side, the federal government was heavily engaged in deciding how they wanted to deliver the Oceans Act, which had been passed in '97, and how they were going to regionalize that. A lot of the Province's time and attention turned to: "What's the federal government up to and how are they shaping their program?" On the Washington State side, I think that the Puget Sound Action Team was also running out of steam. They were about to transition to the Puget Sound Partnership, and then the governor was turning her mind to, "What about the outer coast?"

While the ECC was initially effective in establishing communication lines and building relationships, it suffered in later years when its formal meetings became less frequent. As Tom Laurie, Washington coordinator for the ECC, explained: "It's a pretty porous border. The problem of the ECC is that it's built as if we only needed to talk to B.C. twice a year, when in fact, it's happening all the time, and that is when it needs to happen."

Changing policies and political administrations have also affected the Gulf of Maine Council. While the Council has been successful so far at opportunistically adapting its process to fit new priorities, the U.S. National Ocean Policy and Implementation Plan[38] and the Canadian Ocean Action Plan have the potential to produce institutional changes that will undercut the GOMC.

Ownership That Weathers Political Transitions

Both the GOMC and the PSGB Task Force were buffeted by changes in their political landscapes. New national administrations came and went; new governors and premiers were elected at the state and provincial levels. It is possible that the Task Force's origins as a high-level political initiative made it more challenging for them to navigate the new political context as new political leaders took over. Shifting policy priorities quickly introduced ambiguity about the PSGB Task Force's direction. Some Task Force members became uncertain about their role and responsibilities and began questioning the value of continued involvement.

Ownership and commitment to the PSGB process seemed largely to reside at the ECC and premier/governor levels. When transitions occurred at these levels, new priorities emerged, and commitment to the old process wavered. Kathleen Drew offered one explanation for the demise of the Task Force: "There was not any focus from the governor's or the premier's office. It had kind of settled into a level of bureaucracy that we did not think was going to accomplish high-level goals."

Jamie Alley explained the benefits and challenges associated with their high-level genesis:

> One of the important features that people don't remember as well as they should is the importance that the British Columbia–Washington Environmental Cooperation Council and those things that were under its purview reported to the premier and the governor, rather than the heads of the agencies. That really helped to give it a profile in the first phase from the early '90s through to the end of the twentieth century. I think things ran out of steam because some of those relationships between governors and premiers sort of fell apart.

While the GOMC was largely created and hence "owned" by midlevel managers in the region who saw it as an effective vehicle for advancing their work, the PSGB Task Force was created by high-level officials that eventually left office. The EPA's Michael Rylko commented that one thing "that kept us a little off balance was the political wave that came through in the last decade. It was a good time for them and not so much a good time for us, and then it was a good time for us and not so much a good time for them, just on a national political level."

In 2008, the Canadian Parliament was dissolved unexpectedly, causing a new election and postponement of some government activities, including international work. Agencies in both the province and the state were reorganized several times during the Task Force's tenure, affecting continuity among participants. In Washington, what began as the Puget Sound Water Quality Authority became the Puget Sound Action Team, and then the Puget Sound Partnership, with expanding mandates. New leaders often want to leave their mark with new programs, rather than by adopting their predecessors' initiatives.

The PSGB transboundary initiative might have weathered these changes had it been successful at creating the conditions that sustained the GOMC: an effective structure and set of motivations and accomplishments that encouraged ongoing participation. However, without these, when the top-down inducements stopped, collaboration stopped. "They did not find traction," commented EPA's Michael Rylko. "It seemed to have petered out over time," commented Kathleen Drew. The PSGB effort did not survive its transition from initiation to sustained work on issues in the transboundary ecosystem.

Creativity and Commitment in Navigating Funding and Other Bureaucratic Barriers

The unique institutional and procedural challenges of working across a national boundary need to be faced with an extra measure of creativity; whether that occurs is largely a function of the level of commitment of the individuals involved in the initiative, and the degree to which they receive support or opposition from leadership. In the Gulf of Maine, there was sufficient will to think outside the box in addressing critical challenges. In Puget Sound Georgia Basin, while some participants tried valiantly to keep the initiative afloat, they were unable to rally sufficient commitment from others to find ways forward.

Many PSGB Task Force participants lamented their inability to effectively fund their transboundary work even at the most basic level. As Kathleen Drew observed, "Our budgets would not allow us to travel out of the state much less out of the country. That's a real challenge." They were never able to find a way to secure or distribute funding to incentivize partner activities. Part of their frustration was rooted in bureaucracy associated with aligning budget cycles, making it difficult to implement work plans. EPA staff member Michael Rylko explains:

> When we first signed our statement of cooperation, we had an annual work plan, just a one-year horizon. We didn't recognize until we started implementing it, that our fiscal work years cut that in half. We really didn't have a whole work year. We had the beginning of our work year and the end of theirs. It doesn't sound like a big deal, but you couldn't align fiscal decisions. It was ridiculous. That was one problem. When we looked more closely at the province and the state's bilateral agreement, they had fiscal years that were also six months apart, but in the opposite seasons from our federal ones. We had a new fiscal year starting every season among the four of us. That encouraged us to look at a two-year work plan. But even then, you see the challenge. It's hard to integrate a formal process when your respective processes are sort of out of sync.

Chris Townsend of the Puget Sound Partnership similarly commented: "The Task Force doesn't bring in money, and it doesn't make spending money across the border easier. There's no mechanism right now to spend money, and no easy mechanism to spend money across the border." Without the ability to invest in on-the-ground projects so that participants can see measurable change, it is extremely difficult to sustain collaborative efforts, even without the complication of an international border.

In navigating similar funding obstacles as those confronted by the PSGB Task Force, the Gulf of Maine Council created an innovative administrative arrangement so that funding could be solicited and managed across the border. Funding was obviously needed to support the Council's work, but a pressing question was who could receive and manage the needed funds. Because the GOMC was a voluntary organization that straddled two different countries, two parallel associations were established in 1998, one on each side of the border, to manage funds and contracts and receive grants and contributions for the GOMC: the Association of Canadian Delegates to the GOMC, and the Gulf of Maine Association (GOMA), a U.S. 501(c)(3) nonprofit entity. The GOMA board of directors includes both U.S. and Canadian representatives. As they describe, "The Canadian Association processes contracts from Canadian funding sources and transfers funds to be managed by the Gulf of Maine Association. Both Associations comply with their own bylaws and nonprofit/charitable organization guidelines in their respective countries."[39]

The GOMC has been able to develop a diversified funding portfolio, and opportunistically targets multiple sources of funds. Their budget, Keeley commented, "is a patchwork quilt," and annually ranges from $500,000 to $1,000,000, cobbled together from annual dues, congressional earmarks, and Canadian agency contributions. Grant proposals have been written to various competitive programs on both sides of the border; significant funding has been received for restoration projects. Additional financial support has come from private groups, individuals, and foundations. "We are opportunistic feeders," Keeley explained, "looking for funds and writing proposals. Episodic funding—one-time funding—probably accounts for a couple hundred thousand dollars a year."

The GOMC was also fairly effective at adapting to other opportunities and challenges over time. They established working groups to tackle individual issues and engage others with expertise. They developed and revised action plans that helped to guide and inform member activities. With time their organizational structure and activities became more sophisticated and refined as they learned what was needed and what was possible. For example, the five successive five-year action plans evidence an expanded under-standing of the Gulf ecosystem and more strategic and sophisticated goals and objectives. David Keeley described the evolution of the group's focus:

> In the first five-year plan, we were just lucky to get three states, two provinces and the federal agencies to agree. . . . It's really in the last two plans where we began to insert measurable objectives. For ex-ample, "Over the next five years, we'll see a three percent increase in the rate of restoration of tidal salt marshes from 780,000 acres to 1.2 million acres." Previous to that it was, "We want to be restoring habitats." Kind of mom and apple pie.

Conclusion

The Gulf of Maine Council on the Marine Environment and the Puget Sound Georgia Basin International Task Force initiatives shared many characteristics. Both were voluntary, transboundary structures meant to enhance ecosystem-scale considerations in marine resource management through improved cross-border communication and coordination among resource agencies and ministries. Governors, premiers, and national gov-ernments sanctioned both, but only one of the processes endures. Their differing trajectories highlight several critical attributes of sustained and ef-fective transboundary collaboration in ecosystem management.

People collaborate when they perceive an incentive to do so. The early motivations of participants were many and varied in both the Gulf of Maine and the Puget Sound Georgia Basin. Both initiatives started with great promise. Capitalizing on that promise, however, required attention to the unique challenges facing marine ecosystem-based management within a transboundary ecosystem. A strong sense of place and shared sense of re-sponsibility for the broad ecosystem are prerequisites. Visible accomplish-ments that matter to those involved help to sustain engagement. An effec-tive organizational structure that maintains focus and promotes progress is essential. Sustained commitment at all levels is needed so that inevitable political transitions can be weathered.

While the Puget Sound Georgia Basin International Task Force ap-pears to have begun with similar motivations as the Gulf of Maine Council on the Marine Environment, they encountered many obstacles to sustain-ing those motivations. The initiative never fully bridged the border that bi-sected the Salish Sea, instead focusing attention primarily on priority activities on separate sides of the border. While several of those involved at the management and implementation levels had embraced the transboundary ecosystem-based management objectives and were committed to furthering those objectives, the revolving door of participants "assigned" to the Task Force created a context with varied understanding and commitment to the process. New governors and premiers brought new priorities and initiatives to the region. The parallel national processes between the U.S. EPA and Environment Canada in the PSGB region introduced a duplicate set of meetings and activities with similar objectives. What was expected of the Task Force became unclear, and eventually it was disbanded.

Chapter 3

Mobilizing a Multistate Partnership in the Gulf of Mexico

In the Gulf of Mexico, an innovative multistate partnership has focused attention and energy on an ecosystem of national, regional, and local importance. While large-scale efforts involving more than one state may not have the complication of an international boundary, as described in chapter 2, they still need to navigate complicated jurisdictional factors to initiate and sustain collaboration. The Gulf of Mexico Alliance (GOMA) is a voluntary arrangement that has no authority to mandate action or regulate uses. However, it has provided an opportunity for the five Gulf States to identify and pursue shared objectives at an ecosystem scale by pooling expertise, attracting funding, and finding synergies within their individual state policies and programs.

Before establishment of GOMA, the region had received comparatively little federal funding and attention relative to other marine and coastal areas, such as the Chesapeake Bay and Puget Sound. The relative obscurity of the Gulf of Mexico in congressional budget debates was surprising given the physical and economic importance of the Gulf, since it is the ninth largest water body in the world. The Gulf's coastline extends along five American states, an expanse totaling over 47,000 miles, including the shores of all barrier islands, wetlands, and inland bays.[1] It drains 60 percent of the country's fresh river water, which arrives at the Gulf's shores in thirty-three major river systems.[2] The Gulf has one of the largest shrimp fisheries in the world, and it hosts ports and shipping lanes that move bil-

---

Chapter coauthored by Sarah McKearnan and Steven Yaffee.

lions of dollars of goods—including oil and gas—between the coast and inland cities and towns.

Signs that the Gulf's resources are under intense pressure had been proliferating for decades. A large area of oxygen-depleted water appears off the coast of Louisiana each year, killing fish and other marine life. The Gulf's signature coastal habitats, such as marshes and wetlands, are deteriorating, harming the coast's wildlife and its protection from storms. Several species are listed as threatened or endangered, among them sperm whales, some species of sea turtles, Gulf sturgeon, and smalltooth sawfish. And fish stocks that represent an important contribution to U.S. fisheries are dropping in abundance. National periodicals (e.g., *Time* magazine) have taken notice, publishing articles that sound warning bells (e.g., "The Gulf's Growing 'Dead Zone'"[3]).

The best explanation for why this large marine ecosystem had failed to capture the attention of Congress can be found by looking at the history of local efforts to protect its resources. Until the multistate Gulf of Mexico Alliance was established, earlier efforts were dispersed and lacked regional coordination. Environmental agencies in the Gulf States and a small collection of academic and nonprofit institutions worked on Gulf issues in separate spheres. Elected leaders did not see a critical need to coordinate their diverse programs, or to lobby Congress as a group for funding to address the Gulf's environmental threats at an ecosystem scale. The Gulf of Mexico Program, led by the U.S. Environmental Protection Agency, had been in existence since 1988 but was largely seen as a top-down initiative of one federal agency. While the Program had some success at initiating cross-state collaboration, it struggled at building a shared regional identity or sense of ownership of ecosystem-scale problems and management strategies.

That history took an abrupt turn in 2004. Spurred by Florida's governor, Jeb Bush, all five Gulf State governors began talking about how a new regional initiative might catalyze a higher level of attention to the Gulf in their states and in the country as a whole. Together, the five governors launched the Gulf of Mexico Alliance. Then came the violent storms of 2005—more than thirteen hurricanes, including the infamous Katrina and Rita. Those storms put the Gulf Coast squarely in the national spotlight because of the immense human tragedy and dislocation they caused, and also because it was clear that a lack of coordinated ecosystem-based management had left these areas more vulnerable than they should have been. The storms became the governors' rallying call to begin working across state borders.

Four years after that fateful storm season, the Gulf Coast again experienced a human and environmental catastrophe. In mid-2010, the disabled

Deepwater Horizon well, owned by British Petroleum, spewed some-where between 94 and 184 million gallons of oil into the Gulf's waters in a span of three months.[4] As BP and many governmental agencies began to address the impacts of that unprecedented spill, the benefits of having a robust cross-state collaboration in the region seemed indisputable. The young Gulf of Mexico Alliance provided an organizational foundation for complex recovery and restoration efforts at an ecosystem scale, and a set of relationships that facilitated the work ahead.

How did a region notable for its lack of coordination in the face of serious ecological and economic issues become organized and begin to act on ecosystem-scale problems? How has it navigated tricky state–state and federal–state relationships to build a shared sense of ownership that con-tinues to motivate action? How has it sustained collaboration as political leadership has changed and agency budgets have been cut?

The Environmental Protection Agency's Gulf of Mexico Program Initiates Cross-State Collaboration

The first efforts to promote a regional approach to ecosystem management in the Gulf of Mexico occurred in 1988, when the U.S. Environmental Protection Agency (EPA) invited the Gulf States to get involved in its new Gulf of Mexico Program. Modeled after its other regional programs to pro-tect large freshwater and marine ecosystems in the Great Lakes and the Chesapeake Bay, the Gulf of Mexico Program (GMP) was envisioned as a way to catalyze a "regional partnership of federal, state, local, and public entities committed to improving the environmental health of the Gulf in concert with economic development."[5] It would create a new forum where federal and state agencies could collaborate with nonprofit organizations and other stakeholders on actions to protect and restore Gulf resources, all incentivized by EPA funding for "targeted strategic action."[6]

For the seventeen years between its official launch and the formation of the state-led Gulf of Mexico Alliance, the GMP pursued public education, scientific investigation, and protection and restoration projects with some success: restoration of 6,662 acres of habitat, development of uniform public health advisories for shellfish consumption, detection and tracking of offshore algal blooms, and development of demonstration projects to address the impacts of on-site sewage systems.[7] Perhaps even more impor-tantly, it created a forum where senior staff from different state agencies sat side by side and talked about ecosystem-scale issues in the Gulf.

Many of those now centrally involved in the Gulf of Mexico Alliance believe that the GMP was important in preparing the ground for a state-led ecosystem-based initiative. For example, Larry McKinney, lead for the Alliance's Ecosystems Integration and Assessment Team, and the director of the Harte Institute for Gulf of Mexico Studies at Texas A&M University, believes it fundamentally shifted relationships between the state and federal actors that had a stake in the long-term health of the Gulf. "It was the first time that EPA invited the states in," McKinney explained. "And it was the first place where all the state agencies came together to serve on committees."[8] Nonetheless, the GMP was never able to gain sufficient traction to become the go-to place for marine ecosystem-based management. While GMP still exists and plays an important facilitative role in the Gulf of Mexico Alliance and other programs in the region, it was not until the state-led Alliance was created that significant focus and coordinated activity took hold at the state level.

Impetus for the Gulf of Mexico Alliance

In April 2004, Florida governor Jeb Bush sent a letter to his fellow Gulf State governors with a bold idea: all five Gulf States should join together in a partnership to tackle the Gulf's growing environmental problems. Addressed to Governors Bob Riley of Alabama, Kathleen Blanco of Louisiana, Haley Barbour of Mississippi, and Rick Perry of Texas, the letter argued that the best way to sustain a healthy and economically strong Gulf Coast was for the Gulf States to work across borders in a well-coordinated regional initiative. Although there was already a federal program working to enhance regional coordination in the protection and restoration of Gulf resources, Bush argued that the states should form their own initiative.

All four governors agreed to Bush's proposal. In the winter of 2005, they met for the first time to discuss the Gulf as an ecosystem needing their coordinated assistance. They formed the Gulf of Mexico Alliance in February, and in April, federal agencies convened their own intra-agency working group to support the Alliance's future work. A scant twelve months later, the governors and the working group jointly released the first ever Gulf of Mexico Action Plan.

The speed with which the Alliance formed and got to work is remarkable, especially given the fact that this occurred during the massive disruption and dislocation caused by Hurricanes Rita and Katrina. What were the circumstances that led the governors to turn their collective attention to these resources off their shores? Since EPA's Gulf of Mexico Program already existed with some success at fostering cross-state dialogue, why did Jeb Bush decide to propose a brand new initiative? What were the motivations behind his proposal?

Two major reasons explain why a new initiative was developed. First, Jeb Bush, and several entrepreneurial advisors leading his Department of Environmental Protection, saw a unique political opportunity in 2004 to bring new federal resources to the region. Second, the Gulf of Mexico Program's very identity as a creature of the Environmental Protection Agency may have inevitably constrained how well it could build bold state leadership to begin tackling some of the Gulf's worsening ecological problems. Florida wanted a regional collaboration that was clearly in the hands of the states themselves.

The Pursuit of Federal Resources

In Florida and the other Gulf States, the previous decade had witnessed growing discontent about the lack of federal funding for addressing the Gulf's environmental problems. State leaders were frustrated that the Gulf of Mexico had gone virtually unnoticed in the federal budget process, despite its ecological problems and the measurable impacts they were having on the economy, both locally and nationally. State leaders had noticed that the Chesapeake Bay, Puget Sound, and other large marine ecosystems had received a steady flow of federal funds.

Unfortunately, EPA's Gulf of Mexico Program was not able to reverse the Gulf's fortunes in the federal budget process. Although the program garnered enough funds to maintain a program staff, issue small grants, and manage a few projects of its own, its budget was tiny in comparison to similar federally funded ocean and coastal partnerships in other parts of the country.

Margaret Davidson, the director of the National Oceanic and Atmospheric Administration's (NOAA's) Coastal Services Center, an office that provided extensive support to the Alliance during its formative years, points out that the federal program's geographic structure may have contributed to the difficulty of securing large federal appropriations. It straddles two of EPA's fourteen regions—regions four and six. Davidson suggests that this may have made it difficult for the program to secure the kind of focused support and advocacy from state congressional delegations that it likely would have received had it been fully situated in a single region. Without aggressive efforts on the part of the delegations in all five states, the program was destined to have limited resources for addressing large-scale ecological problems.

Governor Jeb Bush believed that a new partnership led by the Gulf States had the best chance of getting the federal government to elevate the Gulf in its environmental funding priorities. He explicitly mentioned this possibility in his 2004 letter to Governors Blanco, Barbour, Perry, and Riley: "If our state governments take the initiative, we can ensure the effort is steered primarily by the states bordering the Gulf—those most knowledgeable and affected by the conditions of the Gulf. I am hoping the federal government, seeing our partnership and commitment, will help us pursue our priorities."[9]

Phil Bass, at one time the state policy director for the Gulf of Mexico Program and a federal representative on several Alliance teams, explained that the potential to better compete for limited and much sought after congressional appropriations was one of the main arguments that Florida used when trying to persuade other Gulf States of the value of collaborating on ecosystem issues. He reported that Colleen Castille, the director of Florida's Department of Environmental Protection, first raised the possibility of forming the Alliance in a meeting of state department directors organized by GMP: "When Colleen broached the subject, the first response was 'but we already have a Gulf Program and we are all involved in it. Why do we need another one?' She argued that this was an opportunity. If we can provide more and stronger state leadership, we can get some of the resources the Gulf needs."

In fact, Davidson suggested that the director of the Gulf of Mexico Program, Brian Griffiths, also thought that a new state-led initiative was the best way to get resources flowing to the region: "Brian Griffiths was looking at all of these programs getting a ton of money (the Chesapeake, Great Lakes, Puget Sound) and the Gulf not getting any money. He was talking to [Florida DEP staff member] Kacky [Andrews] about trying to make something happen, legitimize his program and get more funds in."

Confidence in the potential success of a state-led initiative was motivated in part by recent developments in the George W. Bush administration. In September 2004, a U.S. Ocean Commission appointed by President Bush released its final report recommending development of a national ocean policy. The report argued that the current state-by-state approach to marine management was not working, and that an ecosystem-based approach was urgently needed to coordinate goal-setting, scientific research, and management actions across jurisdictional and organizational lines. "The voluntary establishment of regional ocean councils . . . would facilitate the development of regional goals and priorities and improve responses to regional issues," the report noted.[10]

In December 2004, the Bush administration followed up on the Commission's recommendations by releasing a U.S. Ocean Action Plan. This report was even more pointed in its support for regional ocean governance throughout the country. Its list of planned short-term actions included the following: "Support a Regional Partnership in the Gulf of Mexico," and it committed administration officials to meet with representatives of the Gulf States to explore "partnership opportunities."[11]

The fact that Florida governor Jeb Bush was the brother of the president likely enhanced his own personal hope and confidence about the prospect of receiving federal funding. There could be no denying that the region's prospects for tapping federal assistance had never looked better.

The Pursuit of State Control

Another key motivation for Jeb Bush and his staff was that a new Gulf of Mexico Alliance could be fully directed by the states. While the existing Gulf of Mexico Program was intended to engage all five Gulf States at the highest levels of their leadership, it was still fundamentally a federal program. Senior managers from EPA steered its day-to-day work, with input from state leaders and other stakeholders.

Phil Bass acknowledged that the Gulf of Mexico Program faced challenges as it tried to get state leaders to the table. The smaller states—Louisiana, Mississippi, and Alabama—were fully engaged. They sent the heads of their environmental, coastal, and fish and wildlife agencies to key meetings. It was harder, he reported, to secure the same level of participation from Florida and Texas; they sent junior staff rather than agency heads.

A new regional partnership independent of EPA's Gulf of Mexico Program would have many advantages for the states. They would have the ability to align the work of the Alliance with their own interests; they could select the issues they wanted to work on, organize the structure of the initiative in the way that they wanted, and make key decisions.

Shared Concerns and New Opportunities Prompt Gulf State Engagement

Considerable outreach was needed with the directors and senior staff of the major environmental and coastal agencies in Texas, Alabama, Mississippi, and Louisiana to persuade them to embrace Florida's idea. Several factors help explain why the four other states ultimately did decide to support Florida's proposal, and invest substantial staff time to get it started. First, Florida's arguments about the benefits of launching a more state-centered program were clearly influential. They had seen the difficulty of getting uniform participation across the Gulf in EPA's Gulf of Mexico Program. Bass believed that "a compelling issue for the smaller states was—if it brings Florida and Texas to the table, we are for it."

The arguments about the prospects for securing congressional appropriations also resonated. In the core group that participated in early meetings about the concept of the Alliance were Brian Griffiths of the Gulf of Mexico Program and Margaret Davidson from NOAA's Coastal Services Center. By their very presence, they signaled that the federal government would likely support this new partnership and help it grow.

Finally, there was increasing media attention to environmental degradation in the Gulf, and citizens and constituencies in each state wanted action, especially on the issues that most affected coastal towns and cities. For example, an expanding dead zone was resulting in dramatic declines in shrimp catch, while red tides and high levels of microbial pathogens in coastal waters were causing beach and shellfish bed closures and threatening local coastal economies. Gulf state governors were increasingly in the spotlight on their management of coastal and marine resources, as reporters began asking how these problems would affect the economies of the states.

The hurricanes in the summer of 2005 left little doubt that the Gulf States shared significant issues in common. They were vulnerable to storm damage, and articles in popular periodicals suggested that global warming might make coastal storms even more destructive. In a prescient moment, Senator Mary Landrieu (D-LA) stood up before her colleagues in Congress and said, "We are telling you and begging this Senate and this Congress to recognize benefits Louisiana provides to the nation. . . . If Louisiana does not receive help, the wetlands will disappear, and the people of Louisiana will be sitting ducks for future floods and storms."[12] All five Gulf States were vulnerable: one of the major points that Jeb Bush's senior staff used to sell the concept of a state-led alliance was the need to preserve the capacity of Gulf ecosystems to provide services like storm protection.

The seriousness of these problems, their potential to strain the economies of the Gulf's coastal communities, and the growing concern about them in the public at large all suggested that the time was ripe for aggressive state leadership to save the Gulf. So the Gulf State governors agreed to launch the Gulf of Mexico Alliance together. Importantly, the Gulf of

Mexico Program agreed to support it. It offered staff support to help the Alliance convene the meetings needed to get up and running, and it offered grants explicitly targeted toward advancing its work.

First Step: Establishing Goals and Prioritizing Issues

The five Gulf State governors formally kicked off the new Gulf of Mexico Alliance in February 2005. GOMA aimed to increase regional collaboration among the five states of Florida, Alabama, Mississippi, Louisiana, and Texas in order to enhance the ecological and economic health of the region. While Mexico was not invited to join the Alliance at the start, the governors recognized the potential for their new organization to serve as a forum for increased binational cooperation with the six Mexican states on common problems such as red tide.[13]

The goal of achieving sustainable Gulf economies is emphasized in many of the materials about the Alliance. After the record-setting hurricane season in 2005, there was a keen awareness of how vulnerable the Gulf Coast's cities and towns were, and how much they needed ecosystem services like storm protection from wetlands. The Alliance began with a strong commitment to protect the economic vitality of the Gulf Coast by protecting its ecological health, and ensuring that the tourism and fishing industries would not be forever damaged and diminished by problems like pathogen contamination on beaches, and hypoxia in key fishing grounds.

At the summit meeting that formally launched the Alliance in the spring of 2005, the governors announced an agreement to address five priority issues through regional collaboration. They also charged their agencies with the ambitious task of completing an action plan to address those priorities within a rigorous deadline of one year. The action plan would be the vehicle for identifying which scientific studies and programs in these five issue areas would most benefit from cooperation across state borders. After the release of its first action plan in 2006, the Alliance added a sixth issue—coastal community resilience—in keeping with its deep concern about adapting to and addressing ecological problems that impact coastal communities. There were six priority issues at that time:

> Water quality for healthy beaches and seafood
> Environmental education
> Nutrient impacts to coastal ecosystems

Habitat conservation and restoration
Ecosystems integration and assessment
Coastal community resilience

Notably absent from the initial set of priority issues selected by the governors were any that were likely to trigger sharp contention, such as how to manage the fishing industry to address depleted fishing stocks.[14]

Leadership on priority issues was divided among the states. Each state developed a white paper on its chosen issue, outlining what the issue was, why regional cooperation was needed, and what kinds of scientific investigations or actions were needed to make progress. These white papers became a platform for dialogue about how the states should combine their efforts, and what resources they would need.

The priority issues created a framework that the Alliance uses to define its strategies. The first action plan is tightly organized around the initial five issues. For each issue, the plan lists a "long-term Alliance partnership goal," and then a small list of specific strategies. For each strategy, the plan presents desired thirty-six-month outcomes (the duration of the plan), and a statement referred to as the Action Blueprint and Commitments. The second action plan has a somewhat different organization but offers the same kind of rigorous organization of goals, strategies, and outcomes for each issue.

Developing an Organizational Structure to Sustain Collaboration

At its core, the Gulf of Mexico Alliance is a voluntary forum for exchanging information about the Gulf and the problems that impact its ecological health, discussing and debating solutions to those problems, and planning coordinated actions. It has no authority to compel changes in management; rather, authority lies with the individual Gulf States. It makes recommendations to state and federal agencies and depends on member agencies to implement actions. Without explicit authority and given a history of uncoordinated action dominated by individual states, how has GOMA gained traction?

One answer to this question lies in the structure adopted to formalize and enable collaboration among the states and federal government (fig. 3-1). This structure balances involvement of higher- and lower-level officials and state and federal agencies, and it provides a focus on the six prior-

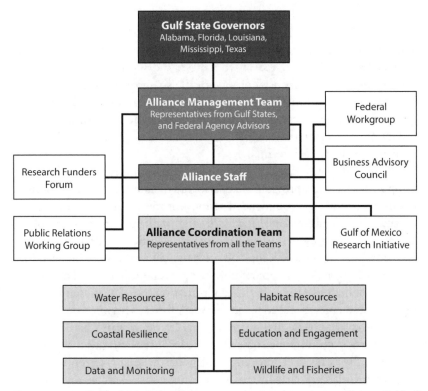

Figure 3-1. Gulf of Mexico Alliance, organizational structure. (From Gulf of Mexico Alliance, http://www.gulfofmexicoalliance.org/about-us/organization/.)

ity issues. Numerous "teams" were created, each comprising representatives of all five states and at least two federal agencies.

The Alliance Management Team

The Alliance Management Team has the most important decision-making role. It is the vehicle through which the governors of the five Gulf States stay apprised of the effort and provide it with high-level guidance. Each governor has appointed two designees—a regular representative and an alternate—to represent him or her at the Alliance Management Team's meetings. These gubernatorial representatives are heads of key environmental agencies, such as Florida's secretary of the Department of Environmental Protection, Texas's commissioner of environmental quality, and Mississippi's director of the Department of Marine Resources.

The Six Priority Issue Teams

The Alliance Management Team provides policy-level guidance to six priority issue teams, which are the day-to-day workhorses of the initiative. Each priority issue team is focused on one of the six priority issues. Each Gulf state has taken responsibility for the work of one of the priority issue teams. In practice, one or several state leads appointed by the states (usually senior program managers within their environmental, coastal, or fish and wildlife agencies) facilitate each team.

State leads take charge of getting their state's priority issue team to develop an annual work program. They also lead their teams in deliberations to reach agreement on recommended actions for the governors' action plans. Finally, they are accountable for facilitating implementation of the plans, and tracking progress on specific recommended actions addressing their issue. In addition to these leads, the priority issue teams now all have full-time coordinators, also appointed by the states and funded by the National Oceanographic and Atmospheric Administration (NOAA), to provide staffing to team members and to help push work forward between meetings.

State leads convene their teams frequently, often as much as every two weeks. Participation can be somewhat fluid from meeting to meeting, but every priority issue team meeting usually has at least one representative from each Gulf state, usually a manager or scientist from an environmental, coastal, or fish and wildlife agency. In addition to representatives of governmental agencies, there are often independent research organizations, universities, and nonprofit organizations represented.

The Alliance Coordination Team

Finally, a new team was added to this detailed organizational hierarchy after the Alliance released its first action plan. Called the Alliance Coordination Team, its purpose is to form a communication bridge between the members of the priority issue teams and the most senior Alliance decision makers that sit on the Alliance Management Team. It includes all of the priority issue team state leads and federal cofacilitators, as well as four designated coordinators, whose job is to attend Alliance Management Team meetings and bring forth issues and perspectives from the priority issue teams. The Alliance Coordination Team keeps the Alliance Management Team apprised of what the priority issue teams are working on, and tees up issues and decisions when priority issue teams need direct Alliance Management Team input.

More fundamentally, the Alliance Coordination Team is a way to limit the demands placed on high-level officials while providing adequate guidance to the priority issue teams. Steve Wolfe, coordinator of the Water Quality Priority Issue Team, commented on the communication challenges that existed before establishment of the Alliance Coordination Team: "As we were wrapping up the first action plan and starting to crank up the creation of the second action plan, the thing that kept plaguing us was the difficulty of getting clear direction from the Alliance Management Team about what things they felt were important for the new plan—how it should be presented, what structure it should have. . . . It was hard to get a clear understanding on whether they were OK with the direction priority issue teams were heading in, or wanted to make changes. It was not a tight communication channel." Phil Bass has seen firsthand how this change has improved overall performance. "Folks on the management team are very busy—they are secretaries of state agencies," he said. "They don't have a lot of time to give. Having this group to communicate with has really helped the priority issue teams."

The overall structure seems to provide an appropriate level of balance between top-down direction and bottom-up work. The Alliance Management Team/Alliance Coordination Team has spelled out the schedule the priority issue teams need to adhere to for their work products, and has articulated expectations for the overall content of the action plans. However, they have allowed the teams autonomy to produce their own recommendations in their specific issue areas, and they avoid commenting extensively on the substance of these contributions. This has allowed the priority issue teams to get onto the right footing by avoiding lengthy debates about their scope of work, a process that can exhaust teams quickly and erode their morale. And it has allowed priority issue teams to have real ownership over their work products, strengthening their collaborative orientation.

Federal Participation

Federal agencies are also involved in all of the Alliance teams. There are federal representatives who serve as ex officio members of the Alliance Management Team, and federal representatives who attend Alliance Coordination Team meetings. In addition, each priority issue team has two federal cofacilitators—one from a relevant office (e.g., the Gulf of Mexico Program) of EPA and one from a relevant office of NOAA. The cofacilitators provide assistance to the state leads. This federal presence at priority issue team meetings helps the federal agencies stay abreast of the day-to-day work so they can determine how to plug in their support and resources to aid implementation. It also gives them an avenue for providing input into particular decisions where federal agencies have a vested interest, for example, because of their impacts on the 404 or 303(d) regulatory process for water quality impacts.

In a move that may create a good model for other regional ocean partnerships, the participating federal agencies also convened a separate Federal Workgroup to coordinate their support for the Alliance. It is not considered part of the Alliance management structure, but its representatives are highly involved in the various Alliance teams. The Federal Workgroup has grown significantly since its inception in the spring of 2005. Thirteen agencies participate, including NOAA, EPA, the National Aeronautics and Space Administration (NASA), and the U.S. Navy.

Careful Attention to Team Composition

Some Alliance leaders believe that the composition of the priority issue teams has been critical to their success. Three factors in particular seem to have contributed to their ability to work together in productive ways. First, convening team meetings and workshops that bring together scientists from the federal and state levels has been very fruitful. In many instances, these scientists had not thoroughly compared and discussed what they know and need to know about the Gulf, despite the fact that they work on many of the same issues. They harbored preconceptions about each other's organizations and scientific work that reduced the likelihood of collaboration. Working side-by-side to advance the missions and work programs of the individual priority issue teams has changed the dynamics between the scientists, and enabled more integration of expertise and resources to accomplish things. Larry McKinney described this phenomenon: "The most positive thing about the Alliance is that it has built relationships that have resulted in a tremendous improvement in the science we are producing and our ability to access that science. We have realized that there is strength in all agencies, federal and state. . . . Now our scientists appreciate each other's views, and trust that those other folks are trying to do their best."

Second, the decision to involve other agencies and research organizations—including university departments and place-based organizations like the Rookery Bay National Estuarine Research Reserve and the Dauphin Island Sea Lab—has also been productive. These organizations often apply for grants to follow through on team recommendations, allowing the Alliance's research priorities to channel the research done year to year.

Third, the decision to sit scientists side-by-side with agency managers with responsibility for managing major programs and projects is an unusual one, and it has given the priority issue teams some of their distinctive capabilities. In many collaborative ecosystem management processes, the technical experts meet in their own workgroups, where they forge technical recommendations that are transmitted to separate policy groups. The Alliance has taken a different approach. While the Alliance Management Team comprises only policy people, the teams where almost all of the work and deliberation occurs, the priority issue teams, have asked agency managers to work very closely with scientists on the development of research agendas and the selection of recommended actions to enhance the health of Gulf ecosystems.

Those who lead the priority issue teams believe that this diverse participation has made them more effective. The input of scientists has kept the teams grounded in an understanding of what kinds of questions should be asked and answered before the Alliance recommends particular actions for managing the Gulf ecosystem. At the same time, the agency managers—those who are the ultimate consumers of the information priority issue teams are collecting—help to limit scientific research that will be less useful to decision makers.

The excitement that the process generates is evident in Kim Caviness's description of a particular meeting her nutrients team organized to bring together scientists doing nutrient investigations in Saint Louis Bay with the agency staff responsible for regulating nutrient inputs: "Everyone was amazed to find out about all the work that was being done. They said things like: 'I didn't know that that research was being done,' or 'I didn't know that modeling was being done.' . . . Everyone just wanted to learn what other people knew and understood better." Many of the other teams report similar breakthrough moments.

A Targeted and Practical Approach

One key factor promoting the success of GOMA lies in the targeted approach taken in the early stages of the initiative. For example, many participants in the Alliance believe the decision to launch with a clear strategic agreement on priorities, rather than a lengthy process to determine what those priorities should be, laid a strong foundation for success. It built political will among the states to participate, created the possibility of declaring victory early in the process, and prepared the way for expanding the scope of the initiative and the ambitiousness of its goals after it was firmly established.

NOAA's Margaret Davidson, who participated in many of those early conversations, commented that the severe storms of 2005 provided the inducement to begin with a practical and doable set of strategies. The storms occurred just after the governors had agreed to form a new regional partnership, but before any work had begun. Recounted Davidson:

> During that winter, deeper conversations took place. We had a lot of plates spinning on sticks, but then we asked what do we really want to do here? Before that it was a mom, pop, and apple pie kind of discussion. . . . "We'll eliminate water quality problems, clean up HABs, etc., do all kinds of amazing things." In January, we got practical.

The architects of the Alliance agreed that the best way to build strong and visible support for their regional collaboration would be to begin with a discreet and manageable set of goals. Phil Bass, at the time director of the Office of Pollution Control in Mississippi's Department of Environmental Quality, explained:

> As we had a series of phone calls, we realized that we as states had been competing for resources for years, and that model had not proven very successful. . . . We talked about the fact that the five states really agreed on most of the issues surrounding the Gulf. We wanted to somehow manage this thing so that we started out working on only those issues where we had commonality, where we had agreement. Since there were other ways to deal with issues of contention that were already established, if we could leave those off the table and deal with only those things where we had consensus, then we could accomplish a whole lot. That is the thing that really brought us together as states.

Leaving contentious issues off the table may have helped to make this early agreement on priorities possible. For example, the Alliance did not select Gulf fisheries as one of its five priority issues, even though there are several species protected under the Endangered Species Act, and others that are considered overfished by the National Marine Fisheries Service. Alliance leaders concluded that fisheries management was the responsibility of other agencies, namely the Gulf of Mexico Fisheries Management Council, a body appointed by the National Marine Fisheries Service to set take limits in accordance with national standards. GOMA wanted to avoid muddying the waters by getting involved in an issue under the formal jurisdiction of another organization. To ensure communication and coordination between the two bodies, the Gulf of Mexico Fisheries Management Council officially joined GOMA in 2011 and is a participant on the Alliance Ecosystems Integration and Assessment Team. In turn, an Ecosystems Integration and Assessment Team member attends regular Fisheries Management Council meetings.

Tight Deadlines and Small Successes

The governors set out a very short time frame for producing an action plan: just one year. With such a tight deadline, the priority issue teams had to stay focused and limit the scope of their planning to what could be agreed upon in a single year. One result was the priority issue teams relatively quickly emerged with a tangible product of their efforts, setting the Alliance apart from other ecosystem-based collaborations that have taken years to produce strategic plans.

The governors also directed the Alliance to produce a plan that would make progress within a short (three-year) time horizon. As a result, the priority issue teams produced a plan that was practical and achievable, with small lists of beginning steps for each issue. Steps included producing interactive habitat maps and launching a web-based network of environmental educators that could share existing materials and messages for educating the public. There were also steps that could be accomplished with very limited funding, since it was unlikely that grants or congressional appropriations would be available within a scant three years. As Steve Wolfe, Florida's coordinator for the Water Quality Team, recounted: "Our basic thinking was that to get support and have the Alliance be a continued success, you had to have accomplishments. There was a feeling that long-term goals and long-term plans don't get anything done and tend to aggravate people."

The manageable to-do list created a low bar for the governors and other state leaders to clear before they could declare that the collaboration was a success. By January 2008, less than two years after the release of the action plan, the Alliance issued a Mid-Term Accomplishments Report. The report showed that, of the seventy-three actions, sixteen were complete and fifty-one were in progress. Phil Bass summarized the strategy:

> We believed strongly that we could best build success by having some successes. We tried to design a plan that was real, that included small

steps that we felt we could accomplish collectively whether we got another nickel of congressional funding or not. . . . We were able to take those small steps and grow this partnership by building some teams with great expertise and great energy.

By starting small and swiftly showing some small successes, the Alliance was able to strengthen the resolve among federal and state agency managers to pursue regional collaboration over the long term. While team leaders initially had to work hard to get people to their meetings, after the first action plan, participants started pouring in the doors. McKinney described how the momentum snowballed in his Ecosystems Integration and Assessment Team. "At our last priority issue team meeting, there was no room; we had fifty people there."

An Adaptive and Accountable Approach

As momentum developed and federal and state leaders started to believe in the potential of the Alliance, its leaders carved out a more ambitious agenda for future work. The second action plan, released in 2009, was a five-year plan and had a more explicit long-term vision for what should be accomplished twenty years down the road. The time horizon for the plan was extended from three to five years in part because the Alliance wanted to secure more grant funding, and grants are often issued in five-year cycles. The actions themselves also aimed higher; the Alliance was ready to commit to doing more now that it was starting to see increased funding and support from the federal and state agencies. Responding to the high priority of disaster prevention and recovery in the region in the wake of the 2005 storms, the Alliance also added coastal community resilience to their set of priority issues.

The third action plan, released in 2016, recommitted the five states to a regional collaborative approach and highlighted the learning and adaptation that had occurred over the Alliance's history: "Action Plan III is a reflection of a decade of experience addressing issues that directly affect the Gulf ecosystems and economies. The Gulf of Mexico Alliance has shown that it can restructure its priorities and organization to better serve the changing needs of the region. The teams' ability to come together across scientific and technical boundaries through the new crossteam initiatives are [*sic*] further evidence of the Alliance's evolution."[15]

Evolving Strategies and Organization

This evolution from the first plan, with its very manageable to-do list, to the second plan, with its expanded and more ambitious goals and actions, to the third plan with a revised set of priority issues and crossteam activities, has been very intentional. A restrained start allowed the Alliance's various teams time to get organized, achieve some small successes, and build morale and a deeper will to participate. As their collaboration has grown, Alliance leaders recognize that they must demonstrate continued successes beyond those that relate to getting up and running, or taking easy steps that constitute low-hanging fruit. McKinney put it this way:

> Our actions related to science have gotten more ambitious, and we have gotten more concerned with measurable results. In the first stage, we were forming. Now we need to deliver, or people will drift away. . . . We have to show impacts on improving ecosystem health— show politicians that we are being effective and are worth putting dollars into. If we do, we will be recognized, and we will get the resources we need.

Organizationally, the Alliance has adapted as well. The Alliance Management Team realized that its regional partnership would not achieve long-term sustainability until it evolved from a loose set of teams to a real organization with dedicated staff resources and an annual budget of its own. Accordingly, they established themselves as a 501(c)(3) nonprofit organization. This decision was accelerated by a change in NOAA's procedures for awarding grants to regional ocean partnerships, a change that made it impossible for the individual Gulf States to receive and manage grants on behalf of the priority issue teams they lead.

At an August 2010 meeting of the Alliance teams in Biloxi, Mississippi, a new constitution was approved that transformed the Alliance into a formal, centralized organization. The sixteen-page constitution carefully detailed the purpose, structure, membership, and roles and responsibilities of those involved. The State of Mississippi agreed to house the new headquarters and EPA loaned it an interim executive director (Phil Bass) to help with startup. Their 501(c)(3) status enables GOMA to receive grants that can only be awarded to nonprofit organizations.

The Alliance also added its Business Advisory Council in 2012 in order to increase and formalize its involvement with the industries that rely on the Gulf, in particular the tourism, oil and gas, fishing, energy, agricultural, and manufacturing sectors. The advisory council is intended to help establish partnerships with industry, enhance communication with the Alliance Management Team, and provide advice to them. Another objective in establishing the Business Advisory Council was to "develop an informed business constituency to increase awareness and understanding of the interdependence of ecosystems and economies" and, thereby, deepen their sense of stewardship in the Gulf.[16]

Accountability

The Alliance has also made a strong commitment to holding itself accountable for implementation of its plans. In addition to the governors' two action plans, which are painted in broad strokes, the Alliance has developed Tier 2 action plans to provide more detailed descriptions of recommended actions. The Alliance's annual work plans for each priority issue team and the accompanying implementation matrices track very specifically who is to be doing what and by when. Using these matrices the teams can maintain a birds-eye view of how they are doing relative to their goals. In November 2014, as it began its strategic planning process for Action Plan III, the Alliance proudly noted that it had accomplished approximately 95 percent of the actions in Action Plan II.[17]

The Alliance holds "all hands" meetings every couple years, in which all the teams come together and reflect on what has been accomplished and what remains to be done. It also publishes midterm accomplishments reports, external documents that describe to stakeholders and to the public at large how the action plans are being implemented.

An Early Focus on Developing Information, Tools, and Networks

A common focus of GOMA's priority issue teams has been on building a better understanding of Gulf ecosystems and the stressors that threaten ecological health and economic vitality of the Gulf Coast. Filling gaps in understanding to support better decision making is no doubt a logical first step toward improved management. However, choosing to invest in science and tool development can also be seen as a less threatening step forward, one that is consistent with the voluntary and enabling character of GOMA.

Integrating Dispersed Sets of Information on Habitat and Water Quality

One of the major strategies in the first governors' action plan was to develop an "accurate and comprehensive inventory of Gulf coastal habitats." This was no easy feat, since data about coastal habitats were dispersed across many databases, located in many different federal, state, and regional agencies, and no one knew where all this information was or how to find it. Moreover, comparing different data sets was complex, due to different methods of data collection and interpretation. The same situation existed with water quality data, and the Alliance embraced a general strategy of coordinating and standardizing the collection of water quality data done by state and federal agencies. They aimed to reduce duplication of effort in data collection and the inefficiencies and extra costs it produces. A second purpose was to improve the quality of data available to NOAA for building an effective Gulf Coastal Ocean Observing System.

The members of the Alliance Management Team and the individual priority issue teams share a strong sense that the Alliance has done some of its most important and groundbreaking work as it has sought to coordinate the collection, storage, and analysis of scientific data across borders. Many of the team leads point to the cost savings that have resulted from organizations comparing their work plans and making adjustments to ensure that efforts to collect data dovetail and build on each other. Cost savings in turn allow them to accomplish more. McKinney provided a good example from the Ecosystem Integration and Assessment Team:

> I've been amazed that at every priority issue team meeting one of our agencies will give a report on the aerial photos they just took of a region, and another will say, "We *just* did that." I've seen the same plane fly over the same area on the same day for different agencies. That's great for that company, but not so good for the agencies. One of the most valuable things we are doing is increasing collaboration between scientists to save costs, improve quality, and add to the science we have. Once we are doing something together, we can do more. . . . If two agencies put their funds into the same pot, we can collect more photos or do new areas, or increase the sensitivity of the images, etc. Everyone comes out ahead.

Since the priority issue teams involve resource managers and scientists, information collection has been focused on science that informs management.

Developing Common Approaches to Setting Nutrient Criteria

The Gulf States agreed to work together to improve the regulation of nutrients flowing into the Gulf. The economies of all five states are affected by this vast volume of nutrients, and the various problems—from coastal outbreaks of red tide to the hypoxic "dead zone" off the coast. At the time the Alliance was launched, all five states were confronting an EPA requirement to ramp up capacity to regulate nutrients by developing state-level nutrient criteria. The states wanted to develop criteria that were grounded in high-quality science about the unique nutrient conditions and dynamics in the Gulf. They agreed that their new regional partnership provided an opportunity to jointly work through how to accomplish this.

A sensitive balance needed to be achieved between developing tools and making decisions. Kim Caviness, lead for the Nutrients Priority Issue Team and director of the Water Quality Division of the Mississippi Department of Environmental Quality, noted that the Alliance did not seek to weigh in on what particular nutrient criteria each state should propose to the EPA. Rather, the Alliance hoped to help the states forge some common methods for setting criteria, so that proposals made by the individual states would have more credibility and weight with the regulatory agency. Caviness proposed that the Nutrients Priority Issue Team should take advantage of their cross-state forum to begin systematically piloting and assessing the most effective strategies for reducing nutrients while finding synergies among their individual activities:

> In my experience, we have agencies doing lots of little things everywhere. There isn't a focus or planned approach to implementing BMPs [Best Management Practices] or doing actions, trying to step back and say, "Let's plan with the limited resources we have and start trying to come up with ways we can leverage." . . . Instead of spending 50K in three different small areas where it might not make a difference, if we put it all in one problem area, then we might really see a difference.

As the Nutrient Team's focus expanded to include pilot efforts to reduce nutrients, the State of Mississippi overhauled the team's membership to include not only agency staff who have responsibility for designing nutrient investigations or regulatory criteria but also staff from nonpoint-source programs and the U.S. Department of Agriculture Natural Resources Conservation Service. Setting its sights high, the state embraced the goal of first determining more systematically which best management practices are most effective, and then using that new knowledge to devise a comprehensive five-state nutrient reduction strategy.

This evolution of Mississippi's leadership on nutrients illustrates the wisdom of giving each Gulf state the responsibility to lead the Alliance's work in a single-issue area. The state team leads have, for the most part, embraced their opportunity for leadership with enthusiasm.

Building Networks for Enhanced Collaboration

Besides information sharing and tool development, the Alliance has also been active in building networks to promote additional collaboration. For example, the strategy adopted by the Alliance to make progress toward educating the Gulf States' population about issues facing the Gulf was to create a network of environmental educators spanning all five states. Named the Gulf of Mexico Alliance Environmental Education Network, it was seen as a coordinating entity that could identify all the different educational programs and activities already under way, and then increase their accessibility across the region, especially in the states that had fewer resources to devote to environmental education. The vision was to hire a full-time coordinator for the network who would work on behalf of all five states.

Similarly, the Alliance committed to establishing a Gulf of Mexico Alliance Regional Restoration Coordination Team, after the 2005 hurricane season prompted the states to recognize, more than they ever had before, the potential value of cross-border coordination to protect and restore wetlands and other coastal habitats. Again, early strategies focused on sharing and integrating information, with the purpose of planting the seeds of future Gulf-wide coordination. The Regional Restoration Coordination Team was to be a forum where the states, federal agencies, and other private-sector partners could begin discussing what areas and sites in the Gulf should become regional priorities for conservation and restoration.

Political Will

One of the factors that has kept the agencies and their leadership working on the Alliance in spite of past differences lies in the level of political will mustered at both the state and federal levels. The five governors were willing to associate themselves closely with the Alliance. In 2005, they gathered together at the summit meeting that formally launched the Alliance to publicly announce the five initial issues that would guide its work; their personal participation in the meeting shows the political investment they were willing to make in it. The two key Alliance products released since its inception were the Governors' Action Plan for Healthy and Resilient Coasts, and Governors' Action Plan II. The governors are the final decision makers on the content in these plans, and hence they are the ultimate authority and source of legitimacy for GOMA.

This level of political will for a regional initiative is rare in marine ecosystem-based management and would be achievable only if the Alliance met the political objectives of the governors and other high-level agency officials. The governors were undoubtedly motivated by the fact that the initiative was framed as a gubernatorial initiative led by Jeb Bush, whose prominence within the Republican Party and ties to his brother's administration made it more likely that the Alliance could generate federal resources. The governors also appreciated the idea of beginning with a limited scope of issues of shared concern. This was a well-defined project that they could describe to the media and to voters in their states. It was one that they could embrace without significant political risk, because its disciplined focus held out a promise of quickly achieving some accomplishments. Lastly, it was a project that could potentially attract federal funding not only because of the presidential-level support but because their combined congressional delegations might enable the Alliance to mobilize quickly to get something done.

State-level political support was matched and reinforced by federal-level support. Strong federal involvement was driven by political will at the highest level of the Bush administration. The administration had recently released its new U.S. Ocean Action Plan, articulating strong support for collaborative multistate ocean partnerships. Within the Executive Office of the President, NOAA's Coastal Services Center, and EPA's Gulf of Mexico Program, senior managers believed that Jeb Bush's pitch to his fellow Gulf governors to mobilize regional study and action for the Gulf had historic importance, and federal agencies should do everything they could to help. Indeed, in his new position as EPA's state policy coordinator for the Gulf of Mexico, Phil Bass reported that, in the winter of 2005, James Connaughton, then the head of the White House Council for Environmental Quality, convened representatives from NOAA, EPA, and other key agencies, and communicated the administration's commitment to help the Gulf States with their new partnership. "I wasn't in those meetings but I think they were told by CEQ we expect you guys to give this 100 percent of your effort and help the states succeed," Bass explained.

This level of top-down executive office direction is rare and no doubt reflective of the relationship between President Bush and Governor Bush. Shortly after that meeting, and only two months after the formal launch for the Alliance, the federal agencies organized the Federal Workgroup described above. The directive to pull together the Workgroup with broad representation of federal agencies came directly from CEQ's director, James Connaughton. The Federal Workgroup became the main vehicle for delivering federal support and staff resources to make this fledgling effort roll forward. "All this staffing was needed to help these guys stand up and sort out their foci, and begin to make it choate," said Davidson.

Navigating Tricky State-State and State-Federal Waters

One of the major challenges facing marine ecosystem-based management initiatives lies in the jurisdictional complexity of marine resource management. Authorities and functions are dispersed across levels of government and different agencies; their individual missions and interests are often in conflict. One of GOMA's major successes has been to work to acknowledge the complexity of political and organizational motivations and capabilities associated with a multilevel governmental system. To succeed in the Gulf region, they needed to develop a process that created a strong sense of state ownership while acknowledging federal capabilities and regulatory roles.

Fiscal pressures following the devastating storm season of 2005 had drained state coffers, and many state environmental agencies were having difficulty meeting their responsibilities given cuts to their budgets and staffing. Many were wary about taking on something new in that fiscal climate. Some in the Gulf States were also hesitant to embrace the value of working closely with their sister states along the coast. As NOAA's Margaret Davidson explained,

> There was a long, checkered, and unsuccessful history of regional alliances in the Gulf of Mexico. . . . Some issue-specific processes had worked, but more broad-based state efforts had not, and the states had a reputation of not being able to work and play well with each other. A major reason is that there are profound sociodemographic, institutional, financial, and cultural differences, particularly between Florida and Texas, and the northern Gulf of Mexico states. As I used to say, you've got the two big book ends and the little books in the middle. . . . Even the way they pursue their shrimp fishery is very

different. Florida and Texas have large commercial fleets owned by doctors and dentists, and Mississippi, Louisiana, and Alabama have smaller vessels, smaller fleets, family-owned operations—it's a way of life rather than a tax deduction.

These differences, combined with a lack of previous history of working cooperatively with their Gulf neighbors, caused some senior agency staff to initially be skeptical about the value of sending their most valuable people to a set of regional meetings.

Tensions between the states and the federal government also needed to be overcome. "There was tremendous distrust between federal and state agencies," explained McKinney. "We basically didn't like each other. Individually we got along fine, but as agencies, there was not much cooperation." He suggested that one driver stemmed from the tendency of the federal agencies to push for uniform regulatory approaches in every area of the country, when the Gulf States (and other states as well) want more customized approaches to environmental management that reflect unique local and regional conditions. He also suggested that federal agencies have, in the past, lacked respect for the science produced by state agencies. "It was kind of a parent-child relationship," he noted.

A Structure That Builds State Ownership

Given these jurisdictional tensions, GOMA carefully fostered regional collaboration in a way that gave state governors and agencies what they needed in terms of a sense of control and ownership. At the outset, having individual states fully and visibly assume the mantle of leadership on specific issues that they cared about created the right conditions for the Alliance to succeed. This approach was chosen as the Alliance was forming and selecting its five priority issues. Each state was able to identify and take responsibility for its own issue of greatest interest and concern.

Structuring the Alliance work teams in this way built a strong sense of ownership in the initiative among all five Gulf States. Each state assigned a senior state agency manager to pull together and lead a priority issue team with a range of experts from the other Gulf States and from academic and nonprofit organizations. These state leads have worked hard and invested significant time to build agreements among their team members about what ought to be done on their state's issue.

Most likely, the power of peer-to-peer competition has been valuable as well. The agency managers who lead these teams simply do not want to be seen as lagging behind on their work to address a key ecological problem threatening the Gulf, while other state leads are praised for the progress they have made. When a reporter asks, "What has your Alliance team accomplished this year?," the state leads want to be ready with an answer. The five governors that they answer to undoubtedly share this desire to avoid any questions about their commitment to the Alliance provoked by a lack of demonstrable progress on their teams.

The flip side of this negative motivator is a powerful positive one. States can point to how their leadership on a given priority issue has led to real change. They see funds flow from federal agencies, universities, and other organizations to underwrite actions recommended by their team. They see how they can work with state agencies in other states to efficiently use limited dollars and staff, so that they can do more to address their issue than they could as individual states. And they see positive attention paid to their accomplishments, not just within the community created by the Alliance, but sometimes well beyond it: in the media and in the larger national community of practitioners working on marine ecosystem-based management.

Phil Bass highlighted how key this dynamic has been. "We have given states an opportunity to be regional and national leaders," he noted. "All of us tend to like that. Most scientists are introverts, and it's difficult for us to beat our own drum. But when you collectively, as a state, can be recognized either regionally or nationally as a leader on a particular issue, you take a lot of pride in that."

Strong Federal Involvement, without Federal Dominance

Many federal agencies have participated in the Gulf of Mexico Alliance. More important than the fact of their participation has been the way they have participated. From the outset, they have accepted and supported the Gulf States' desire for the Alliance to be state led. They have given the states a wide berth to shape the direction and priorities of the effort, while also offering significant support and assistance for accomplishing work. They have led with a light touch.

The first signal that federal agencies would adopt a new kind of role came during the initial conversations about forming a new partnership in 2004. The EPA's Gulf of Mexico Program (GMP) had already been in existence for more than ten years, and it was designed to promote precisely the kind of regional collaboration that Jeb Bush was proposing to his fellow governors. The federal program could easily have resisted his proposal, calling it duplicative and inefficient. But GMP's director, Brian Griffiths, strongly supported the effort to get something more explicitly state-led under way in order to draw more federal resources to the Gulf.

Certainly the high-level attention to regional ocean management following issuance of the U.S. Ocean Action Plan helped raise the priority associated with the Alliance, as did Bush administration contacts with Jeb Bush. Regardless, the federal agencies stepped up and offered critical seed funding to get the process started. The agencies had no new appropriations to work with, but they found ways to tap existing budgets. NOAA took on what Davidson refers to as the secretariat role, helping convene the many meetings that needed to take place, including distributing agendas, documenting key conversations, and offering "straw dog" documents for collective revisions. Davidson estimates that this administrative function has cost NOAA's Coastal Services Center about $400,000. EPA also supplied key administrative support, and currently manages the Alliance Coordination Team.

Just as important, the federal agencies have become reliable behind-the-scenes partners as the Alliance has formulated and implemented its action plans. One way they have fostered a close working relationship with the states is to avoid forms of participation that could be perceived as attempting to exercise control over the initiative. Thus the Federal Workgroup has no formal decision-making role regarding the goals and priorities of the Alliance. It is the state-led Alliance Management Team that selects those goals and priorities and approves the content of the action plans. The federal agency officials serving on the Workgroup attend meetings of the Alliance Management Team, but they are ex officio members and do not vote on key decisions. Likewise each priority issue team has a federal cofacilitator, but these individuals are there to help support the process, not to dictate its outcomes.

Federal agency participants consider their primary job to be aligning federal resources and expertise to assist the Alliance in accomplishing its regional work. After every Alliance team meeting, the Federal Workgroup convenes to identify ways that the group can follow up on specific regional needs or action items that the Alliance Management Team has discussed. Over the ten years that the Alliance has been meeting, the group has supported the Alliance in multiple ways, including funding the priority issue team coordinators and providing grants to support priority projects.

Even though the federal agencies have taken a backseat role, they do not, according to Davidson and Bass, feel that they are providing "blind" support. They are able to gently influence the Alliance's direction and work products while avoiding concerns among state leaders that they are dominating or taking over the process. Davidson commented, "Gubernatorial appointees from the Gulf States lead the Alliance Management Team, and they make the management decisions for the Alliance. But part of our job is to keep issues in front of them, and gently push them to make decisions on certain issues in a certain time frame." Describing how the action plans were formulated, Bass explained,

> The states didn't sit down in a closed room without the federal agencies being engaged and say, "Here's what we are going to do." The plan was developed collaboratively with a lot of federal input, but with state leadership. . . . Our federal agencies have been true partners, and there has been a realization, especially with EPA and NOAA, that the state priorities aren't that different than their own priorities, and working together we can accomplish a whole lot more than we can by sitting back and dictating, "This is what you are going to do and how you are going to do it."

Davidson believes that this light touch—deferring to state leadership while offering a helping hand—is the defining feature of federal involvement in the Alliance. But it does not come easily to all of the federal agencies. In their role as regulators, many are more accustomed to issuing directives and strong guidance to their state counterparts, rather than asking how they can be helpful. A few of the federal agency managers who were among the first to get involved in the Alliance, such as Davidson and Bass, have played a critical role in coaching their federal colleagues about the importance of behind-the-scenes leadership. As Davidson described, "For some feds, just that idea that state priorities might cause you to shift federal priorities was an adjustment."

The state participants sometimes face an uphill battle when they seek to win support for their actions from federal agency managers who are not sitting at the table. One of the Alliance teams working on pathogens, for example, has tried to persuade EPA to consider using different indicators for pathogen contamination in different Gulf ecosystems. This approach would represent a departure from the current regulatory regime that uses one indicator for the entire Gulf. While some of the regional staff members, especially those within the Gulf of Mexico Program, have been supportive of the Alliance's proposed approach, representatives from EPA's national office were skeptical. Ellen McCarron summarized this dynamic and the challenges it has created for the Water Quality Team, which she leads for Florida:

At the local federal regulatory level (like EPA region IV and VI) we certainly have engagement from these offices, as well as the Gulf of Mexico Program itself. . . . On the national level, however, because they deal with national-scale issues, it's not quite as easy to turn the heads. It's going to take a longer time to convince folks at the national headquarters level of the need to make these local changes, even though the local offices and all of the states are in complete harmony about the need to develop better pathogen indicators.

A Process That Created Trust and Cooperation

When Alliance leaders are asked what has contributed most to their success, they always mention the growing willingness and capability of the participants to work closely together. When the Alliance first started meeting, many of the participants, particularly the state representatives, harbored skepticism about the value of close coordination with other agencies and organizations. The somewhat wary posture of the states was evident in the Alliance's first meetings. Priority issue team leaders reported that, in those early days, as many as 75 percent of their participants were representatives of federal agencies, and sometimes states did not send anyone. The agencies may have wanted to see the value the Alliance could deliver before investing staff resources that were already in short supply.

By the time the second action plan was being developed, that skepticism was waning. Membership of the teams was growing steadily, as people decided this was something in which they should get involved. More importantly, the interaction between team members was beginning to shift. The growing understanding and trust among the members of all the priority issue teams created a foundation for achieving a high degree of team productivity in a short period of time. The teams forged consensus recommendations for addressing ecosystem assessment, water quality degradation, environmental education, and habitat loss. They delivered those recommendations quickly (in just two years for each action plan). And they leveraged the efforts and resources of a wide array of state agencies, nonprofit organizations, and universities sitting at the table to begin implementation.

What enabled this trust and cooperation to flourish? At the most basic level, it was simply getting some people who did not know each other very well into the same room together. But the fact that the Alliance organized some meetings is not by itself enough to explain why its members began working together so effectively. Given the challenging nature of the prob-

lems being addressed and the diversity of organizations represented, discussions could just as easily have devolved into conflict and impasse.

Critical to initiating and maintaining momentum was a slowly evolving recognition that the states and federal agencies had shared goals, and
they would do better "hanging together, rather than hanging apart." But
this recognition was the result of much of the hard work by the Alliance
and was not preordained. The support and financial incentives offered by
federal agencies were particularly helpful. EPA and NOAA organized many
of the early meetings, and volunteered the staff time necessary to pursue
some of the Alliance's first substantive projects.

Whether it is a result of the shared interests of team members, their
personalities, or the culture they come from, these teams seem to have
created a strong sense of community and shared purpose that has greatly
facilitated their productivity. One team—the Water Quality Team—recognized how important this sense of community was when they decided to
split their expanding group into four smaller groups. The intent was specifically to maintain a team size that allowed for continued camaraderie
among members.

Conclusion

In May 2014, the Gulf of Mexico Alliance celebrated its ten-year anni-
versary. Three hundred people attended the celebration where Founders
Awards were given to those instrumental in establishment of the initiative;
more than forty-five individuals who had been active Alliance members for
over five years were honored. Two weeks later, Alliance executive director
Laura Bowie remarked on the positive energy evident at the celebration:

> The collaborative spirit is very much alive within our community, and
> it is in this spirit that the Alliance embarks on its next 10 years!
>
> While we are linked physically by the Gulf itself, what is unique
> about the people in the Alliance is that we believe that collaboration
> brings exponential benefits. We have found the formula for build-
> ing relationships, building trust and building inclusive networks of
> people interested in doing good things for the Gulf.[18]

The Alliance has produced some impressive accomplishments. It has
greatly improved understanding of ecological problems as diverse as hypoxia, mercury in seafood, and the loss of coastal habitats that provide

critical ecosystem services, such as storm protection and support for key fisheries. It has established an efficient and coordinated process for building more knowledge about these problems, and enhancing the capacity of state and federal agencies and others to make wise decisions about how to address them. If nothing else, the Alliance has succeeded in engaging five contiguous coastal states, with diverse political dynamics, local economies, and state-defined priorities, in a strong and focused regional collaboration that has endured for over ten years. And for many of the individual scientists, managers, and policy makers, it has been transformative.

Like all marine ecosystem-based management initiatives, the Gulf of Mexico Alliance is a work in progress, and whether it continues to have success will depend on its ability to sustain its high level of participant motivation and political will through transitions in political and agency leadership. As Steve Wolfe, Florida's coordinator for the Water Quality Team, commented: "When it started there was a lot of enthusiasm right up to the Governor's offices. . . . But there is constant turnover of the state people who are involved in the Alliance. When we get a new governor, with new staff, it's hard. How do you get them fully vested in?"

Large-scale marine ecosystem-based management initiatives that bridge state-state or state-federal boundaries must be ever vigilant to the unique interests and concerns of each jurisdiction. They must evidence accomplishments that bring value to those involved and encourage their sustained involvement and support. They must also be deliberate about their organization and how it is managed in order to maintain focus and progress. While challenges and periodic miscues are inevitable, the Gulf of Mexico Alliance thus far has found a way to effectively navigate these challenging jurisdictional waters.

Chapter 4

Balancing Top-Down Authority with Bottom-Up Engagement in the Florida Keys and Channel Islands

Formal marine protected areas (MPAs) are considered by many to be the holy grail of marine conservation. Whether they are called marine sanctuaries, marine reserves, no-take zones, or the like, MPAs are generally established by law and have specific regulatory and management authorities. Many have an explicit mandate for ecosystem-based management, and their ability to restrict use enables protection at a level not achievable by most marine conservation initiatives.

However, a government agency that has the authority to designate or manage an MPA does not necessarily have the power to exercise that authority at will. MPAs are seldom established on a blank slate; they reside within a complex institutional environment with preexisting local, state, and federal jurisdictions and interests. Without the concurrence and support of those affected by decisions, conflict can preclude action. Hence management of MPAs requires carefully constructed bridges between government agencies, organizations, and individuals with responsibility or concern for marine resources.

National marine sanctuaries (NMSs) in the United States provide a rich set of experiences from which to draw lessons about ways to navigate this complex domain. The history of management in most sanctuaries demonstrates that federal authority goes only so far in achieving ecosystem-level action. Most NMSs have crafted mechanisms to work through complicated jurisdictional issues among state and federal agencies. All engage citizens and stakeholders in advisory councils. They balance their top-down authorities with bottom-up processes, and in doing

75

so, deal with scientifically complex issues embedded in an emotion-laden societal context.

This chapter draws from over twenty-five years of experience in the Channel Islands and Florida Keys National Marine Sanctuaries. Both developed management plans and marine reserve networks that have resulted in improvements in ecosystem health. In the Keys, the number of ship groundings on sensitive coral habitats has declined, and populations of heavily exploited species have rebounded within no-take zones. In the Channel Islands, greater biodiversity and fish biomass are evident in protected areas, and kelp forests have expanded.

Both of these sanctuaries have seen rising levels of public understanding and support. Surveys published in Florida as part of an ongoing monitoring effort show public attitudes becoming more favorable toward the sanctuary. In fact, residents in Monroe County, Florida, expressed support for an expansion of marine zoning to cover 20 to 25 percent of the sanctuary.[1] In California, the mechanisms used for monitoring and stakeholder engagement in the Channel Islands NMS were adapted later in designing a statewide network of MPAs established under the California Marine Life Protection Act.

The progress made in these two sanctuaries does not mean that conflicts and challenges no longer exist. Some fishermen in both areas remain opposed to the sanctuaries. Still, the management approaches, structures, and relationships put into place in these and other sanctuaries have enabled conflict to be managed in a manner that allows resource management to advance. How did these sanctuaries leverage the power inherent in their legislated authorities by working with government agency partners and stakeholders to manage conflict and access needed knowledge and resources? How did they achieve an effective balance between top-down and bottom-up management?

Biologically Diverse Places Facing Multiple Stresses and Threats

In 1972, Congress passed the Marine Protection, Research and Sanctuaries Act (later renamed the National Marine Sanctuaries Act [NMSA]), which among other things established the National Oceanic and Atmospheric Administration's (NOAA's) National Marine Sanctuary Program. The act authorizes the secretary of commerce "to designate and manage areas of the marine environment with special national significance due to their conservation, recreational, ecological, historical, scientific, cultural, archaeological, educational or aesthetic qualities as National Marine Sanctuaries." The NMSA provides for multiple uses of sanctuary resources, unlike national parks to which they are often compared. Today, the system includes fifteen marine protected areas covering more than 600,000 square miles, including sanctuaries in the Great Lakes and American Samoa. Two of the earliest sanctuaries to be established under the NMSA are in California's Channel Islands and the Florida Keys.

Channel Islands

The Channel Islands National Marine Sanctuary resides within the largest marine protected area network in the continental United States and contains one of the most ecologically diverse environments in the sanctuary program. While two of the Channel Islands were federally protected as a national monument as early as 1938, NOAA established a marine sanctuary in 1980 under the authority of the NMSA. It encompasses 1,252 square nautical miles of nearshore and offshore waters surrounding the northern Channel Islands (San Miguel, Santa Rosa, Santa Cruz, and Anacapa Islands) and Santa Barbara Island.

The sanctuary contains a globally unique and unusually diverse assemblage of habitats and species and was designated by the United Nations Educational, Scientific and Cultural Organization (UNESCO) as a biosphere reserve in 1986. Vast forests of giant kelp provide food, attachment sites, and shelter for an estimated five thousand invertebrate species and more than 480 species of fish, including the commercial species of albacore, bass, mackerel, salmon, and swordfish.[2] Four species of sea turtles can be found in the sanctuary. Every year more than twenty-seven species of whales and dolphins visit or inhabit the sanctuary, including rare blue, humpback, and sei whales. It is also a culturally significant area, particularly for the Chumash Indians, who have inhabited the region for more than ten thousand years.

Today, the primary stressors to the ecosystem are overfishing, kelp harvesting, degraded water quality from vessel traffic, anthropogenic noise impacts on marine mammals, and related losses of biodiversity. Storms and other effects of climate change threaten the ecosystem, and ocean acidification has become a concern of sanctuary managers. Ship strikes on endangered blue whales prompted changes in shipping.[3] The growing population in Southern California has resulted in rising demand for recreational and commercial fishing, tourism, and energy, each of which has the potential to damage marine resources in the Channel Islands.

To deal with these and other issues, the sanctuary provides a structure through which a wide array of community stakeholders and government agencies engages in management discussions and contributes to the development of management plans. Over 20 percent of the sanctuary's waters have been established as more protective MPAs, most of which are no-take marine reserves. Significant research and monitoring within these protected areas have increased understanding of the ecosystem and of the initial effects of MPA designation.

The Channel Islands NMS uses an ecosystem-based approach to management to fulfill its NMSA mandate to protect, manage, and restore marine resources.[4] According to Sean Hastings, the resource protection coordinator for the sanctuary, "We try to look at the issues and challenges and resource management threats holistically, looking at who all the parties at play are and what the natural history and ecology and biology of the situation is. With that information, we work through a community-based approach using our advisory council."[5]

Florida Keys

The Florida Keys NMS was established by Congress in 1990 and, like the Channel Islands, resides within a complex jurisdictional context. Stretching 220 miles southwest from the tip of Florida to the Dry Tortugas islands, the marine sanctuary covers 2,900 square nautical miles of coastal waters, overlapping with four national wildlife refuges, six state parks, and three state aquatic preserves, and incorporating two previously designated marine sanctuaries.

The Florida Keys support a biologically diverse ecosystem—an underwater tropical rain forest. More than six thousand species of plants, fishes, and invertebrates live along the shore and under the surface of the water in highly interconnected and interdependent habitats; changes to one community of organisms can profoundly affect another.[6] The coral reef is the third largest reef system in the world, and the most extensive living coral reef in North America. One of the world's largest seagrass beds, covering thousands of acres, lies beneath the waters of the marine sanctuary. As one of the richest, most productive, and most important submerged coastal habitats, seagrass offers food and nursery habitat for commercially and recreationally important fish and invertebrates.

Prodigious fishing grounds can be found in the water around Florida's Monroe County, which encompasses the Keys. In 1990, nearly twenty million pounds of finfish, shellfish, and other organisms were landed in the county, with a dockside value of $48.4 million.[7] The most valuable catch was the spiny lobster. In 1995, Monroe County accounted for 91 percent of the total spiny lobster harvest in a fishery that is located mostly in waters under state, not federal, jurisdiction.[8]

The rich and distinctive ecosystem drives the two most important economies in the Keys: tourism and commercial fishing. In 2007, tourism was the number one industry in the Keys, with over $1.2 billion being spent annually by over three million visitors.[9] As a result, the health of the ecosystem is under stress. Fish and other animal populations on the coral reef have been dramatically altered.[10] Increasing commercial and recreational vessel traffic is also having an effect. For example, the number of privately registered recreational boats increased sixfold between 1965 and 1995. Climate change is adding to the stress on the ecosystem; coral disease and bleaching events are increasing in frequency with the rise in ocean temperatures.

The Florida Keys NMS has sought to address the drivers of ecosystem stress through scientific research, coordination among numerous public and private entities, and outreach and education. The Keys was the first place in the United States to adopt marine zoning and create no-take zones, which currently cover some 6 percent of the sanctuary's waters. An extensive water quality protection program involves monitoring, education, and recommendations for compliance. In one of the simplest strategies adopted by the marine sanctuary, more than seven hundred buoys are being used in the Keys to protect sensitive habitat areas.

The Tipping Point for Action

Establishment of an MPA tends to be a high bar to reach. Without substantial public support and political leadership, most MPA proposals are quickly defeated. Even those that reach the high bar are often battle scarred after navigating the contentious federal–state, state–local, business–environment, and science–politics divides. While distrust and opposition can constrain forward progress of an MPA proposal, a tipping point motivating action seems to occur when widespread concern, political leadership, and acknowledgment of interdependent interests are present.

Something needs to move places that would benefit from a marine ecosystem-based management approach beyond the status quo. More action at larger scales involving a larger number of players requires an energizing event and a leader to motivate change. Often the trigger for action has come from a perceived sense of crisis facing an iconic place that empowers individual champions and political leaders to press for action. Over time, recognition that problems are larger, more interconnected, and more complex creates the potential for a marine ecosystem-based management approach to emerge. A tipping point can occur when there is recognition that effective action requires a coordinated set of responses because no single entity alone can address the myriad ecological and social issues needing attention.

Ship Groundings and Oil Spills Trigger Awareness and Concern

A crisis in a treasured place invariably sparks a response. While they are vastly different places, both the Keys and the Channel Islands are iconic land- and seascapes that are highly valued locally and nationally. Agency officials, stakeholders, and communities came to view them as threatened. In the Channel Islands, oil and gas development pressures sparked concern. In the Florida Keys, the crisis was a concern for the health of coral reefs, one that was elevated by several ships running aground in the fall of 1989. Prior concerns had led to creation in 1963 of the world's first underwater park, John Pennekamp Coral Reef State Park. Two smaller federal sanctuaries were created,[11] but pressures on the ecosystem were unabated. One study found five of six coral locations between Miami and Key West had lost between 7.3 and 43.9 percent of their coral cover between 1984 and 1991.[12] A major die-off in seagrass was documented.[13] Long-time divers noticed the degradation. Long-time fishermen remarked on a decline in the populations of reef fish.

Large-scale protection was finally made possible, however, by a series of random mediagenic events when three ships ran into the reefs. In late October 1989, a 155-foot freighter ran aground in the Florida Keys, slicing 200 feet across a shallow coral reef in the Key Largo National Marine Sanctuary. Five days later, a 475-foot cargo ship also ran aground, significantly damaging another portion of reef. Then, in November, a third ship ran aground, this time a 470-foot freighter.[14] In an eighteen-day span, fragile coral reefs had been damaged by three unrelated incidents of ships running aground. Although ship groundings in the shallow waters of the Keys were not unusual, the series of one after another triggered intense media coverage and public interest. Images from television news helicopters circling overhead were beamed into homes across the nation. As Sean Morton, acting superintendent of the marine sanctuary, commented, "When you have a couple in a row, people ask, 'Well, why does this happen, and how can we prevent it?'"

Political Leadership Seizes on Crisis to Champion Action

Political leadership was needed in the Florida Keys to shepherd protective legislation through Congress. The media attention and sense of crisis sparked by the ship groundings provided political cover for those who sought greater protection for the Keys. A month after the ship groundings, U.S. Rep. Dante Fascell (D-Miami), a longtime supporter of South Florida's environment, introduced legislation to protect the coral by creating a marine sanctuary and managing human activity in the waters of the Keys. U.S. Sen. Bob Graham (D-Fla.) sponsored legislation in the Senate. A bill was passed with bipartisan support, and about one year after the groundings, on Nov. 16, 1990, President George H. W. Bush signed into law the Florida Keys National Marine Sanctuary and Preservation Act.[15]

In the Channel Islands, similar pressure to create a national marine sanctuary was triggered in part by the 1969 Santa Barbara oil spill. Ultimately, that elevated sense of threat was used to secure political leadership to advance sanctuary designation. Clearly visible from towns on the California mainland, the Channel Islands were viewed by many as the "Galapagos of North America" for their mixture of cold- and warm-water marine life. In general, Californians care passionately about their coastline and tend to be knowledgeable and supportive of progressive initiatives designed to protect it. But expanded federal protective action was seen as threatening by oil and gas interests as well as some fishing groups and state agencies.

The blowout of the Union Oil Company's drilling rig on January 28, 1969, resulted in a spill of more than 3.2 million gallons of crude oil and served as a trigger for development of a national environmental movement. In the four years after the blowout, Congress passed numerous environmental laws, including the National Marine Sanctuaries Act in 1972, and a coalition of interests used this law to press for greater protection of the waters around the Channel Islands. A coalition of mayors, city councils, and county supervisors nominated the Channel Islands for sanctuary designation in 1978.[16]

The presence of active oil and gas leases within the proposed sanctuary almost derailed the process since environmental groups were wary of the precedent that might be set by allowing drilling in a protected area. Richard Charter, director of a local government coalition on ocean issues, pushed back. "I remember saying in meetings, 'Just do it! Just create the sanctuary!' I'm still amazed it happened."[17] On September 22, 1980, six months after President Jimmy Carter created the Channel Islands National Park to protect the Islands' lands, he approved designation of the Channel Islands

NMS. In the end, suggests Charter, the societal "posttraumatic stress" from the 1969 oil spill was enough to propel the sanctuary through the designation process.[18]

Recognition That a Problem's Scale Transcends Individual Jurisdictions

A perception of imminent threat to a valued resource provides a trigger for action, but who is responsible for taking that action? Overlapping jurisdictions create both ambiguity and complexity. In both Florida and California, a dawning recognition that the problems facing marine resources were larger and more complicated and warranted more ambitious solutions triggered concern. It became clear that the scale of the problem transcended individual jurisdictions, and everyone was interdependent. Effective action could only come through a unified response. As Dante Fascell, the Democratic congressman from Miami, commented, "If we are going to save this reef, and if it is going to provide both ecologically and economically, it is going to take the combined efforts of all the agencies at all levels of government, including the people. Nothing is going to work unless the people support it."[19]

In Florida, concern for the health of the coral in the Keys had been building for several decades. In fact, when the groundings occurred, Congress had already been asked to order a feasibility study to examine expanding marine sanctuaries in the Keys. It was clear that the relatively small areas of protection that had already been established were not enough. A new approach was needed that embraced complexity. On top of dealing with the varied interests of fishermen, dive operators, and other marine users, the underlying threats to the entire ecosystem were varied. Add to that dynamic a complex web of jurisdictions and regulations that were already in place around the Keys. Multiple agencies played a role in regulating the waters and shores in the Keys, including existing fisheries management regulations, the existing and smaller marine sanctuaries, and the existing Everglades National Park and Biscayne National Park that were adjacent to the area.

As the acting Florida Keys NMS superintendent, Sean Morton, commented, the new approach had to be holistic:

> All of those things combined for an awareness that there does need to be more management and more connection between all these other pressures on the ecosystem and you need to take a more holistic view. You can't just do fisheries management and not look at other things

that are destroying the reef and the habitat. . . . If you went out there and blocked (coral) off and did nothing but restoration, well, okay, we've got a whole bunch of new coral. In a few years, they'd all be dead because you haven't looked at water quality and what kind of water input is going on out there.

Dealing with Jurisdictional Complexity through Partnerships and Co-management

Partnerships and co-management arrangements were developed in the Channel Islands and Florida Keys that employed the authorities and capabilities of the federal and state governments. Indeed, federal–state relationships were transformed from an obstacle to a resource, as state officials were used for enforcement and outreach and state authorities were employed in concert with those of the federal sanctuary. For example, co-management with the State of Florida was instrumental in lending legitimacy to the marine sanctuary and demonstrating that the state had a significant stake and role in its success.

The partnership works because the goals of the marine sanctuary and state are aligned, as can be seen in the critical area of water quality. Although the marine sanctuary's authority stops at the shoreline, goals such as improving water quality require significant political and capital support from Monroe County. The involvement of the state gives the marine sanctuary a partner with more extensive authorities. As early as 1974, the state recognized the Keys as an "area of critical concern," issued restrictions on building permits, and required Monroe County to draft a Comprehensive Master Plan for development, but the county's plan failed state scrutiny. As the county was under pressure to refine its master plan, the marine sanctuary was designated. Through its Water Quality Protection Program, the marine sanctuary provided technical assistance to the county and identified additional sites of wastewater infiltration into the ecosystem. The state then established effluent standards for wastewater treatment systems in the Keys, which were key to fulfilling the county's master plan.[20]

Clarifying Jurisdictions and Convening Partners in the Channel Islands

The Channel Islands National Marine Sanctuary sits in a complex jurisdictional context in which a multiplicity of state and federal agencies possess conflicting responsibilities and interests. Wrangling over state and federal jurisdiction goes back many years, and required several Supreme Court cases to establish who had authority over living resources and undersea oil reserves. The sanctuary is managed by NOAA as part of the National Marine Sanctuaries Program, but it works closely with four entities that have jurisdiction within the sanctuary boundary: the National Park Service, the California Fish and Game Commission and California Department of Fish and Game (now Fish and Wildlife), and the National Marine Fisheries Service, which approves and enforces fishery management plans, developed by the Pacific Fishery Management Council.[21] In addition, the U.S. Fish and Wildlife Service shares jurisdiction with the National Marine Fisheries Service for implementing the Marine Mammal Protection Act and the Endangered Species Act.[22] The U.S. Environmental Protection Agency regulates water quality in the sanctuary. The U.S. Coast Guard has broad responsibility for enforcing all federal laws and regulations in the sanctuary.[23] Multiple other state and federal units have interest in how the sanctuary is managed, as do Ventura and Santa Barbara Counties and numerous municipalities.

Sorting out who has authority for what in this jurisdictional morass can be complicated. Differing missions and priorities challenged coordinated management. As Matt Pickett, the former sanctuary superintendent, explained,

> On paper, we have the mission [to implement ecosystem-based management]. But whether we have the authority is kind of the question. With sister agency NMFS [the National Marine Fisheries Service] being the primary fisheries management agency, our efforts to work in that arena are often cut short. Also, EPA has water quality jurisdiction. On paper, we're ecosystem-based management mandated. It's a little harder to actually pull off in reality.

The lack of clarity on which agencies possessed authority to close areas to fishing slowed and complicated the process to designate the sanctuary's marine reserve network. Once it was determined that the Department of Fish and Game had authority in state waters and the Pacific Fishery Management Council and National Marine Fisheries Service in federal waters, the sanctuary then had to work with both agencies to get them to understand that the National Marine Sanctuary Program operates under a legislative mandate to protect and manage the entire ecosystem. Unlike the sanctuary, the Department of Fish and Game and the National Marine Fisheries Service have fishery management mandates, not ecosystem management mandates. The sanctuary, however, cannot fully implement ecosystem-based management without coordinating with those agencies. According to Channel Islands Sanctuary Advisory Council member Dianne Black, "It's been a long, complex effort to really get a handle on ecosystem protection with all those agencies involved. There sometimes appear to be some turf issues that prevent the best decisions from being made or the most rational decisions from being made."

One way in which jurisdictional coordination has been fostered is through establishment of formal sanctuary advisory councils (SACs) that provide a forum for interagency communication and collaboration as well as engagement of interested citizens and stakeholders. Key local, state, and federal contacts are voting members of the Channel Islands NMS SAC, which gives them a direct influence in sanctuary management.

Additionally, formal interagency enforcement agreements have been negotiated so that the National Park Service conducts most enforcement of regulations, with some being conducted by the U.S. Coast Guard and the Department of Fish and Game. Although California has the responsibility to regulate the activities within the marine portion of the national park, National Park Service rangers are deputized as state game wardens and carry out enforcement activities.[24] The National Park Service also conducts monitoring activities in the nearshore portions of the park.

To support these structures and understandings, the sanctuary under-stands that it needs to motivate its partners, which means the sanctuary has to show its potential partners how it can help them. As Sean Hastings, the sanctuary resource protection coordinator, explained,

> We're used to being a small program with pennies, and just immers-ing ourselves in these big issues, showing people that we make a dif-ference because we bring folks together. Other agencies have single-species or single-constituent or single-habitat focuses, and we say, "Hey, we kind of manage the whole place. You may have the primary [jurisdiction over a single resource], but let's get together and let's do it this way." I think folks like that. I think they like someone being the convener. . . . By the nature of the size of our budget and staff, we are coordinators. We are not doing the actual work, but we bring it together. Because of the size and diversity of our areas and mandate, we can't be the experts on everything. So we coordinate with experts. We pull the research community together to drum up questions that need to be asked, and then get them out there. They take the data and package it, and then we find a way through volunteers and others to distribute it.

Formal Co-management Arrangements with the State of Florida

In the Florida Keys, an equally complex set of agency jurisdictions and concerns prompted creation of an innovative co-management arrangement. With 65 percent of the marine sanctuary located in state waters, Congress recognized that a coordinated effort was needed with the State of Florida. The size of the marine sanctuary required resources to be leveraged across levels of government. A partnership was also necessary to allay political concerns as opponents of the marine sanctuary feared the loss of control over resources in the Florida Keys.

The partnership is conducted between NOAA and the Florida Department of Environmental Protection (DEP). It is governed by a Co-Trustees Agreement for Cooperative Management signed in 1997. Co-management puts the state on an equal footing with NOAA in ensuring the health of the reef, one of Florida's most recognizable and important resources. The marine sanctuary's policy and management committees also include partnerships with federal, state, and local agencies.

The Co-Trustees Agreement specifies that neither NOAA nor the marine sanctuary superintendent can unilaterally amend the management plan or make substantive changes to sanctuary regulations without review or approval by the State of Florida. The governor of Florida has the power to seek changes to the management plan and can object to and invalidate portions of it. The agreement also clarified and codified earlier pacts, specifying that the management plan would apply in both state and federal waters, and provide consistent and cooperative regulations regarding fisheries, submerged cultural resources, and enforcement within the sanctuary boundaries.[25]

Day-to-day operational decisions are made by a sanctuary management team, which includes representation from the State of Florida, through its DEP. Other members include the sanctuary superintendent, program manager and policy coordinator, and regional managers of the upper and lower portions of the sanctuary.[26] Historically, the manager of the lower region has also been a DEP official. A resource management team, which creates policies on resource management, includes the sanctuary superintendent, U.S. Environmental Protection Agency, Florida DEP and Fish and Wildlife Conservation Commission (FWCC), and Monroe County Marine Resources Department.

Enforcement of marine sanctuary regulations is conducted through a partnership with the State of Florida. NOAA does not have staff resources sufficient to enforce regulations across such a large area. Other agencies, such as the U.S. Coast Guard, have the authority, but are immersed in more pressing duties, such as interdicting smugglers. Seventeen officers of the Fish and Wildlife Conservation Commission are cross-deputized in both national marine sanctuary and state fish and wildlife regulations. Making sure they do not put their national marine sanctuary enforcement responsibilities on the back burner, NOAA pays the State of Florida to cover Fish and Wildlife Conservation Commission deputy salaries.

A provision for this enforcement partnership was spelled out early in the planning process. As Interim Superintendent Morton commented, "They know NOAA came through to make sure that they're out on the water, doing their jobs. Money talks. They wouldn't be there if we didn't fund them, especially in this economy." But there is another benefit of having state law enforcement officers on the water, where they have a high level of interaction with marine users, conducting frequent water patrols and routine boardings and inspections.[27] According to interviewees, the officers, wearing the insignia of the state Fish and Wildlife Conservation Commission, are more familiar and trusted than NOAA personnel.[28]

Navigating Conflict and Informing Management through Stakeholder Engagement

Many marine ecosystem-based management initiatives bog down in conflict and a lack of motivation once the initial flurry of activity has subsided. Rather than being resigned to it, Channel Islands and Florida Keys sanctuary managers recognized that opposition was often rooted in distrust, fear, and lack of control. They tackled these concerns head-on in their management process by providing meaningful roles for concerned citizens and stakeholders that enabled them to contribute their knowledge, perspectives, and ideas. Working relationships were established through a structured sanctuary advisory council (SAC) process that diminished distrust and fear and provided real opportunities to influence management decisions.

Opposition Rooted in Fear of Federal Regulation

Public opposition was a serious obstacle in the Florida Keys NMS. To successfully manage the marine sanctuary, NOAA had to overcome Monroe County residents' deeply ingrained fear of federal regulation. While residents of the Keys supported prohibitions against oil development and large-vessel traffic, they protested vigorously when they learned Congress intended to create a marine sanctuary with restrictions that would also impact their use of the water. As Doug Jones, a Monroe County commissioner, commented at a congressional hearing about the coral reefs: "This is all we have left. To give it up to federal protection is ludicrous. . . . We are not going to destroy it."[29]

At the time of the debate, incomes had been rising in Monroe County as more and more tourists visited the Keys each year. But an older, more hardscrabble way of life was still important to the sense of place of many Keys residents. Many were eking out a living by extracting natural resources they felt belonged solely to them. That sense of ownership, as expressed in Jones's testimony, had run deep for decades. In the late 1960s, for instance, residents aligned with development interests to oppose the creation of the Biscayne National Monument. Opponents obtained bulldozers and plowed a "Spite Highway" seven miles long and six lanes wide across the forest on the island in the bay, hoping to cause so much environmental damage that the federal government would decide there was nothing left of value to preserve.[30]

In 1982, anger at federal authorities flared again, though this time in a more theatrical way. Residents of Key West, upset with the federal government, staged a mock secessionist ceremony proclaiming the formation of "The Conch Republic." Fishermen, treasure hunters, real estate interests, and others who were against federal regulation formed a Conch Coalition (long-term residents referred to themselves as Conchs) and hung signs and banners denouncing NOAA. The first superintendent of the marine sanctuary, Billy Causey, was hung in effigy, twice in the same day.

Establishment of the marine sanctuary tapped into some residents' fears of having their way of life attacked by outsiders, feeding their belief that any regulation was too much. NOAA was not helped in its efforts to build trust by including provisions in an early draft management plan that suggested the marine sanctuary would assume authority over everything from airplane overflights to local decisions on land use.[31] "The handwriting is on the wall," said John Knudsen, who earned a living hunting tropical fish. "They want to make it a playground for the rich. They want to turn this into Disneyland on the water, and then there's not going to be any room for weird, smelly fishermen who have made their living here for years."[32]

Sanctuary Advisory Councils Provide a Forum for Addressing Concerns and Managing Conflict

Effective use of SACs was key to shifting public opposition in both the Florida Keys and the Channel Islands. The opportunity for SAC members

to discuss issues and offer recommendations replaced fear with some measure of control and ownership. Indeed, their effectiveness as a mechanism
for sharing information and promoting dialogue between groups in the
Keys and Channel Islands led the sanctuary program to establish SACs at
all national marine sanctuaries.

In Florida, the SAC was mandated by the Florida Keys National Marine Sanctuary and Preservation Act of 1990 and was created in 1992. The
twenty voting SAC members include representatives of nongovernmental
interests, such as conservation, fishing, and tourism, along with a representative of Monroe County. The SAC has ten additional nonvoting members,
including the NOAA sanctuary superintendent and representatives of most
of the federal and state agencies with interests and jurisdiction in the Keys.
More than two hundred community members have served on the SAC.

The Channel Islands SAC was established in part because of pressure
from local commercial fishing interests who saw the advisory council as
a mechanism for providing input to the sanctuary's management during
a plan revision process. Although some fishermen saw the sanctuary as a
potential threat to their livelihood, they felt that if changes were going to
be made, they wanted the ability to voice opinions in the early stages rather
than at the end of the planning process. The SAC was created in 1998 with
ten voting seats for representatives of community interests, such as recreational fishing and education, and nine voting seats for representatives of
federal, state, and county governments. The Channel Islands superintendent participates as a nonvoting member, as do representatives of two other
national marine sanctuaries in the region.

A CAREFULLY STRUCTURED PROCESS

Each of these SACs has an explicit structure and process; they are not
informal or irregular chat sessions. Both meet in public bimonthly. Each
has a charter that lists its roles, objectives, and decision rules. Notable
elements of the Channel Islands decision rules, for example, include the
preference for a consensus approach to decision making, where "all voices
should be heard and creative solutions should be sought to resolve issues
and craft advice that encompasses the diversity of viewpoints."[33] If minority views emerge on the SAC, the protocol states that all views are important, and minority views should be recognized and communicated to the
sanctuary superintendent.

Each SAC established working groups to address specific issues or topics best handled by a smaller group. For example, the Channel Islands SAC

is supported by seven working groups: the Research Activities Panel, Marine Shipping Working Group, Conservation Working Group, Sanctuary Education Team, Commercial Fishing Working Group, Recreational Fishing Working Group, and the Chumash Community Working Group. Each working group is chaired by a SAC member and composed of both SAC members and persons outside the council.[34] The chairperson of the working group typically is responsible for inviting noncouncil members who have expertise in the particular issue to serve on the working group. Each working group has a sanctuary staff liaison.

The SACs serve as a conduit for two-way information flow: information about sanctuary issues disseminated to all stakeholders, and information about community concerns advanced to government resource managers. They also become links outward to the broader constituent community. For example, the Florida Keys SAC held more than thirty public meetings during the 1997 management planning process. It also established ten working groups to focus on specific aspects of the proposed plan, such as zoning. Its role was one reason NOAA received so many public comments—6,400 in all—during the planning process.[35]

No authority, but real influence

By all accounts, the SACs have been successful at supporting the sanctuaries and helping them to navigate difficult decisions. They serve as a forum for airing and resolving differences among user groups before the disagreements burden managers. In the Florida Keys, several SAC members led the prosanctuary campaign before the vote on the county referendum, and lobbied the governor and other state officials to approve the management plan. As the authors of an independent assessment of the National Marine Sanctuary Program concluded, "It is not an exaggeration to say that NOAA almost lost the chance to create the sanctuary—perhaps forever. The advisory council—as a group and through individual efforts—saved the bacon."[36]

Keys residents began to see that the SAC's advice was taken seriously by managers, giving it legitimacy and credibility as a source for collaborative decision making. Sean Morton, the interim Florida Keys NMS superintendent, commented that he presents new initiatives to the SAC at a very early stage in their development. "We never start any process without probably a year of workup with the advisory council, to just even frame how we're going to approach any new activity."

Similarly, in describing the Channel Islands SAC, member Dick McKenna explained,

It brings in a large representation. I'm very pleased with the tenor of the deliberations, and I'm finding it quite educational myself. I look at it as trying to address all of the issues, but not in isolation. Everybody, basically, has a say in this. It's the use of the islands and the waters, the preservation of the ecology and the species. It's very all encompassing. The marine protected areas are one of the fundamental issues that are addressed, but the local fishermen and the sportspeople and all these other folks have a say too. It's not like everybody agrees on everything, but the process is quite evenhanded. That's a credit to NOAA. The National Parks is there as well, but the NOAA folks who run [the SAC] are doing a pretty good job of bringing everybody in for their particular part, and it comes across really well.

Like all SACs, the Channel Islands SAC is solely advisory and has no authority, but its influence on sanctuary management is significant. Typically, sanctuary management goes with the recommendation of the SAC, or a majority of the SAC if consensus was not reached. As Sean Hastings, the sanctuary resource protection coordinator, commented,

The Advisory Council we support is a very effective way to involve the affected stakeholders and the community at large. Where we lack expertise on staff, we bring in scientists and economists and have them help us pull data and information on whatever the issue may be—marine reserves, ship strikes—and feed that into the community process. I can honestly say our advisors have their fingerprints over everything we do.

Balancing Top-Down Authority with Effective Bottom-Up Process

Authorities granted by law are not unimportant to NMS management. In particular, the explicit authority to create and enforce a sanctuary management plan appears to put sanctuary leadership in the driver's seat. However, while the law provides authority, the power to exercise that authority is more elusive. For the sanctuaries, the SACs are an important tool for navigating contentious issues and securing bottom-up concurrence. Although some might view the SACs as simply a public engagement mechanism designed for managers to communicate issues, get feedback, and placate public opposition, that interpretation would inaccurately describe the situation in the Keys and the Channel Islands. Without a real and tangible effect, participants would lose interest or contest and undermine sanctuary management decisions.

The opportunity to inform a management decision that can get implemented, and the fear of being excluded, motivates stakeholder participation in the SACs. The SACs provide a ready platform upon which significant engagement in planning activities can be undertaken. In both the Channel Islands and the Florida Keys, SAC-established working groups tackled the contentious issue of marine reserve planning, thereby instilling a degree of ownership and support for designation of no-take reserves. The careful design of this bottom-up process embedded in top-down requirements enabled the sanctuary to act on its authorities.

Establishing Marine Protected Areas in the Channel Islands through a Stakeholder-Based Process

Many observers believe that, without the SAC, the network of marine protected areas in the Channel Islands would not have been established. The presence of a structured, representative body of stakeholders provided a ready forum to tackle this issue. Just before the SAC was established, a small group of recreational fishermen and representatives of the Channel Islands National Park approached the California Fish and Game Commission. The fishermen and park officials were aware of declines in marine species in the region but took note of more resilient populations of species within the state no-take reserve. The group proposed setting aside 20 percent of the nearshore waters within one nautical mile of the Channel Islands as no-take marine reserves. As Matt Pickett, the former Channel Islands NMS superintendent, explained, "They [the recreational fishermen who approached the California Fish and Game Commission] wanted to look at the possibility of reserves for restoring recreational fisheries, not necessarily for protecting the ecosystem. It was more like, 'we have to do something about the declining sport fishing opportunities.'"

A partnership between the California Department of Fish and Game and the sanctuary was formed to explore the issue. The sanctuary superintendent, Ed Cassano, felt it would be a great task for the newly formed SAC. Satie Airamé, formerly the policy coordinator for Partnership for Interdisciplinary Study of Coastal Oceans ("a long-term monitoring and research program designed to understand the California Current Large Marine Ecosystem"[37]) recalled, "The primary motivation was that local people were seeing changes in marine ecosystems and declines in specific fish species. They brought the issue to management, and management was responsive and set up a process to implement change that would help address problems. It was very much a grassroots process at the beginning. There was no legislation requiring it."

The SAC provided a mechanism by which different interest groups could be organized to address this issue. The SAC formed a marine reserves working group to integrate scientific and socioeconomic considerations and develop a recommendation on the marine protected area (MPA) network. The working group included five SAC members, academic and government representatives, and ten additional members selected by the SAC to represent a range of community interests.[38] The SAC wanted to achieve a relative balance between consumptive and nonconsumptive interests on the working group. Neither sanctuary staff nor California state officials played a role in selecting the working group members.[39]

The SAC also appointed members to two other bodies, a science advisory panel and a socioeconomic panel, which provided guidance to the Marine Reserves Working Group. The science advisory panel was composed of sixteen scientists with expertise in MPA science who served as volunteers. The SAC selected members based on criteria that included their local knowledge and their lack of a published "agenda" on the reserves.[40] The science advisory panel developed an ecological framework and created design criteria for the marine reserve network.[41] The socioeconomic panel was staffed by NOAA economists to provide analyses of social and economic implications of the MPA options under consideration.[42]

The sanctuary and the Department of Fish and Game jointly sponsored the process, hosting and chairing meetings, providing staff time, and devoting funds for facilitation. For two years, Marine Reserves Working Group members met monthly and received input from both expert panels as it considered the appropriate number, size, shape, and spacing of reserves. The working group developed and analyzed more than forty proposals.[43] Robert Warner, a member of the science advisory panel, explained that establishing the MPA network "was a highly iterative process back and forth between us and the stakeholders, and in my mind a very successful one because of lots of exchanges of information. There was interaction all the way along the line." As Bruce Steele, fisherman representative on the Marine Reserves Working Group, commented, "We had a lot of GIS and economic support modeling. They spent a lot of time with us where we got to sit down and look at maps and move area closure concepts around, and push the button to see how that came out with economic effects. I think that was a valuable tool in the process."

Although all Marine Reserves Working Group members ended up

agreeing on the value and necessity of establishing marine reserves, the actual size of the MPAs proved to be one of the biggest points of contention. One notable recommendation of the science advisory panel was that reserves should protect 30 to 50 percent of each habitat type, an ecosystem-level consideration.[44] That recommendation, however, prompted working group members to focus on reserve size to define the success of the process. As the working group process facilitators comment in their final report, "While efforts were made to avoid focusing primarily on reserve size as the basis for a recommendation [to the SAC], input from the science panel largely defined the success of the reserves in terms of size." A consensus agreement on a single option was not possible, the facilitators noted, "because the gains to one or more stakeholder groups are construed as losses to other groups and because stakeholder options away from the negotiating table appear better to each side than compromise on this issue."[45]

Some individuals noted that the recreational fishing representatives were the only working group members paid by their constituency to serve on the group. Because it had been decided that a recommendation for reserve design would be forwarded to the SAC only after consensus, a few members were able to keep the group from consensus. As Robert Warner, a member of the marine reserve science advisory panel, explained: "The thing that slowed the process down the most was there were essentially lobbyists as part of the stakeholder group that were paid to have a particular position. It's very difficult to change their minds, because they're not paid to change their minds."

In May 2001, unable to proceed, the Marine Reserves Working Group presented the SAC with the information it had developed and a composite map, showing two marine reserve options with areas of overlap. Individuals who represented consumptive interests could not support marine reserves that constituted more than 12 percent of the sanctuary. On the other hand, individuals representing nonconsumptive interests proposed setting aside 29 percent as no-take marine reserves.[46]

The SAC recommended that the sanctuary superintendent and California Department of Fish and Game work with the community to develop a preferred option for a marine reserve network that would be "consistent with the MRWG's [Marine Reserves Working Group] consensus agreements."[47] As they worked to meet a SAC-imposed deadline to finish in August, the sanctuary superintendent and Department of Fish and Game officials adjusted boundaries of proposed MPAs to satisfy the top priorities of fishermen and conservationists.[48] Finally, they submitted a final recommendation and several other options developed through the Working Group process to the California Fish and Game Commission, which held public hearings before making its decision.

In October 2002, the California Fish and Game Commission selected its preferred option and established the network of MPAs in state waters. NOAA proceeded with their discussions to extend the MPAs into federal waters. When NOAA finished its reserve designations in 2007, the entire MPA network was the largest in the continental United States.[49]

While some viewed the lack of a final consensus on the marine reserves as a process failure, most viewed the process as an exemplar for how to effectively blend bottom-up engagement and problem solving with the exercise of top-down authority. Striving for consensus, even if consensus was not achieved, nonetheless elevated the discussion and narrowed the range of disagreements between the stakeholders. The process identified major points of agreement, clarified points of disagreement, and provided a well-vetted basis for the Fish and Game Commission and NMS superintendent's eventual decisions. In the words of one staff member, the council's willingness to try something that had never before been done on the West Coast and to "open themselves up, make honest recommendations, and thrash through the disagreements" showed what could be accomplished through advisory councils.[50] Ultimately, the marine reserves ended up being closed to fishing under three different pieces of legislation: state reserves were closed by the California Fish and Game Commission under state law. The Pacific Fishery Management Council closed the sea floor in federal waters under the Magnuson-Stevens Act. The Channel Islands National Marine Sanctuary closed the water column under the National Marine Sanctuaries Act.

Adapting Marine Zoning in the Florida Keys to the Reality of Conflict

A comparable effort to designate MPAs in the Florida Keys also demonstrates the importance of a bottom-up process to the federal sanctuary's ability to exercise its authority. Initial efforts at developing a management plan that included no-take zones were seen as top-down decisions formed by government scientists and managers. This reaction was partly a residual effect associated with the level of alienation that persisted after the sanctuary was created by Congress despite the opposition of many Keys residents.

This feeling of disenfranchisement was reinforced by the way in which only government agencies were initially involved in management planning. In 1991, the Interagency Core Group was established to engage federal, state, and local agencies with direct jurisdictional responsibility in the marine sanctuary. That body developed policies and directed the process of developing the management plan. Then, sanctuary planners held a series of workshops in 1991 and 1992, focusing on topics that would become key elements of the plan, such as education, mooring buoys, and zoning. A strategy identification work group of forty-nine local scientists and management experts generated the initial set of strategies and details for implementing the management plan.[51]

By the time the SAC was established and met for the first time in February 1992, many local residents were critical of details of the planning that had already been conducted by government staff.[52] Commercial fishermen were the most alienated user group. A survey of fishermen revealed the following: "They perceived themselves not to be part of the process that developed zone location, size and governing regulations. Three-fourths of fishers (surveyed) believed that they would be unable to state their opinions about zones once they were established."[53]

With input from the Interagency Core Group, sanctuary planners laid out a first draft of the no-take zone locations, and then brought the plans before the SAC.[54] Those plans already represented a reduction in the amount of no-take zones, down from the 20 percent of the marine sanctuary that was sought by some environmentalists and considered by planners at one point. Amid community outrage, however, the SAC found the concepts lacking in details, and formed a zoning work group that reviewed habitat maps, aerial photography of the areas, and data on use of the waters. The SAC redrew the boundaries, and its recommendation encouraged NOAA to eliminate two of the three ecological reserves from its final management plan, reducing no-take areas to less than 1 percent of sanctuary waters.

From this experience, NOAA recognized that it needed to change its approach to community engagement; it took a more collaborative, bottom-up approach when the time came to revisit the subject of an ecological zone near the Dry Tortugas. After NOAA initiated the discussion on the ecological zone in 1998, the SAC named a twenty-five-person working group of stakeholders, which included fishermen, divers, environmentalists, and federal and state officials. A 110-square-mile no-take zone had been listed and then dropped from the original management plan because of community outrage. About one hundred fishermen operated in the area. NOAA waited to reinitiate discussions on establishing an ecological zone in the area until after the furor had been reduced from a boil to a simmer. The agency, however, knew it would have to build extensive community support to implement any zone. This time the public would be involved at the very earliest stages of planning, long before any proposed boundary lines had been committed to paper.

Considerable thought was put into designing a process to deal with potential conflict. An extensive set of ground rules governed community discussions to facilitate the development of a consensus on an ecological zone. All disagreements among the members would have to be, as they were instructed, "worked through." Members who held out from the rest were told they might have to explain how they would be negatively affected by a proposal, and put forward alternatives.[55] An extensive listening phase was begun. Members of the SAC-appointed working group enlisted their personal networks to seek out fishermen, even walking the docks, going from boat to boat, seeking out information from fishermen about how they used the Tortugas area.[56] The working group used GIS mapping techniques to plot areas of heavy use against areas of habitat. Before drawing up boundaries of a no-take zone, members rated criteria in order of importance, such as sustainable fishing or socioeconomic impacts on fishermen, which would help them decide how to draw zone boundaries.

In May 1999, working group members voted unanimously to recommend a 151-square-mile zone, split into two parts. Because the zone would effectively extend the boundaries of the marine sanctuary, NOAA would have to work with other agencies with adjacent jurisdictions, including the National Park Service, Florida Fish and Wildlife Conservation Commission, and Gulf of Mexico Fishery Management Council. In developing the zone, the working group considered the ecosystem, not jurisdictions. The zone would protect some of the healthiest coral in the Keys as well as a diverse range of fish habitats. By July 2001, the no-take zone was fully implemented. As stated in the meeting minutes of the working group:

This alternative and this process represent a new way of making decisions. We have tried to build trust and reach agreement. In the past, extreme positions are staked out, and are then compromised away for a final result. This time, effort was made to address all concerns to see if the group can come up with a decision they can all live with and support. The goal is to get away from strategic positioning with extreme options.[57]

One of the fishermen who served on the working group, Tony Iarocci, explained his support for the no-take zone:

When we first heard about marine reserves there was a lot of fear. But once people got involved in the Tortugas project, the fear started to fade away. I'm now convinced that the Tortugas Reserve will help deal with overfishing and protect a critical breeding ground for the fish. That's why I am here (at the signing ceremony) today instead of out fishing.[58]

Conclusion

There are few places in the world where government authorities, exercised in isolation, have sufficient power to impose and enforce MPAs. While this power might seem indisputable, in practice, all government agencies function in a social and political context that must be considered if protected areas are to be an effective marine ecosystem-based management strategy. Overlapping government jurisdictions must be respected, with attention given to the specific roles and responsibilities of each. Whether it is designating large-scale protected areas such as a national marine sanctuary, or smaller-scale reserves or no-take zones within a sanctuary, top-down authorities must be carefully balanced with bottom-up concurrence.

One of the lessons in both the Channel Islands and the Florida Keys is the tremendous value of having a credible, carefully structured, and effectively managed process like the sanctuary advisory councils that can incorporate diverse perspectives in a sustained manner. Having this ready forum provided the needed bridge between sanctuary officials and the broader community of interests that had a stake in sanctuary management. While consensus among diverse stakeholders may prove elusive, processes that are structured to at least *strive for* consensus can narrow the range of disagreements and inform decision making by bringing new knowledge, concerns, and ideas into consideration.

Both the Florida Keys and Channel Islands National Marine Sanctuaries have been able to promote an ecosystem-scale perspective and achieve procedural and ecological improvements. They have done so by engaging a wide spectrum of governmental and nongovernmental interests with authority or a stake in how the ecosystem is managed. In so doing, they have instilled a sense of ownership and shared responsibility for the sanctuaries and their resources.

Chapter 5

Motivating Engagement in Voluntary Programs in Narragansett Bay and the Albemarle–Pamlico Estuary

Chapter 4 described the unique attributes and challenges associated with formal top-down marine protected area initiatives that have regulatory teeth. This chapter shifts to the opposite end of the spectrum and examines top-down policy initiatives that possess no regulatory authority. These initiatives encourage and enable ecosystem-scale conservation through planning and capacity building. While simple in concept, these initiatives can be particularly challenging in practice. Top-down initiatives that are both voluntary and "not invented here" often languish in the face of indifference, competing priorities, and outright opposition. While some places welcome the opportunities inherent in having "the feds" convene a discussion of issues of shared concern, for others it is just one more thing on an already full plate. Hence these initiatives need to find ways to motivate engagement, instill ownership, and enable action.

This chapter draws lessons from more than twenty-five years of experience of the National Estuary Program in pursuing precisely these objectives. The National Estuary Program (NEP) was created by the U.S. Environmental Protection Agency (EPA) to foster a regional-scale perspective on water quality management in large coastal estuaries. Although the Clean Water Act had significant success improving water quality due to point sources of pollution, nonpoint source pollution was a much tougher nut to crack. The NEP was an effort to promote science-based, collaborative planning at the large-watershed level and reduce the multiple sources of nutrients and contaminants that degrade water quality in large coastal estuaries.

While the Clean Water Act grants the states and federal government significant regulatory authority to improve water quality, the regional NEPs are top-down but nonregulatory. Unlike most other EPA programs, the NEPs' role is to *enable* action, not *force* it. The NEPs' four "cornerstones" are a watershed focus, science integrated into decision making, a collaborative approach, and public engagement.[1] NEPs employ a consensus-based, stakeholder-inclusive process to develop watershed-scale plans. With their relatively small staffs, the programs facilitate plan implementation by coordinating federal, state, and local activities; building partnerships; creating information; and incentivizing action through small grants programs. NEPs are conveners who facilitate connections and dialogue that otherwise is unlikely to occur.

As collaborative structures designed to promote basin-scale perspectives across state lines, NEPs are one of the longest-standing tools for promoting an ecosystem-based management approach. The United States had experimented with river basin commissions in the 1970s, and remnants still exist, but all were challenged by jurisdictional conflicts and a lack of political will.[2] How have the NEPs addressed these challenges? How have critical federal–state–local relationships played out? How do the NEPs motivate and sustain engagement in a process that lacks regulatory authority? What are the ways in which they have tried to instill ownership and enable action at the state and regional levels?

The Albemarle–Pamlico and Narragansett Bay National Estuary Programs

Of the twenty-eight NEPs created to date, programs focused on the Albemarle–Pamlico watershed in North Carolina and Virginia and the Narragansett Bay watershed in Rhode Island and Massachusetts were among the first NEPs established. Their more than twenty-five-year history provides significant lessons about how a federally funded, ecosystem-scale, nonregulatory enabling structure can function. Each has faced significant challenges, yet they both play an important role in their own watershed.

The Albemarle–Pamlico Estuary

The Albemarle–Pamlico estuary contains the largest geographic area of any NEP. Bordered by the state of North Carolina with portions of the watershed extending north into Virginia, the Albemarle and Pamlico Sounds constitute the second-largest estuarine system in the United States (excluding Alaska, and second only to the Chesapeake Bay estuary). North Carolina has the longest tidal shoreline on the Atlantic Coast after Maine, and originally contained nearly eight million acres of high-value wetlands, concentrated in the Albemarle–Pamlico region. These areas have been reduced by 25 to 50 percent due to land use change, primarily by residential development and agriculture.[3] The sounds are socially and ecologically vital and provide habitat, natural communities, and ecosystem processes that together form the estuary network.

The 31,478-square-mile (81,527 sq. km) Albemarle–Pamlico watershed encompasses almost 9,300-miles (14,967 km) of freshwater rivers and streams. The lower portion of the Roanoke River floodplain contains the largest and least-disturbed bottomland forest ecosystem in eastern North America. Over two hundred animal species, including the endangered red wolf (*Canis lupus rufus*), and three hundred species of plants have been recorded. The National Audubon Society has designated approximately one million acres in the Albemarle–Pamlico system as an Important Bird Area.[4] The creeks and embayments of the estuarine system provide nursery areas for aquatic species that are important to over seventy-five species of fish and shellfish. The Albemarle–Pamlico estuary represents half of the juvenile fish habitat from Maine to Florida.[5]

Habitat has been significantly altered, which has affected numerous species of economic and other concerns. Submerged aquatic vegetation provides vital habitat for many aquatic species. Before the 1990s, submerged grasses grew so thickly that paths had to be cut to pass between open river and the shore.[6] Now in many places the grasses are gone, along with the young fish and shellfish that were once common. Wetland areas have been cleared and drained, and planted as extensive fields of soybeans, wheat, and corn. Though much of the marshland is now protected, it is estimated that 25 to 50 percent of wetlands have been either lost to development or so significantly altered that their function is severely impaired.

Water quality in the sounds has been significantly affected by nutrients from municipal wastewater treatment plants and agricultural and urban runoff. Large algal blooms have resulted from high nutrient levels and have generated anoxic conditions that decimate fish and shellfish populations. The declining water quality, disease, and barriers to anadromous spawning areas have significantly affected fisheries. Landings of catfish, striped bass, river herring, American shad, croaker, bluefish, flounder, weakfish, white perch, bay scallops, and oysters have all declined. To make matters worse, the region is especially susceptible to sea level rise given its low-lying topography. A 2010 study published by the North Carolina Department of Environment and Natural Resources (NCDENR) predicted sea level to rise from 2010 tidal means by 1.3 to 4.6 feet (0.4–1.4 m) along North Carolina's coast. An updated 2015 analysis lowered these estimates to 0.05 to 0.26 meters over thirty years, but still concluded that sea level rise would cause "more frequent flooding of low-lying areas."[7]

In response to these issues, and faced with the opportunity provided by the EPA NEP, the Albemarle–Pamlico National Estuary Program (APNEP; later renamed the Albemarle–Pamlico National Estuary Partnership) was established by the EPA and the state of North Carolina in 1987 to "identify, restore, and protect the significant resources of the Albemarle–Pamlico estuarine system."[8] Key regional goals include improving water quality, habitat, fisheries, and stewardship of the region's natural resources.

The Narragansett Bay Watershed

Narragansett Bay and its watershed are much smaller than the Albemarle–Pamlico but still contain highly valued ecosystems that cross two states. The estuary itself is 192 square miles in area, of which 95 percent are in the waters of Rhode Island, with the balance in the waters of Massachusetts. The greater watershed of Narragansett Bay is 1,707 square miles, 60 percent of which is in Massachusetts and 40 percent in Rhode Island.[9]

Many habitat types are found in and around the bay, including open water, salt marshes, subtidal bottom habitat, and brackish waters. A complex intertidal zone of sandy beaches, mud and sand flats, and rocky areas contains areas of submerged aquatic vegetation with macroalgal and eelgrass beds throughout. The estuarine habitats foster an abundance and diversity of wildlife, including shore birds, fish, crabs and lobsters, marine mammals, clams and other shellfish, marine worms, sea birds, and reptiles.[10] Although shellfish remains an important commercial fishery, warming water temperatures due to climate change are causing significant shifts in the commercial species in the bay.[11]

The watersheds that feed the estuary provide critical inputs of nutrients, sediments, and other materials, but also bring pollutants from upstream, affecting the ecology of the estuary and surrounding bay. Currently, excess nutrients are the most significant form of pollution affecting the bay. Agricultural and urban development creates large amounts of stormwater runoff, which carries nutrients from the land. While human waste, heavy metals, and other toxic compounds were significant pollution sources in the past, improved wastewater pretreatment and the decline of manufacturing in the Northeast have helped to diminish these sources. However, these contaminants can still be found in the sediments or mud of the rivers and upper bay, where they create problems for fish. Stormwater and runoff are now most likely the greatest sources of toxics and a major source of bacteria in Narragansett Bay.[12] The infrastructure necessary to support industrial and population growth resulted in increased impervious surface, dredged waterways, railroads, and sewage systems, which have affected the ecology of the region.[13]

Concerns about water quality and fisheries in Narragansett Bay pre-dated establishment of the EPA National Estuary Program. Indeed, the Narragansett Bay Project was established in 1985 as one of four initial pilot programs investigating the health of large important estuaries, under the joint sponsorship of EPA and the Rhode Island Department of Environmental Management. The Project was charged with developing a management plan based on a study of the bay and its resources.

When 1987 amendments to the Clean Water Act provided EPA with the authority to identify nationally significant estuaries threatened by pollution, land development, or overuse,[14] Narragansett Bay was one of the first to receive this designation, and the Narragansett Bay Estuary Program (NBEP) was born. According to its mission statement, the program's goal is, "To protect and preserve Narragansett Bay and its watershed through partnerships that conserve and restore natural resources, enhance water quality and promote community involvement."[15]

Creating Management Plans That Prompt Action: The Goldilocks Dilemma

To nudge action, nonregulatory top-down initiatives need to be more than a simple policy pronouncement. They need a task that provides focus, resources with which to undertake that task, and incentives for agencies and organizations to participate. The NEPs had to carefully navigate these waters. They did so by creating a collaborative planning process in which participation was voluntary but which had the potential to generate new resources and capabilities and greater efficiencies in state agency management. Although they have struggled at times, their experience and accomplishments contain valuable lessons for similar initiatives.

Each NEP is responsible for developing a Comprehensive Conservation and Management Plan (CCMP) that establishes priorities for activities, research, and funding. This plan serves as a blueprint to guide future decisions and addresses a wide range of environmental protection issues.

The CCMP is based on a scientific characterization of the estuary and is developed and approved by a broad-based coalition of stakeholders who seek to balance economic and ecological goals.[16]

NEP planning is inherently challenging. In attempting to provide guidance and promote accountability without enforcement authority, a CCMP has to be framed somewhere between a very broad statement of goals and a very detailed statement of work plans. Too broad and there is no clear direction or accountability, too detailed and there can be limited buy-in and overload. The porridge has to be not too hot and not too cold, but just right. And both APNEP and NBEP were challenged in finding this "just right" balance.

The 1994 Albemarle–Pamlico Management Plan: Too Broad?

The Albemarle–Pamlico plan was developed through a process of extensive scientific assessment followed by stakeholder-based drafting and decision making. The Albemarle–Pamlico Estuarine Study sought to determine the extent of environmental problems in the estuary and to determine how the sub-estuaries might be preserved and managed to maintain environmental integrity and maximize the use and pleasure people derive from them.[17] More than one hundred reports were generated through the initial EPA investment.

The planning process was overseen by a ninety-five-member management conference that was composed of a policy committee, a technical committee, and two citizens advisory committees, one each from the Albemarle and Pamlico Sounds. These initial committees included representatives from government agencies, university researchers, and the public. Members represented a variety of interests, including agriculture, forestry, development, industry, and fishing, as well as environmental groups and local elected officials, including representatives from Virginia.[18]

Published in 1994, the plan identified five overarching management goals, each of which contained one or more objectives with associated strategies and management actions. In addition, "critical steps" identified measures to be taken to implement the management action. Potential economic costs, evaluation methods, and funding strategy (if known) were also included.[19]

However, some participants felt that conflict in the collaborative process led to a "lowest-common-denominator" plan. For example, the agricultural community protested the plan's recommendation that twenty-foot vegetated buffers be required along all streams and water bodies in the region. Subsequently, this recommendation was removed from the plan. As last-minute resistance led to removal of offending language from the CCMP, the plan became broader and less specific. Proponents of the draft who had been engaged throughout the process were disheartened by last-minute weakening of the plan. The result was that the CCMP was neither strongly opposed by interest groups nor strongly supported by participants that had been enthusiastic about the plan throughout its development.[20]

Wilson Laney, cochair of the APNEP Science and Technical Advisory Committee (STAC), remembers the 1994 CCMP as an "agreement on goals and objectives which everyone ultimately signed off on" but that was short on detailed strategies:

> What was unfortunate, from my perspective, was that the early drafts of that document had a whole lot more specific and definitive actions proposed. As it went through the approval process, it tended to get watered down, so that by the end of the process what was published as the CCMP had a tendency to be extremely broad and general and not very controversial. It turned out to be a document everyone could agree on simply because no one's ox got gored.[21]

The program director, Bill Crowell, acknowledges that, "some aspects of the 1994 CCMP were very vague. It may call for our program to support something, but 'support' is very broad, and it didn't really articulate what that meant, whether it was financial or helping with grant writing or otherwise." And, because it started as a broad set of agreements and was not revised for more than fifteen years, the CCMP also became less relevant to partner groups as time passed.

The 1994 Narragansett Bay Estuary Program Plan: Too Detailed?

The development of a CCMP for Narragansett Bay followed pretty much the same process as that seen in the Albemarle–Pamlico NEP. A seven-year sequential process involved scientific research and assessment followed by a consensus-based stakeholder process. A hierarchy of advisory committees governed the planning process, including an executive committee consisting of the regional EPA administrator and the director of the Rhode Island Department of Environmental Management, who exercised ultimate decision-making authority. Established in 1985 as the primary decision-making body, an NBEP management committee had broad representation of a diverse group of managers and users of Narragansett Bay.

These included federal, state, and local officials from Rhode Island and Massachusetts; representatives from marine, land development, and metals industry trade organizations; environmental and commercial fishing organizations; and academia. Subcommittees helped to do the work of the management committee.

Research was coupled with an effort to reach agreement about goals for Narragansett Bay through an open planning process. Public opportunities to participate in the planning process included conferences, public hearings, and a comment period on the draft CCMP.[22] The executive committee provided final plan approval, with implementation falling to the various federal, state, and local agencies. The intent was that these agencies would each incorporate plan elements into their own management processes.

Approved in 1994, the initial CCMP focused largely on reductions of detrimental inputs to the bay that had been identified through the research projects. For example, the CCMP identified toxics, nutrients, combined sewer overflows, on-site sewage storage, nonpoint sources of pollution, and boater discharges as major sources of impairment that would be addressed by the efforts of the NBEP. The CCMP also highlighted the need to protect critical habitat and areas of concern.[23] The plan was then designed to address these concerns, with work plans prescribing a wide variety of actions. Indeed, the final CCMP contained a set of five hundred recommendations for implementation outlined specifically for each participating environmental agency and aimed at accomplishing these goals.

Some participants felt that, once the plan was created, it had limited effect partly because the document was far too detailed to provide guidance that the partner agencies could adopt in their own settings. As such, commented Margherita Pryor of the NBEP management committee, once the CCMP was released "it was practically abandoned. Nobody wanted to own it." Toward the end of the CCMP development, participants were so frustrated with the process they just wanted it to be done. This precluded the kind of engagement required to achieve broad-based support of the final document and the actions it prescribed. As director Richard Ribb recalled,

> It just didn't fly too well. There wasn't as much buy-in because it was [too] prescriptive. At that time we didn't have the tools that [we] do now to work with a process such as this. We didn't have facilitators, we didn't have email . . . and I think we didn't have the skill set to manage a stakeholder process as well as what we have all learned to do now.

2012 Plan Revisions: Just Right?

In recent years, both NEPs have worked to update their management plans. The APNEP policy board approved its CCMP in March 2012,[24] and the governor of North Carolina, Beverly Perdue, issued an executive order in November 2012.[25] The executive order renamed APNEP as the Albemarle–Pamlico National Estuary *Partnership* and established the implementing structure for the CCMP to include a policy board, an implementation committee, and a science and technical advisory committee.

The new plan defines a set of three overarching management goals with ecosystem outcomes and indicators for each. It clusters a set of sixteen objectives and fifty-eight actions under five headings: identify, protect, restore, engage, and monitor. The plan embraces adaptive management and highlights the importance of an EBM approach: "The shift from management methods presented in the previous CCMP (1994) is most notably evident in the integration of ecosystem-based management practices. Ecosystem-based management (EBM) includes consideration of human and natural systems, an adaptive management framework, and meaningful engagement with the region's citizens to find environmental management and policy solutions."[26]

In dealing with the breadth versus depth issue, Bill Crowell, the APNEP program director, indicated that the 2012 plan was more "action oriented," but did not include specific directives. In his view, the plan was intended to be "a much more dynamic document so that the basic framework will be within our plan and how we implement various actions [will] come out of an annual work plan. What our priorities will be in any given year relates to the larger CCMP. Hopefully this will be much more open to an adaptive management approach. If this is not working, we'll try something else. Or if this is working we'll provide feedback to show that it's working."

An updated NBEP plan was finalized in December 2012. It was strategically constructed on the foundation of preexisting plans and activities in Rhode Island and Massachusetts that had been adopted by both governmental and nongovernmental organizations. The updated CCMP defines "a realistic, consensus-based priority-driven plan for achieving a sustainable future for Narragansett Bay Region. . . . [It] outlines a collaborative framework to apply ecosystem-based management principles for planning and action."[27] The plan identifies four overarching goals: protect and restore clean water; manage land for conservation and community; protect and restore fish, wildlife, and habitats; and, manage climate change impacts to human and natural systems. Under each of these goals, the plan identifies a set of actions and priority actions. In total, 27 priority actions are identified among the total of 119 actions.

Rather than the highly detailed 1994 plan, the newer CCMP was intended to create a much broader framework for action. As Director Ribb explained, the updated CCMP was

> not so far down into the weeds of the exact implementation steps, because a lot of that should be worked out in individual organizations. As long as they are paying attention to the goals, sub-goals, the objectives and action recommendations . . . that's as far as you want to get down to it. You don't want to get down to "This department and this agency will do this by May of next year, with this resource.". . . Our CCMP from 1992 looks like the Bible, the newer [one] look[s] like *USA Today*.

NBEP plans to monitor implementation activity under the updated plan and provide progress reports at regular intervals. As the plan states: "By defining key goals and actions and establishing a system for tracking progress in meeting goals, plan implementation will increase accountability and allow us to assess progress toward common goals."[28]

Converting Plans to Action Requires a Sustained Process

One of the major lessons of the CCMPs was that the planning process needed to be about more than just development of "a plan." Without motivation and opportunity to implement plan provisions, the documents primarily become habitat for microorganisms. The CCMP process provides a mechanism for developing relationships and understanding problems and potential solutions, but it needs to be sustained in order to facilitate implementation. In the original conception of the NEPs, the federally funded programs were to underwrite CCMP development and then leave it for the states to implement the plan. Indeed, NEPs are authorized by the Clean Water Act to develop plans, but they lack regulatory power to hold agencies responsible for implementing the plans. APNEP program director Bill Crowell commented, "We use our governor's executive order to get some authority, but it is just advisory."

In many places, this approach did not leave a cohesive organization in place to promote implementation. In the case of Narragansett Bay, the lack of an implementation body in place immediately after completion of the CCMP resulted in lost opportunities to make progress. State agencies did not buy in, and many of the recommendations became quickly outdated by the time federal funding arrived to leverage implementation. Director Ribb explained:

> [The] biggest lesson is having a group like this that is dedicated to ongoing care and feeding of these types of partnerships . . . continuity of funding and people that made progress. . . . It's a mistake to fund a watershed effort and walk away, which was the original intent of the NEP process. . . . You [need] a big picture national policy instead of expecting the states to just continue on with this.

Consistent with the original image of the NEPs as a mechanism to develop plans, federal financial support for the NEPs was only allocated for plan development. No funding was provided specifically for plan implementation. States were expected to incorporate and support the implementation of the plan themselves, but, as Margherita Pryor explained, they "were precluded from having some core group to implement it." In the early years of implementation (1993–2000), the staff of the NBEP was funded through its affiliations with state agencies and other financial partnerships. When 2001 amendments to the Clean Water Act allowed EPA to administer grants for CCMP implementation, federal support was brought back into the equation. However, the funding, for the most part, was only sufficient to fund staff and administration of the NBEP, with little left over to invest in individual projects.

Gaining Traction

If the plans have no power and the NEPs have no authority, how can they gain on-the-ground traction? Much of the leverage of the programs comes from their ability to incentivize action through small grants and pilot programs; facilitate collaborative grant-seeking so that partners can secure more funding; and enable action by developing information, relationships, and the capacity of other organizations in their regions.

Incentivizing Action through Pilot Programs and Demonstration Projects

Pilot programs and demonstration projects have an ability to catalyze action of a scale beyond the amount of dollars that they represent. They model success, catalyze groups of partners working on tangible projects, and enable the NEP to get something done that a partner wants. For example, the APNEP citizen's advisory committee distributes funding for demonstration projects in the coastal region. In 2009, $50,000 in grants was awarded focused on projects that demonstrated more sustainable practices in the areas of rainwater harvesting, reducing stormwater runoff, and renewable energy. The APNEP website highlights these projects through an interactive map that displays project sites and provides brief summaries and photos of the work.

When funding has been available, the NBEP has run a small Watershed Action Grants program that provides money to groups such as schools, nongovernmental organizations (NGOs), and universities to carry out small projects that advance the goals of the CCMP. Since many of these partner groups have missions consistent with the NEP but lack organizational and financial capacity, small grants help them build capacity while also producing tangible results that can be showcased to members and donors. These small accomplishments build an awareness of the benefits of the NBEP that can snowball over time. As Director Ribb explained, "This helps bring people to the table, and once they start seeing the benefits of working in these partnerships it becomes a much bigger thing."

Funding Leverages Participation; Participation Leverages Funding

Both NEPs are limited by the amount of available funding, and this challenge is likely to worsen as funding for government programs is cut. As APNEP director Crowell noted, "Funding for our entire program area comes down to an operating budget of $500,000 to $600,000 per year. Which means if I wanted to actually buy an acre of land on the water, for restoration purposes, I couldn't afford it with just our operating money." As the largest NEP, the scale of their program area compounds the effect of limited funding. Crowell muses, "If we were a smaller NEP, you'd probably see more [demonstration projects]. But since we're scattered out across two states, you have to look wider. If we were doing all our program work in one county, I think we'd be a bigger presence in that one county. It's a scale issue."

One of the ways that the NEPs have dealt with their own limited capacity to fund projects is to use their ability to link partners across the watershed for leverage in attracting other people's money. For example, APNEP has connected partners with federal funds. Bill Crowell notes, "Our partners in DENR will say, 'we don't have funding to do this, but we know this needs to be done,' or 'we have funding for a small part of our project but it needs to be part of a bigger one.' They can come to us and we will help find other partners or be able to facilitate a discussion or bring groups together with various pots of money to have a bigger project."

NBEP plays a similar role. Indeed, much of the program's strategy aims to pull in outside resources by writing grants for projects staff have targeted as fulfilling NBEP objectives and priorities. A 2009 EPA programmatic review found that "the NBEP has played a leadership role in leveraging almost $6 for every $1 it receives in Section 320 funds."[29] This funding is often used to leverage participation and collaboration by other organizations and state agencies in the region. The more federal resources the NBEP can bring to the table, the more incentive state agencies and local NGOs will feel to participate in the program. As Director Ribb explained:

> We try to bring together expertise around an issue and then we ask, "How do we build relationships and partnerships to implement that? Who are our strategic partners in this? How do we as a program provide value to this? What federal resources can we attract and weave into this package?" [Development of partnerships] relies both on strong connections to the local stakeholder community and on connections to federal resources.

Its ability to attract federal funding enables NBEP to have greater influence in planning efforts in and around the bay. Additionally, because the program is federally funded, it can take a longer-term and broader geographic perspective than other programs and can help promote a regional-scale perspective. As Jane Austin, of Save The Bay, observed, "They can fill a niche, even though they are not the most publicly visible actor in the area." "I think one of the things the NEPs do, and what we try to do," explained Director Ribb, "is look at where we can make the most impact, keeping in mind the overall principles of the CCMP."

Creating Linkages through Partnerships and Outreach

Beyond their work linking partners to secure more funding, one of the major ways that the NEPs have an impact is their broader role in convening and enabling partnerships.[30] Staff cite APNEP's ability to bring different agencies and NGOs to the table as a key factor facilitating its impact. In a world of partisan, parochial views, the NEPs can occupy a strategic middle position in which they link agencies and groups sharing common interests or having different interests that are interdependent and require collaboration to get addressed. Encouraging partner organizations to rise above their limited scope and worldviews is what NEPs do best. As APNEP director Bill Crowell explained, "NEPs must work with various agencies to help them take that broader view."

Each of the NEPs has been involved in multiple partnerships in their watersheds. For example, NBEP developed the Coalition for Water Security with support from the Rhode Island Foundation. The Coalition is a group of sixteen environmental organizations formed to address water supply and use issues in Rhode Island, and to serve as the foundation for collaboration in solving environmental problems in the future. The Coalition worked with the Rhode Island Water Resources Board to draft, propose, and support legislation on water supply policy. In November 2009, the Water Use and Efficiency Act passed both state legislatures to become law, primarily due to the partnerships formed around this issue.

Another example of an effective NBEP partnership was the effort developed around monitoring of hypoxic conditions in the Bay. Given the well-mixed nature of Narragansett Bay, most scientists and managers in the region did not believe that it was suffering from hypoxic events. The State of Rhode Island did not monitor for dissolved oxygen, so NBEP's chief scientist, Chris Deacutis, decided to assess whether or not hypoxic events were occurring. In the spring of 1999, Deacutis set up a meeting to organize volunteer monitoring for Narragansett Bay. Though there would be no money available, fifteen scientists showed up interested in contributing to the effort. Eventually, this monitoring partnership was composed of several organizations, which contributed equipment and volunteers. The surveys proved that, contrary to long-standing scientific opinion, hypoxic conditions were present in the bay. The data were used to advocate for legislation requiring a 50 percent reduction of nutrients from wastewater plants by 2012. The goal was achieved, resulting in "noticeably clearer" water in the bay.[31]

APNEP is also involved in a host of partnerships, including a Submerged Aquatic Vegetation Partnership involving various divisions of the North Carolina Department of Environment and Natural Resources, the state Department of Transportation and Wildlife Resources Commission, various universities, the North Carolina Coastal Federation, The Nature Conservancy, and a range of federal agencies.[32] APNEP became the coordinating lead of the Partnership in summer 2004 and invested significant funds in baseline mapping and digital aerial photography of submerged aquatic vegetation. The State of North Carolina had not done extensive mapping of submerged aquatic vegetation at the coast until APNEP mobilized the effort and established a work group to develop a series of flights to do aerial photography to map the vegetation. As Director Crowell explained,

> We got enough partners together and our policy board put in a significant chunk of money that then allowed the other partners to come in. We were able to get photography for the entire coast. APNEP itself doesn't really need that imagery. But we have various partners that have needs for it. By bringing those [partners] together, and getting them to work together, and finding little pieces of money, we can do bigger projects together.

Another APNEP partnership is the Albemarle–Pamlico Conservation and Communities Collaborative (AP3C) initiated in 2007 partly to focus on the impacts of climate change on native species since the Albemarle–Pamlico Sounds region is one of the three areas in the United States considered most threatened by sea level rise.[33] Members include APNEP, Audubon, The Nature Conservancy, and Environmental Defense Fund. In the AP3C partnership, APNEP cohosted a series of seven "listening sessions" on sea level rise and population growth in North Carolina. Held during the summer of 2008, over one hundred residents attended these sessions. The sessions provided an opportunity for citizens to learn about and prepare for rising seas that threaten their environment and the tourism, fishing, and farming economies.[34]

APNEP's role in these partnerships varies but often includes provision of some level of core resources to enable the partnerships to function. For example, APNEP supports a portion of the salary of Jimmy Johnson, the eastern regional field officer for the North Carolina Department of Environment and Natural Resources, who has primary responsibility for developing and implementing the North Carolina Coastal Habitat Protection Plan. The Plan is a mechanism to implement North Carolina's Fisheries Reform Act of 1997, a law that mandates protection and enhancement of habitats supporting coastal fisheries in order to protect habitat and prevent overfishing. The law requires cooperation among three rule-making commissions: environmental management, coastal resources, and marine fisheries and wildlife resources. Johnson coordinates quarterly meetings of the Coastal Habitat Protection Plan steering committee that is made up of two commissioners from each of four commissions. Johnson's position represents the "melding of two different positions, which is becoming more common as states try to cut budgets." Thus the Coastal Habitat Protection Plan represents a state initiative that is being implemented through APNEP.

In the best of worlds, multiparty partnerships create forums that foster coordination and collaborative decision making, partly due to the relationships created through the partnerships. "Business happens among friends," an APNEP participant commented in a 1998 analysis of that process. "It is a lot easier for me now to call up [a state] office to get information."[35] In the submerged aquatic vegetation example, APNEP was able to mobilize partners to work toward common goals, as opposed to taking a piecemeal approach, where one division would work on a small aspect of the larger project and another division on another. APNEP enables stakeholders to work together to reduce overlap and redundancy and to get people working in the same direction on a project. Practically, such conversations allow agencies to articulate their needs and work from a common set of information.

Developing Management-Relevant Science That Enables Priority Setting

One of the major strategies of the NEPs from the start was to enable scientists and researchers to advance understanding of environmental problems and trends in the bays and watersheds. Indeed, the first step in the NEP process is to conduct an assessment. In Narragansett Bay, NBEP funded over 110 scientific and policy-related research projects from 1985 to 1991. Every study was subject to extensive peer review. Additionally, investigators were required to submit all original data for permanent archival storage in the Narragansett Bay data system. This emphasis on science assessments continues today. "We are trying to create a structure where science feeds into good policy," explains Tom Borden, the current NBEP director.[36] "We hope to build a program where all this scientific information can be compiled and synthesized, allowing the NBEP to be seen as a clearinghouse of scientific knowledge about the watershed," Borden commented. "That, in turn, will enable all parties to make more informed decisions on protection and restoration matters."[37]

Both NEPs have done considerable work assembling status and trends information that could be used to inform management. For example, NBEP produced *Currents of Change*, a technical report on the status and trends of the Narragansett Bay region that brings together data from various sources.[38] These sources include state, federal, local, and NGO monitoring programs around the bay and its watersheds. Technical committees reviewed the data and, where possible, reached consensus on their assessment of conditions and trends.

The *Currents of Change* document has several objectives. First, creating the report brings together the disparate sources of data around the bay into a single assessment framework. Second, the report identifies gaps in current environmental reporting and analysis. This analysis seeks to inform future decision making on environmental monitoring and data management. Third, *Currents of Change* was developed to assist NBEP in revising its Comprehensive Conservation and Management Plan (CCMP) to reflect current areas of concern and priorities for action. Finally, the report is intended to guide management decisions and planning efforts at federal, state, and local levels, by providing accurate assessment of conditions and trends.[39] NBEP works to communicate this information to stakeholders and community members and has published a version for nonscientists.

Similarly, APNEP did extensive early work on a 1991 Status and Trends Study to inform its 1994 CCMP.[40] Currently, the APNEP science and technical advisory committee (STAC) "plays a pivotal role in providing APNEP with the scientific and technical support needed to implement the [CCMP.]"[41] The group also develops research initiatives and reviews the scientific components of policy recommendations. Monitoring is a critical dimension of their role, which has involved developing and tracking indicators to monitor progress and promote adaptive management. According to the science coordinator Dean Carpenter, "All NEPs are required to have a suite of indicators to track in support of adaptive management. In addition to the CCMP, which says where you want to go—stating the goals—then you need an indicator component to help you track whether indeed you're meeting those goals, or if not, to help you make corrections."

The STAC developed rosters of indicators to be used in developing a monitoring plan that will in turn be used to assess the status of the Albemarle–Pamlico ecosystem. The 2012 list totaled 150 proposed indicators, with approximately 35 per thematic group. The STAC is responsible for drafting two-page overviews for each proposed indicator. A template was used to summarize information about the proposed indicator, identifying (1) the importance of the measure, (2) management goals related to it, (3) monitoring programs that are providing data, (4) recommended improvements and their costs, and (5) current data sources and references. Rather than having individual experts write an extensive monitoring plan for each indicator, the idea behind the two-page document is to provide an overview to determine the cost–benefit tradeoffs of these indicators.

Even as it refines the suite of indicators to be used in future monitoring activities, APNEP funds ongoing monitoring activities and provides resources that can assist others to be effective at monitoring in the region. For example, the program provides a "Directory of Monitoring Information Sources," recommends a two-volume National Oceanic and Atmospheric Administration guidance document for science-based restoration monitoring of coastal habitats, and offers a website link for laboratory protocols.[42] Program staff members also contribute to monitoring partnerships, such as FerryMon (short for *ferry monitoring*), in which local universities and federal agencies utilize the state ferry system to monitor water quality.[43]

NBEP has also invested in monitoring, including a long-term oxygen-monitoring program focused on understanding hypoxia in the bay. To this end, the chief scientist spends significant time writing grant proposals to bring in federal funds for projects that have been identified by the management committee or other partners in the bay monitoring efforts.

Pursuing funding for science has become an even greater necessity and challenge due to the public sector fiscal crisis of the last few years. With state coffers empty, monitoring efforts are not seen as a high priority. Indeed, managers and policy makers often view monitoring as a black hole that absorbs a lot of money and energy without producing much management-relevant information. "Monitoring often goes on forever without any synthesis or assessments. [It] just sits there. You need to get people involved in synthesis. Have modelers look at the stuff and see if there are trends," explained Deacutis. He has observed that funding priorities are often driven by short-term needs:

> If we had an oil spill, everyone would be talking about oil for the next three years. As a scientist I get frustrated at the short attention span on issues. For monitoring it is difficult to get the higher-ups to commit to long-term monitoring. They don't recognize that things are always changing.

At times, both programs have been criticized for emphasizing development of basic science over management-relevant information. Though millions of dollars were invested in the Albemarle–Pamlico Estuary Study (APES), for example, very few of the reports included interpretation of management implications. The program did not specifically require researchers to provide interpretation, and many felt that it was not their job as research scientists.[44]

Nevertheless, both NEPs are sensitive to the need to relate monitoring and assessment information to stakeholders and policy makers. At AP-NEP, one tool for linking science to management choices has been STAC technical issue papers. These one- to two-page "white papers" are designed to introduce APNEP stakeholders to the topic for which the STAC, in its advisory capacity, is recommending a change from the status quo. Papers include a position, supporting statement, and references.

To achieve management-ready science, stronger linkages between scientists and managers are needed, partly so that managers can better inform the scientists about higher-priority needs. For example, the STAC developed the indicator project, but it will require significant investment by the management advisory committee (MAC) to be successful. APNEP program scientist Dean Carpenter explained, "I've been concerned that the science is getting too far out ahead of the management. We'd like the MAC to help us define management goals that we can tie to our indicators, to determine what is good and bad in the system. The integration of the management component is essential. That's been sort of a rough spot for us heretofore."

Dealing with Disinterest, Opposition, and Turf

As a voluntary program promoting a regional watershed-scale approach, a major challenge for the NEPs is to provide enough benefits to member groups and agencies to trigger interest and engagement, so as to overcome the inclinations of individual participants to pursue their own interests. At times, the collective good requires some sacrifice or change in direction by individual agencies or groups. Even when it is clear that issues like water quality and climate change may cost each participant a great deal in the long term, short-term considerations often outcompete long-term ones.[45] There is a constant tension in a collaborative group between the forces that pull parties away from the table and those that induce members to participate.[46] With both the Albemarle–Pamlico and Narragansett Bay NEPs, the tension shows up as stakeholder disinterest or opposition and as jurisdictional battles between levels of government.

Narragansett Bay: A Two-State Watershed with a Single-State Identity

Although 60 percent of the Narragansett Bay watershed is located in Massachusetts, few communities or state agencies in Massachusetts perceive much relationship to the bay. With NBEP's administrative offices located within Rhode Island, and the bay providing such a prominent feature within that state, there was little shared identity with the ecosystem between Rhode Island residents and officials and those of Massachusetts. NBEP director Richard Ribb struggled with this situation, commenting on the challenges encountered in trying to elevate awareness and concern about the bay on the Massachusetts side of the border.

Membership on the NBEP management committee was one way to connect with Massachusetts, but, until recently, a Massachusetts official held only one seat. Initial efforts to incorporate environmental agencies, NGOs, and stakeholders from Massachusetts into the development of the NBEP CCMP were limited. With the growing recognition of the critical role Massachusetts plays in nutrient loading to the Narragansett estuary, however, engagement of Massachusetts state agencies and stakeholders is essential. To try to increase their participation, NBEP has expanded its focus on river restoration projects, which brings some Massachusetts representatives to the table.

NBEP has also targeted outreach and education activities to elevate public awareness, understanding, and concern about issues in the watershed and thereby prompt state agency involvement. Scientific information and partnership activities are communicated to communities and groups to increase visibility and gain support for activities and policies aimed at improving ecosystem health. Another strategy NBEP has pursued is publication of the quarterly *Narragansett Bay Journal*, which highlights successful activities of NBEP and its partners and communicates current issues facing the bay and its watersheds.[47] A major objective of this publication is to try to foster a broader sense of connection and identity with the bay.

Stakeholder Opposition in the Albemarle–Pamlico National Estuary Program

The challenge of securing effective buy in to NEP action from local governments and some key constituent groups came early for APNEP.[48] Although early citizen committees had representation from diverse interests, several groups soon dropped out of the process. Representatives from local government, agriculture, industry, and fishing interests were conspicuously uninvolved. For example, it was not until 1989 that a local government representative was assigned to the policy committee. Conversely, some thought that environmental views were overrepresented, a perspective that was exacerbated by much higher turnover among nonenvironmental representatives. As a result, longer-tenured environmentalist volunteers tended to rise to leadership positions in the committees, furthering the appearance of a discourse dominated by environmental groups.

Overall, these perceptions may have decreased the credibility of the recommendations formed by citizen committees early in APNEP's evolution.[49] Indeed, a lack of sustained engagement by agriculture and forestry representatives in the APES research and planning phase resulted in last-minute opposition to the CCMP by the North Carolina Association of County Commissioners.[50] While these groups were officially represented on the citizen advisory committees, the individuals either stopped attending or were not successful in expressing their concerns in the drafting phase. Some did not believe that their interests would be adequately heard. For others, behavior might have been motivated by a strategic calculation that it would be more effective to oppose the proposal than to participate in the planning process. Regardless, the net effect was that they opposed the final draft CCMP during the public comment period.

To be fair, there was some confusion about the appropriate role of citizens and their influence on the program. During the APES phase, the technical committee believed that "although citizens' balanced input on public values was important, the public was not qualified to participate in technical decisions."[51] The committee's view was that citizen involvement made the APES a political exercise rather than a scientific one. Conversely, citizens who expected to be equal partners in the process accused the technical and policy committees of "scientific cronyism" and focusing too much on research instead of action.[52] These misgivings about the process left negative impressions with many individuals.

Maintaining effective engagement has remained a challenge in more recent years. As Jimmy Johnson, APNEP's eastern regional field officer, noted, "You find pockets of people that are very attuned to what's going on, but there's also a lot of apathy. There were several meetings where very few people showed up. Out of sight, out of mind, I guess." Johnson cited a recent partnership between APNEP and the Nicholas Institute for Environmental Policy Solutions at Duke University to conduct a series of meetings with elected officials in the northeastern sound counties regarding their ideas, priorities, and thinking about climate change–induced sea level rise and the challenges ahead. Notably, Johnson commented, "Several of the municipality and county commissioners didn't even want to recognize that sea level was rising. They were calling it erosion and different things like that."

Dealing with Conflicting State Agency Agendas and Mandates

Top-down policy initiatives like the NEPs are not created on a blank slate. Preexisting state agency norms, priorities, personalities, politics, and history will invariably challenge the process. Both NEPs have faced challenges managing the relationship between the federal program and the state agencies. APNEP director Bill Crowell acknowledged that their home agency, the North Carolina Department of Environment and Natural Resources, was focused on the issues and places in line with its own missions and mandates, and these mandates are often narrower than the goals of the NEPs: "While the programs try to work together to make sure their rules don't conflict, and they try to share resources and information, there is still not an ecosystem-based entity within our state government that looks comprehensively across the programs and tries to get them to work in concert." Divisions within the department have their own missions tied to statutory and historical mandates. For example, the Division of Water Quality enforces the Clean Water Act, but they do not "look at what kind of land cover we need to protect water quality, and what type of forest we need to have the diverse wildlife that supports functional ecosystems," noted Crowell.

Crowell reflected further on how agency mandates affect APNEP:

> In the EBM framework, various agencies have statutory restrictions about what they're supposed to focus on. They have a mission and they're implementing their mission. They know they need to be doing other things, but they don't have funding or something that's associated with it, because of the restrictions within their mission that could associate with the statute.
>
> So one of the things we've told our policy group—and the staff here know—is we will never be a full EBM program because we have to work with partners that are restricted in certain ways.

The Narragansett Bay Estuary Program has also had to deal with jurisdictional conflict in Rhode Island. State agencies have viewed the work of the NBEP as overlapping with their jurisdiction and roles, and at times have resisted taking action. As Director Ribb noted, "It's a bit of a turf issue. They're saying, 'we do this. That's what we do.' . . . You get a little kick back from that. It's important for [state agencies] to recognize that ecosystem management is not strictly the responsibility of government alone. That's hard for some old school agency people to think that way. You have to overcome that kind of resistance." A legacy of government-directed, top-down, command-and-control regulatory actions often impedes engagement in stakeholder-based collaborative planning and restoration.

Residual perceptions of the program having been instituted from the top down appear to have made achieving buy-in difficult for NBEP. After being selected by EPA, the governor of Rhode Island agreed to adopt the program primarily to gain access to federal funding. Consequently, state agencies were required to participate in the program whether they saw it as beneficial to their agencies or not. EPA staff member Margherita Pryor explained:

We have to recognize that these things take off or not due to a variety of local influences. If you have a strong persistent advocate you will see a different trajectory. You had to be nominated by a governor to be part of the NEP. The earlier programs didn't have that. The ones that came in with a governor's package, with grassroots support, were very successful because they start out that way. When you have a program that [is] sort of dropped into [place], this was one more program that needed to stake out its own influence.

To some degree it was also perceived to be in conflict with Save The Bay. It has struggled all along due to the public perception of Save The Bay as the advocacy group. So NBEP has struggled to define [its role]. "We are not going to do the advocacy, we're going to do the other piece: facilitate, find the science, figure out how science can be applied to management decisions". . . which is a whole other thing.

An example of these jurisdictional conflicts lies in the development of overlapping NBEP and state management plans. A dramatic hypoxic event in 2003 led to a visible fish kill that triggered formation of the Rhode Island Bays, Rivers, and Watersheds Coordination Team (BRWCT), with the aim of better coordinating state agency action.

In 2008, Rhode Island's General Assembly mandated BRWCT to create a systems-level plan (SLP) for state environmental agencies. The SLP was intended to "establish overall goals and priorities for the management, preservation, and restoration of the state's bays, rivers, and watersheds, and the promotion of sustainable economic development of the water cluster." The SLP included a strategy for attaining goals, delineating specific responsibilities among agencies, and identifying funding sources and a timetable for attaining goals.[53]

The state SLP has significant overlap with the NBEP CCMP, which until then had been the guiding document for the state agencies. However, BRWCT did not incorporate the NEP in development of the plan, resulting in two statutory mandates to coordinate actions of state agencies, but without a legal framework for integrating the two plans. The SLP also does not incorporate Massachusetts into the coordinated efforts, which points to the utility of Rhode Island not abandoning the NBEP CCMP entirely.

It is unclear whether NBEP was intentionally left out of the development of the SLP, or if Rhode Island was unsure how to blend the federal and state mandates. However, the result has been a set of juxtaposing plans that are at times in conflict with each other. Jane Austin, of Save The Bay recounts:

> [There are] two statutory frameworks with a big overlap, but no explicit reconciliation. If there had been a thought about this initially, the [NBEP] could have been included on the [BRWTC], or any number of other things. . . . I don't know if this was an explicit decision that they not be included, or if they just weren't sure how to blend a federal program into all the state programs. At some point there was a thought to have the head of the [NBEP] as head of the Coordination Team . . . but there was a lack of support in the state legislature. . . . This has had a negative impact on relationships between the two entities. Not insurmountable, but part of the history in a small state.

NBEP attempted to develop an integrated plan in partnership with the BWRCT. But, as Ribb laments, "We didn't have a good enough plan to make a plan." Clearer ground rules for the process and the earlier involvement of a facilitator might have helped. After two years of work, NBEP decided to pull out of the process and proceed on its own path by updating its CCMP. Differences in the scale and scope of the two organizations' plans and the lack of political support kept an integrated plan from being completed. As Ribb explained, "I think that if the governor had said 'this is a priority to me,' and got involved and said, 'let's figure out how to make this work,' I think that would have helped tremendously."

Organizational Dilemmas: Identity, Location, and Capacity

Finding a viable home for the process is yet another unique challenge confronted by top-down initiatives like the NEPs. If "not invented here," where should they reside? These jurisdictional issues have translated into dilemmas in organizational identity and location for the NEPs. Funding and staffing limitations have compounded these dilemmas. If the programs are enablers of multistate, regional efforts, then it does not make sense for them to be located within state government. But if they are not based in state government and have no enforcement power, then it is unlikely that they can get state agencies to implement the desired direction. And if NEPs are located in state government, being housed in a single agency limits impact. But being housed in multiple agencies creates coordination challenges, and being housed in the governor's office makes the program subject to political maneuvering. There are no easy answers to these organizational dilemmas.

Playing Musical Offices at APNEP

While some feel that APNEP should be located outside of state government in a university or NGO setting, the program has consistently been located within state government but in varying offices. Early on, described Crowell, the program was "buried within the Division of Water Quality. . . . Think back to the mid-'80s, people may [have been] afraid that this will be a new regulatory program, or unfunded mandate. Or it was just new and people were afraid of it to some degree." Prior to 2001, the program was housed in the Planning Assessment unit within the Division of Water Quality. Following an EPA review in the early 2000s, the program was briefly elevated into the North Carolina Department of Environment and Natural Resources office of the secretary of Conservation and Community Affairs. Until the end of 2012, APNEP was administered by the Division of Natural Resource Planning and Conservation as a cooperative program between the state and EPA.

Administration-specific political influence may explain some of the shuffling. An earlier study of APNEP noted that previous administrations were not fully behind the program: Governor Martin's administration (1985–1993) feared it could not control proenvironment elements of the program, and Governor Hunt's administration (1977–1985 and 1993–2001) changed the CCMP to make it more acceptable to constituents, such as agricultural interests.[54] Several staff members felt that the nesting of the program within a North Carolina Department of Environment and Natural Resources division diminished some of the flexibility and influence awarded by its earlier position in the secretary's office. As Director Crowell commented, "We feel that if we're in a division, that limits us to some degree—either in reality or perception. And sometimes, perception is stronger than reality."

Crowell noted that the program's location in a North Carolina Department of Environment and Natural Resources division versus the office of the secretary was a challenge to achieving cross-divisional coordination. When working with people in divisions and agencies for whom APNEP's mission is not a priority, "we often get put to the back burner. And that may be somewhat of a result of where we are. If we were located in the secretary's office, you may—but not always—get a quick response."

Following adoption of the 2012 CCMP, APNEP leadership pressed for a more strategic location to ensure the program would be better situated for impact. In the governor's December 2012 executive order establishing the Albemarle–Pamlico National Estuary Partnership, the program was relocated back into the office of the North Carolina Department of Environment and Natural Resources secretary, who was responsible for administrative and fiscal management of the APNEP office.

Shifting Locations and Complex Funding Mechanisms in NBEP

NBEP has also faced numerous challenges due to its institutional and organizational structure, all of which have made funding, staffing, and creating a coherent identity for the organization difficult. During the initial implementation phase in 1993, NBEP was affiliated with the Rhode Island Department of Environmental Management. This location was difficult for a group that was supposed to be stakeholder based, and it took a long time for the program to escape that regulatory setting. NBEP was later affiliated with the University of Rhode Island's Coastal Institute, and the Rhode Island Natural History Survey.

Annual base funding for NBEP staff and operations has been funneled through three separate cooperative agreements between EPA and each state partner. One grant was allocated to the Rhode Island Department of Environmental Management, used to employ the chief scientist. The second grant went through the University of Rhode Island Coastal Institute, and the third grant ran through the Rhode Island Natural History Survey. Additionally, NBEP utilizes fiscal partnerships with Save The Bay to employ staff members for specific programs and activities. This arrangement has enabled NBEP to avoid state hiring freezes and union constraints on employee selection.

This three-host institutional arrangement has proven problematic for NBEP. As Jane Austin, of Save The Bay commented, it was "[a] challenge to define themselves as a coherent entity in light of divided personnel settings." Though most of the staff is based out of the University of Rhode Island Coastal Institute offices, key individuals are missing, such as the chief scientist. Austin noted that, "a major factor in determining what direction the NEP goes is driven by its institutional structure. If it was a unitary organization, there would be more flexibility in terms of organizing their work across multiple areas." However, Austin did see some benefits of this institutional setting:

[Though it] would be nice not to have the tri-part institutional framework, on one hand, it brings an investment (from state components such as the Department of Environmental Management, University of Rhode Island) in the programs that can't be undervalued. And the NEP would be a lot weaker if it didn't have a significant investment of time and resources from DEM and URI; those are resources the NEP can really tap into.

Additional challenges are found in getting funds to program areas across state lines. Because funding for NBEP is funneled through Rhode Island state agencies, funding activities in Massachusetts is difficult. Fiscal partnerships have been used to get money where it is needed, yet this makes it more complicated administratively.

As the umbrella agency overseeing all 28 NEPs, the EPA conducts five-year program evaluations of each NEP to ensure that adequate progress is being made in implementation of their CCMP. NBEP's most recent program evaluation noted the tremendous challenge they face because of their scattered staff locations, calling it a "unique institutional and jurisdictional situation." In particular, the program evaluation commented on the "duplicative operational tasks associated with having staff under three institutional entities," and the "inconsistency in organizational policies, such as pay scales, leave requirements, and supervisory oversight, resulting from host institution policies and practices."[55]

An external consultant hired by EPA to review the NBEP institutional quagmire and develop recommendations "to strengthen its financial and institutional stability" found an overly complex organization that "results in inefficiencies including multiple layers of oversight, and a lack of clarity regarding who holds the authority to make decisions regarding program administration."[56] An outcome of this formal program evaluation was a major reorganization of NBEP in 2013. A new director and staff were hired, and the program was connected to a new host agency, the New England Interstate Water Pollution Control Commission, based in Lowell, Massachusetts. Along with this organizational shift, and to address the persistent challenge of engaging interest and involvement from the Massachusetts side of the watershed, the NBEP management committee was expanded from twelve to twenty-six members, bringing more Massachusetts perspectives to the table.

According to the new NBEP director, Tom Borden, "The gist of it was rectifying the need to get more representatives from Massachusetts. There had been just one member from Massachusetts, now there are three."[57] Management committee membership has also expanded to include utilities and the Narragansett Bay Commission, which is Rhode Island's largest wastewater system. The objective of these changes, explained Director Borden, "is to bring these people together and really force the various players who are critical to the watershed to work together."[58]

Challenge of Residing under EPA's Regulatory Umbrella

Given the voluntary nature of the NEPs, EPA may not be the best agency in which to house them. Much of EPA's mission is regulatory; the NEPs, however, are charged with engaging state, local, and federal partners in collaborative planning and decision making. This mismatch leads to confusion on the part of nonfederal partners, and it can be undercut by the perception of EPA officials as well. From EPA's perspective, it is challenging to demonstrate the effectiveness of NEP programs, particularly because it can be difficult to track the outcomes of NEP activities in physical and biological terms. NBEP chief scientist Chris Deacutis commented:

> I think people with EPA, within the regulatory sections, find that uncomfortable. They're always asking, "What are we doing to get the TMDLs [total maximum daily load] done." We understand their viewpoint, and do get involved in some of the TMDL bean counting, [but] from a strict engineering approach it doesn't make sense for us to just knock off bean counts. There tends to be this tension because like all bureaucracies, [EPA] wants bean counts that are easy to count, and that have a likelihood of [demonstrating] success in short time periods. . . . The value of the NEPs is that they don't have this bean count approach. So you can turn your attention and focus faster . . . when new situations show up due to new information, or changes within the watershed. You can refocus and say, "Wait a minute this is a big issue."

Funding and Staffing Constraints

Both NEPs have extremely small core staffs. For example, the 23,000-square-mile APNEP area is the responsibility of a full-time staff of four. APNEP regional field officer Jimmy Johnson comments, "We are by far the largest

[NEP]. We cover a huge area compared to most of the other NEPs, which often cover only one county. We have five major rivers and watersheds, two states, and over thirty counties. [Since] the program is only staffed by four people, it is very difficult to be able to do everything that needs to be done in an area that large with such a small staff." Indeed, the activities that many NEPs use to build social capital and momentum in their regions may be limited by the larger distances involved in APNEP. Being able to travel to participate in meetings, cultivate a community-level sense of purpose, and mobilize around local environmental conflicts may all be constrained by the scale of the program.

Another liability of a small staff is the effect of employee departures. At times, APNEP staff turnover and leaves of absence were problematic. For instance, work to revise the CCMP was started but then delayed due to staff departures, and momentum was lost. Similarly, in the middle of a campaign to rally the management advisory committee's role as implementers, the staff project coordinator left the organization. A lag in rehiring resulted in a slow effort to reengage the committee.

Ironically, the small staff and uniqueness of the NEPs can enable them to escape some of the bureaucracy of large government programs. In doing so, they can benefit from the close interaction among diverse professional staff. They also benefit from a significant degree of autonomy and flexibility in defining the specific direction of their programs. Yearly work plans developed by NBEP staff with the overall goals of the CCMP in mind are submitted to the management committee for approval. These yearly work plans allow staff the latitude to identify emerging problems on which to focus attention and resources. They are not restricted to the originally prescribed pathway laid out in 1993, but can adapt to the dynamic conditions of the bay ecosystem. Chief scientist Chris Deacutis describes the NBEP as being "like a small company. A jump ahead of the behemoth companies. Lean and mean and able to move quickly to adapt to problems."

Recognizing the scale of the problems and their own limitations as a small program, the NBEP recognized early on that they needed to build the capacity of other organizations in order to promote action. Their work has included educational workshops and training programs targeted on existing and emerging land trusts, watershed councils, volunteer groups and other environmental NGOs in the Narragansett Bay region. The Rhode Island Land and Water Partnership (RILWP), a partnership founded by the NBEP and the Rhode Island Land Trust Council, has facilitated much of the capacity building. This effort brought together over 40 land trusts, a dozen watershed organizations, and numerous conservation commissions.

The RILWP conducts a yearly Land and Water Conservation Summit for the leaders of community-based conservation organizations and local governments where participants receive training designed to enhance technical and organizational effectiveness. Topics essential for watershed management, land conservation, and organizational development are covered during the Summit.

One way to deal with limited size and tenure of staff is to use volunteers to fill organizational needs, but volunteers have their own challenges. "We work with citizen volunteers, and sometimes things move a lot slower because of it," explains APNEP director Crowell. "We have multiple people across the program area who are busy. They're doing a lot of other things, and to get their time takes time." The science and technical advisory committee cochair, Wilson Laney, commented on the challenge of retaining volunteers: "We've had a real challenge in keeping members on the STAC for the full duration of their term. We have a fair number of resignations, but that's not unique to this program."

Conclusion

Ronald Reagan famously commented that the words, "I'm from the federal government and I'm here to help you," are among the most terrifying in the English language. This comment has been a staple joke ever since. As seen in the APNEP and NBEP cases, navigating a well-intended voluntary process initiated from the top down is fraught with many challenges. With limited budgets, small staffs, and variably supportive home agencies at the state level, the NEPs need to find ways to motivate engagement of agencies and organizations in an estuary's watershed and instill a sense of ownership in the enterprise. They need to build capacity and incentives for actions that benefit an ecosystem which is generally beyond the immediate jurisdiction or concern of state or local managers. The NEPs are not alone in facing these imperatives. Regional Ocean Councils established under the U.S. National Ocean Policy, and National Estuarine Research Reserves established under the Coastal Zone Management Act, among others, are in the same boat.

A major strategy employed by NEPs is collaborative development of a comprehensive plan that identifies critical issues and potential strategic responses. The NEPs seek to engage key players in a nonthreatening planning process that is intended to provide added value to their own state and local management activities. This planning process ideally builds relationships and a sense of shared responsibility for the broader ecosystem. Building partnerships, leveraging funding, encouraging targeted and applied research, and providing information, education, and training are all critical strategies that position the NEPs to foster more coordinated and informed decision making within an estuary ecosystem.

Both APNEP and NBEP have faced challenges associated with their roles as convener, coordinator, and enabler of basin-scale activity. Asking partner organizations to act at a systems level requires them to think beyond themselves, which is intrinsically and organizationally difficult. Mediating among diverse interests and governmental units requires skill at managing the conflict inherent in this role. Doing it with few staff and limited resources in a time of public sector fiscal difficulties is even more challenging.

It is difficult to ascribe specific ecosystem changes to the efforts of the Albemarle–Pamlico and Narragansett Bay NEPs; however, some key ecosystem indicators (e.g., number of fish kills and levels of nutrient loadings) are moving in the right direction, and many of the programs' activities have provided important foundations for ecosystem change: new or better coordinated information, more effective data systems, expanded funding or facilitation of restoration projects, heightened awareness of estuary conditions and challenges, expanded engagement of governmental and nongovernmental groups, and stronger networks of groups acting in a more coordinated fashion. The programs often succeed in moving their regions forward by taking a behind-the-scenes role so that partner agencies and organizations can claim credit. This role is important but nonetheless challenging when individual NEPs come under review and the question asked is, "But what did *you* accomplish?"

Yet, just because it is a difficult role to play does not mean that it is not important. Indeed, as issues like nutrient loadings, invasive species, and climate change take center stage, thinking and acting at an ecosystem scale become critical, and someone is needed to foster the linkages and connections that can sustain effective action. The nonregulatory, collaborative approach advanced by the NEPs is important in encouraging an ecosystem perspective in a highly fragmented institutional landscape. As Margherita Pryor, EPA representative on the NBEP management committee, explained,

> I see this program as a mediating organization between groups that want to do their local plans, and the huge big ecosystem picture. [You] have a group that has scientific and analytical capacity to try and figure out where to target local actions so they contribute to improvement of the system as a whole. I think that is really important.

APNEP director Bill Crowell views the role his program plays in a similar way: "That's where the NEPs have a real niche in government or environmental protection. That they can come from the outside and take the bigger view and bring people together, facilitate those discussions. Develop the contracts or whatever needs to be done. Instate the actions where the others can't."

Individual agencies and municipalities have few resources or motivations to adopt this "bigger view." For that to happen often requires a top-down initiative that is concerned about the broader ecosystem and can bring organization and resources to bear. In the end, of course, it only matters if it improves ecosystem health. And, if nothing else, the NEPs have created a process within which people can convene, identify priorities, monitor progress, and ensure that ecosystem-scale issues are not ignored.

Chapter 6

Influencing Management from the Bottom Up in Port Orford, Oregon, and San Juan County, Washington

In communities throughout the world, fishermen, community leaders, scientists, and agency managers are working together to advance marine conservation. These efforts often emerge in an ad hoc manner, without high-level political endorsement, a legislative or administrative framework, or much in the way of resources. As a result, community-based processes face a unique set of challenges. They require motivated individuals who step up and take leadership, and they need to find ways to establish their legitimacy and credibility so that others take them seriously. They have to be entrepreneurial in attracting resources and building capacity.

The smaller scale of community-based efforts can diminish cross-jurisdictional complexity and associated challenges. However, their lack of authority requires these initiatives to find ways to strategically influence those organizations *with* authority if they are to have meaningful impact. Unlike marine ecosystem-based management (MEBM) initiatives that build on a foundation of government authorities and resources, community-based processes must build their credibility and impact through other means.

The Port Orford and San Juan County Community-Based Initiatives

This chapter describes the experiences of two communities that developed impressive marine conservation initiatives from the bottom up. Following different paths, citizens in Port Orford, Oregon, and Washington State's

San Juan County established formal organizations that were able to tap the energies and concerns of local fishermen, residents, businesses, and government in a way that enabled them to have impact despite their lack of regulatory or management authority. They organized and functioned in a manner that was legitimate and broadly credible. In so doing, they positioned themselves to pursue partnerships with local and state government that ensured their influence.

Port Orford Ocean Resource Team

Port Orford is a small town on Oregon's south coast. Roughly one-quarter of its 1,135 residents are directly employed in the fishing industry. Unlike other harbors in the state that are located alongside rivers and estuaries where their vessels are protected from strong storms, Port Orford's harbor is located on the oceanfront. As a result, all of Port Orford's fishing boats must be hoisted out of the water after each fishing trip; thus all commercial fishing vessels in Port Orford are less than forty feet long. Most ports along the Oregon coast have fishing fleets with a wide range of vessel sizes and gears, such as trawlers, longline, and trolling vessels, whereas Port Orford's fishing fleet is homogeneous and uses no net gear. Port Orford's fishermen exclusively use longline or hook-and-line gear and pots for crab fishing. They fish for a variety of high-value species throughout the year, with over 70 percent dependent on the groundfish fishery, primarily black cod and several species of rockfish. Many of Port Orford's rockfish are harvested and sold live, fetching revenues at least one-third higher than those for dead fish sold in neighboring ports.[1]

In the late 1990s, concerns escalated about declining fisheries along the West Coast, and federal fishery managers imposed new catch restrictions. By 2003, many groundfish fisheries were closed to allow overfished species to recover. According to Port Orford fisherman Aaron Longton, "It was one of these deals where trawlers overcapitalized and fished the resource down so low that there was a crisis. Fishing opportunity was greatly curtailed."[2]

Port Orford fishermen had been increasingly frustrated by the federal fishery management process, which they felt had failed to account for the unique attributes of their small-boat, live-fish fishery. Unlike most other fishing fleets in the state, the Port Orford fishery is largely focused around geographically discrete reef systems near their harbor rather than in the open ocean. However, assessment and management of Oregon's fisheries were largely conducted on a coast-wide basis, at spatial scales too coarse to incorporate and effectively manage these local reef system fish stocks. For example, lingcod had been severely restricted before and after the groundfish closure, but local fishermen reported that lingcod appeared more abundant in Port Orford than was estimated by state and federal fishery managers. The fishermen felt that something needed to be done to incorporate local-scale scientific information on the life cycle and status of targeted stocks into fishery management decision making at the regional scale. The sustainability of Port Orford's fishing community and the resource upon which it depended was at stake.

Recognizing the need and growing support for locally based scientific data to better inform fishery management in the region, the Port Orford Ocean Resource Team (POORT) was established in 2001 by local fishermen and community members. POORT's mission is to "ensure the long-term sustainability of Port Orford's ocean resources and our community that depends on them by uniting science, education, local expertise and conservation." POORT is "dedicated to maintaining access to natural resources by people who are fishing selectively, while promoting sustainable fisheries and protecting marine biological diversity."[3] According to its cofounder, Leesa Cobb, "When we started the organization, fishermen were facing a lot of changes. There had been a salmon disaster coast-wide, collapse of our urchin fishery locally, and we were headed into a groundfish disaster. Nothing that was passing as fisheries management was working for us; that's for sure. People were ready for change."

Acknowledging that the health of Port Orford's fish stocks, community, and economy are interdependent and all equally important, the overarching objective of POORT, in the words of local fisherman Aaron Longton, is to maintain "a healthy environment and a healthy fishing community for a healthy greater community in Port Orford." They have actively engaged the local community in establishing a community stewardship area and local stormwater ordinance. POORT, describes Longton, "collaborates with the conservation and science community, fisheries managers, and fishermen themselves up and down the coast" in assessing and monitoring marine ecosystem indicators. Their efforts were responsible for establishment of the first marine reserve in the state of Oregon. Notably, POORT received the National Oceanic and Atmospheric Administration's 2010 "Award for Excellence for Non-Governmental Organization of the Year," recognizing its innovative community-based approach to sustainable fisheries management. It also received the 2012 "Governor's Gold Award" that celebrates "Greatness in Oregonians."

San Juan County Marine Resources Committee

San Juan County is an archipelago of 170 named islands in the Northwest Straits region of Puget Sound in the state of Washington. Depending on the tide, the island chain encompasses an additional 250 to 530 islands, reefs, and rocks. Its 408 miles of remote shoreline are the most of any county in the nation. The cold, nutrient-rich waters from the Pacific Ocean and intricate tidal currents foster high levels of marine biodiversity. As detailed by the San Juan Marine Resources Committee:

> These waters and shorelines are home to six species of salmon, orcas, Dall's porpoise, Steller's sea lions, river and sea otters, lingcod, several species of rockfish and over 100 species of marine birds. Twenty-two varieties of endangered Chinook salmon use the San Juans in various life cycle stages. Two valuable habitats that provide food and shelter for several kinds of marine life are found throughout the San Juans. Eelgrass grows along 140 miles of our shoreline and one third of the bull kelp in Puget Sound is found here.[4]

Approximately 16,000 full-time or seasonal residents inhabit the islands. People are drawn to the islands' natural beauty, and tourism is an important part of the local economy.

In the 1980s, the National Oceanic and Atmospheric Administration considered establishing a national marine sanctuary in the region at the behest of environmental groups, tribes, and agencies who had expressed concern about the decline of marine species. This proposal was met with broad opposition by all seven counties in the Northwest Straits region, including San Juan County.[5] Most of those opposed were concerned about losing control of local waters to the federal government. There were also substantial fears that a federally administered program would not meaningfully engage local communities or respond to local needs.

In 1994, all seven county councils voiced formal and strong opposition to the sanctuary proposal.[6] As Terrie Klinger, one of the original San Juan County Marine Resources Committee members, recalled, "When NOAA first came and did a feasibility study . . . in the San Juan [islands] there was a lot of support because . . . a lot of people care about the environment, and the marine environment in particular . . . but there was also some very vocal opposition [to] the establishment of a [national marine sanctuary] from a number of very powerful and local people." With Washington governor Mike Lowry unwilling to risk political backlash by supporting an unpopular national marine sanctuary proposal, and given his ability to veto its establishment, NOAA officially withdrew its sanctuary proposal in 1996.[7]

Although the effort to establish a national marine sanctuary failed, there remained recognition in the region that something needed to be done to address the failing health of the Northwest Straits marine ecosystem. Several regional-scale programs already existed in the area, including the National Estuary Program administered by the state's Puget Sound Action Team and work by conservation organizations focused on protecting Puget Sound, but many believed that there was nothing in place that effectively engaged the energy and expertise of local citizens in the conservation and restoration of marine resources.

The San Juan County Commission established a citizen Marine Resources Committee (MRC) in 1996 as a grassroots effort intended to foster local management of marine resources. "Access to beautiful beaches, diverse and abundant wildlife, and stunning views are a big reason why people come to see the San Juans," noted the MRC. "These resources need to be managed for the health of our economy, our enjoyment, and preserved for our children's children."[8] The MRC's mission is "to protect and restore the marine waters, habitats and species of the Salish Sea to achieve ecosystem health and sustainable resource use."

This initiative has leveraged considerable resources and formally represents the county's interests in several policy forums. As chair Steve Revella documented in the San Juan MRC's 2010 Annual Report:

> In partnership with the County's Public Works Dept., the MRC helped the County obtain a $700,000 grant from the EPA [Environmental Protection Agency] enabling a constructed wetland in Eastsound and technical assistance for landowners to help protect the marine environment. We're partnering with the City of Seattle on another EPA project to pilot a certification program to encourage sustainable building practices along the shoreline. The Derelict Vessel Removal program will be restarted, preventing significant pollution.
>
> In keeping with our commitment to engage in local and regional marine protection efforts, we provided input to the Washington Department of Fish and Wildlife's five-year strategic plan and participated in their rockfish advisory group. Two of our members sit on the Puget Sound Partnership's Implementation Committee.
>
> Responding to concerns, the MRC was asked to advise on prioritization of the county's stormwater basins for planning and is working with Public Works to scope out a stormwater monitoring pro-

gram. We commented on the County Council's white paper on oil spills, the number one priority identified by the county.

These accomplishments were made possible by the extensive volunteer hours and personal commitment of the extraordinary people on the MRC.[9]

Informal Beginnings Rooted in Place and Entrepreneurial Individuals

While these community-based initiatives have achieved stature and influence over time, each had humble beginnings. With no mandate or framework provided by others, they were started by individuals in the community who saw a need and began trying to find ways to address it. While pressing issues in a place of shared concern are often what motivate a marine conservation initiative, the fact remains that somebody has to step forward to get the ball rolling.

Both Port Orford and San Juan County had concerned and respected community members who were personally motivated to try to do something to help their communities. In Port Orford, that individual was Leesa Cobb, the wife of a prominent Port Orford fisherman. As she explained, she was already volunteering her time to help local fishermen "figure out their permits and deal with paperwork" during the tumultuous fishing closures. Like most residents of Port Orford, Cobb cared about her community and the marine ecosystem upon which that community depends. Along with Laura Anderson, a graduate student at Oregon State University studying fisheries management, and with a $10,000 grant from Environmental Defense Fund, Cobb began working "full-time for part-time pay" soliciting input from fishermen on their views of fisheries management in the region. Most fishermen were unhappy with the state of fisheries management and felt that finer-scale management, based on local scientific information, would improve management overall. With widespread concern and a desire for change, and with others willing to work with them to try to advance shared objectives, Cobb and Anderson established the Port Orford Ocean Resources Team (POORT) in 2001.

One of the things that community-based processes have going for them is that they are place based. They can build on preexisting local relationships. While POORT's accomplishments are impressive when viewed today, and its governance appears to be a textbook organizational structure, the fact is that the initiative had a very simple beginning. As Mike Murphy,

Port Orford city administrator, recalled, "Port Orford is a small place; everybody knows everybody. I don't think it was destined that way; it just happened. Leesa made some suggestions and [people] said, 'Gee that's a good idea, I didn't think of that.' And everything just kind of worked."

It was the same story in San Juan County where a local port commissioner and county commissioner discussed the idea of creating a committee composed of a diverse group of citizens with the mission to address marine conservation issues at the local level. As county commissioners, they personally knew many of the individuals who had been opposed to the national marine sanctuary proposal but who nonetheless remained concerned about San Juan County's marine environment.

While established by the San Juan County Commission, at the outset, the MRC was anything but formal. Initially, it was simply a group of concerned citizens willing to discuss urgent marine conservation issues and try to chart a path forward. As long-time MRC member Jim Slocomb recalled, "It wasn't an organized enough thing to even call it a vision. I think it falls more into the realm of what seemed like a good idea at the time. Get a few illustrious locals with some knowledge of the marine environment to sit down and take it from there. When I came on the MRC . . . it had no budget, no work plan, no guiding principles. It was just a bunch of people sitting around talking."

Establishing Legitimacy: Two Contrasting Paths

An ad hoc group of citizens concerned about marine conservation issues is unlikely to have much influence. Who are they, and why should managers, elected officials, or other community members pay them any heed? In order to be recognized as a legitimate voice in local, state, or national forums, they need official sanctioning, and the community-based initiatives we examined generally achieved recognition in one of two ways: either through acquiring nonprofit status, or by establishment as a sanctioned committee under their local or state government.

POORT's 501(c)(3) Nonprofit Status

POORT was formalized as a 501(c)(3) nonprofit organization in 2003. As such, it has a board of directors that consists of five commercial fishermen and meets monthly. A community advisory team meets quarterly in a public forum and "provides a formal means for Port Orford community leaders, stakeholder representatives, scientists and agency staff to advise POORT and its project partners in bottom-up efforts in ocean management, science, and marketing."[10] Among others, the mayor of Port Orford, the chairman of the Port Orford Planning Commission, the editor of the local newspaper, and the ocean ecosystem project manager for the Surfrider Foundation are all members of the community advisory team. POORT also has an executive director, Leesa Cobb, and a small staff that sometimes includes an AmeriCorps volunteer.

POORT's 501(c)(3) status, with its required leadership and management structure, raised its stature and established a formally recognized role for the group. The Port Orford City Council, noting that over 70 percent of local boat owners were participating in the POORT process, passed a resolution in June 2006 that formally recognized and endorsed POORT, and pledged the City's participation in the process. The resolution stated, "The City Council of Port Orford, by virtue of the authority vested in this body by the City Charter and the State of Oregon, does hereby endorse the vision, principles, and community-based process of the Port Orford Ocean Resource Team."[11]

POORT's 501(c)(3) status gave the group a legitimate voice in official forums at the local, regional, state, and national level. Moreover, it enabled them to enter into partnerships with other public and private entities and to receive grants. For example, in 2009, Oregon governor Ted Kulongoski endorsed Port Orford's Marine Economic Recovery Plan, making Port Orford eligible to compete against other applicants for federal economic stimulus funds. Over time, POORT was able to secure funds to build a science laboratory, new facilities for the Port of Port Orford's live fish fishery, as well as a marine interpretive center that features the unique and important habitat and fish species found in Port Orford's marine reserve.

Similarly, its 501(c)(3) status enabled POORT to sign a memorandum of understanding with the Oregon Department of Fish and Wildlife in September 2008, which established a collaborative science and management relationship. The memorandum of understanding has enabled POORT to receive priority state funding for ecosystem-based management science projects in its stewardship area and has helped ensure that Port Orford fishermen play a stronger role informing the Department of Fish and Wildlife's management decisions. As explained by Surfrider's Charlie Plybon, fishermen, through POORT, are now able to have their concerns voiced at the state and federal levels. Their questions and data needs are turned into "true science questions" that may be funded by Department of Fish and Wildlife, with research conducted in Port Orford, and then incorporated into the Department's management decisions.

According to POORT board president Aaron Longton, communication now "goes both ways. . . . We are able to give our information to them and share what our needs are and what our experiential knowledge from being out on the water is showing us and telling us." For Port Orford's fishermen, commented Longton, this opportunity to influence the "large immovable object" of management-as-usual "inspires hope and keeps us keepin' on."

By virtue of having a formalized organization, POORT can also act as a convener, bringing together citizens, businesses, organizations, and agencies involved in or responsible for marine conservation activities. POORT regularly hosts Land–Sea Connection Workshops, the intent of which is "to bring together natural resource professionals and land owners within the Port Orford Community Stewardship Area. Participants provide information about their projects and are provided with the opportunity to explore ways to work together towards common goals."[12]

County Commission Advisory Committee Status in the San Juan Islands

While POORT was formalized as a nonprofit organization, San Juan County's initiative was established as a formal advisory committee of the San Juan County Commission (renamed the County Council in 2006). The Council sanctions MRC activities, and any decisions requiring Council action—such as approval of new ordinances or adoption of new policies—are acted on by the Council after it considers recommendations by the committee. Terrie Klinger, longtime County Council member, described the formal establishment of the MRC:

> [San Juan County] pulled together a citizens advisory group that they called the Marine Resources Committee and the County Commissioners endorsed it as an advisory body to them. The original purpose of the San Juan County MRC was to have a group of citizen stakeholders that were quite diverse . . . advise the County Commissioners on matters having to do with the marine environment.

As a formal County Council advisory committee, the MRC has no jurisdiction or authority. It cannot regulate the activities of others. Its role is to offer advice and recommendations of a policy nature to the County Council and to take actions on projects supported by the Council. Specifically, the MRC was charged by the County Commission to advise the San Juan County Council on marine resource issues; participate in local and regional processes affecting marine resource management; develop resources for local marine science, ecosystem preservation, and recovery projects; raise awareness and engage citizens in marine issues; and manage marine preservation and recovery projects. Its mission "is to protect and restore the marine waters, habitats and species of the Salish Sea to achieve ecosystem health and sustainable resource use."[13]

Given its respected role and accomplishments, eventually the San Juan MRC became a model for community-based marine conservation activity in the broader Northwest Straits region. When Congress established the Northwest Straits Marine Conservation Initiative in 1998 to provide an opportunity for local knowledge, input, and prioritization in marine conservation in the region, it adopted San Juan County's MRC model and replicated it in six other counties. In turn, their involvement in the Northwest Straits Initiative has enabled access to an expanded array of funding and support opportunities for the San Juan MRC.

Ensuring Credibility: Science-Based Stewardship and Extensive Outreach

Leaders in both the Port Orford and the San Juan County community-based initiatives acknowledged that, to make a difference and be respected, their proposals and advice needed to be credible. It was essential for them to work closely with scientists, involve resource managers and users, and keep community members informed and on board.

Science-Based Stewardship in Port Orford

POORT recognized early on that it needed to construct its strategies on a strong foundation of science. As the city administrator, Mike Murphy, put it, management decision making must be based on science, "otherwise you're going to lose." Collaborative research between Port Orford's fishermen and university and government scientists is central to POORT's activity. POORT has collaborated with the Oregon Department of Fish and Wildlife and Oregon State University to complete a multibeam bathymetric survey at Redfish Rocks, their then proposed marine reserve, and to develop baseline ecological data. Oregon State University developed habitat maps based on the multibeam imagery collected as part of the bathymetric survey. Similarly, the Department of Fish and Wildlife is conducting a remotely operated vehicle video survey in the Redfish Rocks area to better understand fish behavior and life cycles. In 2008, POORT joined The Nature Conservancy in a study of algal communities, seaweed, and the animals that rely on them in their proposed marine reserve. As part of this study, sixty species were identified, twelve of which had never been recorded in Oregon and one that may be new to science. In June 2013, POORT and Oregon State University signed a memorandum of understanding to establish a long-term relationship for science and education work at OSU's new Port Orford field research station.

Collaboration with scientists has facilitated information sharing and understanding between Port Orford's fishermen and the scientists. The fishermen's knowledge of the reef aids scientists in designing and implementing research projects. Fishermen also assist with data collection and offer charter boat services to scientists. POORT has several ongoing collaborative research projects within and near the now-designated Redfish Rocks Marine Reserve. One project involves tagging key species in the live fish fishery to examine the survival rates and movements of live fish caught but released to provide scientific support for the release of gravid female fish. POORT, local fishermen, and the Department of Fish and Wildlife are also collaborating on a port sampling project to add to biological data collected on nearshore species with the goal of conducting stock assessments on a finer spatial scale.[14]

The scientists' improved relationship with the community has helped to translate research into management and policy decisions. For example, using new scientific information, partnerships, and the guidance of Port Orford's fishing fleet, the City of Port Orford in 2006 designated over one thousand square miles of terrestrial and marine habitat as the Port Orford Community Stewardship Area. Port Orford's Community Stewardship Area is explicitly grounded in ecosystem-based management principles:

[It] is an integrated approach to management that considers the entire ecosystem, including humans. It is driven by the integration of all types of knowledge, information and people to minimize conflict and comprehensively manage natural areas to overcome management problems of the past. The overall goal is to support the health, recovery and diversity of natural ecosystems while also taking into account the sustainable use by humans of the system. In most cases, it uses a science-based approach to manage natural resources on a smaller, place-based scale.[15]

Early in the Stewardship Area planning process, POORT sought the assistance of nongovernmental organizations, foundations, and consultants to help ensure a technically sound and scientifically informed process. The Surfrider Foundation, a nonprofit grassroots organization "dedicated to the protection and enjoyment of our world's oceans, waves and beaches,"[16] provided financial and technical support to conduct participatory mapping of potential areas for protection. The outreach and water quality monitoring efforts provided by Surfrider helped the Port Orford community conceptualize and respect the "land–sea connection," a hallmark of their ecosystem-based management approach. The mapping of commercially and ecologically important fishing territories led by Ecotrust, a Portland-based nonprofit with expertise in geographic information systems and economic analysis, helped identify potential sites for a marine research reserve and stewardship area that would meet POORT's goals of maintaining ecological and economic sustainability. The now defunct Pacific Marine Conservation Council also worked very closely with POORT to draft its stewardship plan.

The Port Orford Community Stewardship Area comprises the geographic scope of POORT's work. As they describe it, "The Stewardship Area is the traditional fishing grounds of our fleet and the upland watersheds that feed into them. In total, it covers 1,320 square miles—385 sq. mi. of terrestrial habitat and 935 sq. mi. of ocean habitat."[17] Fishermen initially suggested a larger area for protection than was eventually finalized in the Stewardship Area, surprising the facilitators of the mapping project, and bucking common stereotypes about fishermen's behavior and likely responses to fishery protection proposals.

As Charlie Plybon of the Surfrider Foundation recalls, in Port Orford, "We started with a need to manage, a need for better management, a need for sustainability" identified by fishermen and the local community. The inclusive organizational structure of POORT and the shared sense of purpose, place, and problems in Port Orford led fishermen to identify ecologically and economically important areas to protect in the ocean and on land. The fishermen's attention to the land and sea interface impressed the outside facilitators. As Plybon described, "We were drawing lines for a Stewardship Area on a map saying, 'Okay, we're going to protect this area.' That was a breakthrough for me [when] these fishermen drew these lines. But then when they drew them up onto the terrestrial system and said, 'We need to protect the watershed as well,' that blew me away; I was just like, holy cow! They get it."

The Stewardship Area plan identified five principles for management:

"Science should drive management; rules must provide the community a secure future; management decisions should reflect local needs; management decisions must maintain economic and ecological sustainability; and recognition comes with participation."[18] While explicitly encouraging collaboration between the community and state and federal agencies, it does not affect established jurisdictions or formal authorities. According to Plybon, "Other EBM [ecosystem-based management] attempts usually come with the idea of strong restrictions, like marine reserves" designed and implemented by outside entities. This leads certain sectors of the public to think "you're taking something away from me and they don't understand the reasons why you're taking that away from them, or they don't understand the reason why it's being managed this way." In contrast, in Port Orford the fishermen were integrally involved in defining the Stewardship Area and discussing management strategies within it, which eventually included a designated marine reserve.

The State of Oregon recognizes Port Orford's Community Stewardship Area as an appropriate management strategy and, through their formal memorandum of understanding, has helped POORT secure funding that supports continued monitoring and research.

Science-Based Stewardship in San Juan County

Like POORT, the first major initiative of the San Juan MRC was to set the groundwork for establishment of a marine stewardship area informed by science and local knowledge. In the 1990s, western Washington was experiencing an economic and housing boom, and most acknowledged that the problems facing the marine environment were occurring as a direct or indirect result of that development. The role of the MRC as an advisory body to the County Council positioned it to influence local land use planning and ordinances. The first order of business was to define the area of interest and conduct an assessment of the status and issues of concern within the area. The MRC identified a countywide marine stewardship area "to facilitate the protection and preservation of our natural marine environment for the tribes and other historic users, current and future residents, and visitors." The county board of commissioners formally created the marine stewardship area in 2004 and "asked the MRC to work with scientists and community leaders to create a management plan that would achieve a healthy marine ecosystem in balance with human use and enjoyment."[19]

The San Juan County Marine Stewardship Area Plan was developed in partnership with The Nature Conservancy using a version of their Conservation Action Planning process to fit the needs of the MRC. At the time, The Nature Conservancy used a "Five-S Framework" to systematically address conservation planning: (1) identifying *systems* (targets) of conservation concern, (2) identifying *stresses* on the conservation targets, (3) identifying *sources* of the *stresses*, (4) determining *strategies* to conserve the priority conservation targets, and (5) determining measures of *success* against which to evaluate and revise the conservation actions. The Marine Stewardship Area Plan describes the initial stages of this process:

> The Committee began collecting available marine resources data and placing this data on maps in order to get a better picture of the county's marine life and the potential measures that would help to protect it and the human activities that depend on it. During the first year following the designation of the stewardship area, the MRC compiled marine resources data, mapped them and developed the concept for a countywide zone scheme. . . . The zone scheme proposed special use areas along county shorelines where resources were found to be especially abundant. The proposal included multiple use and restricted use areas, proposing voluntary protection measures such as no anchoring in eelgrass beds.[20]

The MRC also integrated sociocultural values into the planning process, with its own set of targets and strategies. Jonathan White, San Juan MRC member, explained the importance of a planning process grounded in science: "[The MSA plan] gives us a scientific backbone for some of the measures that we need to do here that might be perceived as draconian by some, but necessary to turn the health of the system around. One of the things we felt from the beginning is that we needed to have [scientific] backing for what we were doing because of the pushback we get from the community." Given the complexity of marine ecosystems and the reality of limited data, considerable interpretation of data was required when assessing the status of indicators and stressors. Consequently, the MRC solicited independent scientific and technical reviews to validate the viability and threat assessment results for their marine biodiversity targets.

The ultimate result of this multiyear endeavor was the creation of a countywide scientifically based marine stewardship plan that identified areas of existing voluntary and regulatory protection from federal, state, and county authorities and that proposed additional areas to be afforded protection. The County Council adopted the plan in 2007.

Extensive Outreach to Ensure Community Understanding and Support

Community-based initiatives must be scientifically sound and credible at multiple levels. Both the San Juan MRC and POORT used extensive outreach and engagement to build their credibility. Credibility rooted in science and extensive community engagement was doubly important for the San Juan County Marine Stewardship Area process because it relies on voluntary activities and compliance to achieve its goals. To this end, draft Stewardship Area plans and ideas were submitted for public comment and input from community members. Environmental managers were involved throughout the process.[21] San Juan MRC member Jonathan White described the wide-ranging collaboration involved in developing the plan:

> We had a number of agencies involved. We [had a] Marine Managers Workshop every year, we still have them every year. We invite[d] managers who have responsibilities in the area to be involved in that and it specifically focused on the marine stewardship area plan. Right from the get-go they helped us do some of the planning over the five years, now they help us to look at the monitoring and what's come out of it. These are regional folks, federal [officials], scientists, parks people, local people, it's quite a group, stakeholders of all kinds. Their input is embedded in this whole thing.

POORT members and staff similarly follow an open and inclusive process that keeps the community informed and engaged. Port Orford's stormwater ordinance was adopted in November 2009 with no public objection, largely because of POORT's extensive outreach efforts. POORT conducted over 170 hours of outreach. Brianna Goodwin, POORT's stewardship outreach coordinator, teamed up with POORT board president Aaron Longton and spoke with as many groups as possible. Along with a fact sheet and answers to frequently asked questions, Goodwin and Longton circulated their materials to the community in formal meetings with the Rotary, the Watershed Council, and the Chamber of Commerce. Goodwin commented:

> When we did our outreach, we started with the issue of surface water pollution and Aaron would smoothly go into how the nearshore environment would affect the fishery. So we have Aaron with a lot of credibility as a commercial fishermen talking about the effects.

He had stories about filleting a fish and finding a cigarette butt in its stomach. And finding golf balls in crab pots.

Together, they also wrote articles in the local paper, held a town hall meeting, and distributed factsheets at restaurants, the library, and the hardware store. As Goodwin emphasized, "Most of the outreach work in Port Orford is informal." POORT staff and board members spoke to community members and answered their questions at the grocery store, a holiday barbecue, and the local diner. In so doing, they fostered understanding of the impacts of unregulated stormwater and the benefits a new ordinance would bring to the community. Their efforts paid off in broad community support for the ordinance as well as for other POORT projects. City administrator Mike Murphy underscored how essential POORT's extensive outreach was to ensuring that community members fully understood and supported the proposal: "If you don't give people a chance to see [your proposals] before public hearings, they will come in with a whole bunch of misconceptions."

POORT was also careful to frame their ideas and approach in a manner that was meaningful to community members, not just scientists. As Charlie Plybon of Surfrider observed:

> I think one of the best things we did was saying "Stewardship Area," not EBM. . . . We all know what stewardship means—it means we want to take care of this. . . . Protection didn't just mean protecting the environment, but protecting the economic stability of natural resource extraction . . . protecting the economy too.

Creating Influence through Mutually Beneficial Partnerships

One way that these community-based initiatives gained influence was by developing "win–win" partnerships with state agencies and local governments. They found critical synergies between what those in a position of authority needed and what the community-based group was able to provide. In each of these efforts, the community-based groups were in a position to provide essential resources, expertise, and support to local, regional, and state authorities; without this support, the agencies were precluded from taking action. In exchange, the community groups were able to secure their own objectives. Partnerships such as these are a critical way for community-based initiatives to gain leverage.

Advancing a State Program through a Local Initiative: POORT's Marine Reserve

POORT's successful efforts at establishing a marine reserve provide a good illustration. POORT was interested in the reserve to advance its own stewardship objectives but possessed no authority to establish one. In turn, the State of Oregon wanted to begin developing a system of marine reserves but realized that, even though they possessed regulatory authority, they needed community support in order to succeed. Both POORT and the state could benefit each other's interests and capabilities if they could make it work.

In 2005, Oregon's governor Ted Kulongoski began a public process to establish a network of marine reserves along the Oregon coast and assigned his Ocean Policy Advisory Council to conduct a background assessment. Intended initially to set the stage for the establishment of a national marine sanctuary, in 2007 the governor directed the Ocean Policy Advisory Council to explore possibilities for a more bottom-up approach to establishing marine reserves, hoping to avoid the inevitable conflicts associated with top-down designation. Citizens and interested parties were encouraged to nominate potential marine reserve sites. The Advisory Council then synthesized these proposals for the governor, state agencies, and local governments in its Oregon Marine Reserve Policy Recommendations report.[22]

With financial and technical assistance from Ecotrust, POORT began conducting focus groups with fishermen in 2006 to identify potential locations for a marine reserve in the Port Orford Community Stewardship Area. POORT provided large maps of the area used by Port Orford's fishing fleet, and fishermen identified economically and ecologically productive fishing grounds. These areas were then converted into polygons through geographic information system mapping software, combined with publicly available habitat data and used to select potential sites that minimized economic harm while maximizing ecological benefits. Throughout this process, according to Aaron Longton, POORT did "a ton of outreach; we spoke to every group that would have us, repeatedly. The garden club, senior center, Women's League of Voters, Rotary, Chamber of Commerce, the list goes on." These outreach efforts were essential for gaining community support and minimizing opposition to a marine reserve proposal.

After much public discussion and input, POORT eventually selected Redfish Rocks as the site for their proposed no-take research reserve, nested within the already established Community Stewardship Area. With the assistance of Jim Golden of Golden Marine Consulting, a small locally based consulting firm that had worked with POORT during the Stewardship Area planning process, POORT prepared and submitted its marine reserve proposal to the Ocean Policy Advisory Council. As described by POORT, the Redfish Rocks area:

> encompasses 2.6 square miles around Redfish Rocks, from the Extreme Low Tide Line (ELTL) to about 20 fathoms. The use of the ELTL instead of the Extreme High Tide Line (EHTL) as the boundary will allow clam digging in the rocky intertidal areas to continue. In addition to this reserve, a Marine Protected Area (MPA) was proposed that extends from the western boundary of the marine reserve to the 3 mile territorial sea boundary. This was added to the proposal to address the issue of increasing ecological benefits and decreasing economic impacts. By closing the area to any net, jig or longline gear, but allowing for the salmon and crab fisheries that use pelagic troll and pots to continue, increased protection for rockfish and other nearshore species with larger home ranges is provided while maintaining historic economic uses.[23]

Of twelve proposals submitted to the Ocean Policy Advisory Council and later to the governor and state legislature, Port Orford's was one of two selected for official designation as Oregon's first marine reserves. Redfish Rocks Marine Reserve was signed into law in July 2009.[24] The Redfish Rocks Marine Reserve proposal had substantial community support that clearly facilitated its designation. Other marine reserve proposals were largely top-down efforts put forward by state and federal agency scientists with little or no community support. According to Mike Murphy, Port Orford's city administrator, the other proposals faced significant community opposition, with communities "fighting them tooth and nail."

POORT Partners with Local Government to Advance a Local Ordinance

The stewardship area defined by POORT includes both marine and terrestrial systems. Recognizing that runoff from upstream watersheds was impacting the marine ecosystem, POORT began discussions with the City of Port Orford about strengthening its local stormwater ordinance. POORT was interested in reducing the impact of stormwater on the marine ecosystem; the City was interested in developing an updated ordinance that met state and federal standards. However, the City had neither the resources nor widespread support for advancing a new ordinance. As city administrator

Mike Murphy noted, like many small towns, Port Orford is "understaffed and overworked." Without jurisdiction or authority, POORT could not develop and enforce a new ordinance, but they could help the city raise funds and build needed local support. In much the same way that POORT capitalized on the benefit their community-based process provided the State of Oregon in the Marine Reserve designation process, POORT sought a mutually beneficial relationship with the City of Port Orford.

In December 2008, Port Orford's city council signed a memorandum of understanding with POORT establishing a formal partnership. Throughout the marine reserve designation process, several of Port Orford's city councilors regularly attended POORT-sponsored meetings as observers. Others served on POORT's community advisory team, including the mayor of Port Orford, the chairman of the Port Orford Planning Commission, and the president of the city council. These existing relationships provided a foundation for this new formal partnership.

Funding from the Surfrider Foundation enabled them to hire an outside consultant to write a grant proposal, and POORT and the City applied for and obtained a technical assistance grant from the Oregon Department of Land Conservation and Development to draft, promote, and pass a revised stormwater ordinance. The new ordinance uses the U.S. Environmental Protection Agency's Best Management Practices for volume, rate of flow, and amount of pollutants to improve water quality by capturing and treating stormwater.[25] Most of the stormwater regulated by the new ordinance will be treated through rain gardens or bioswales. The ordinance that was eventually developed included guidelines and requirements for managing stormwater from new development and provided a solid foundation for future collaboration between POORT and the City. According to city administrator Mike Murphy, the collaboration between POORT and the City of Port Orford on the stormwater ordinance was a "really positive thing," demonstrating that "city government can work with private citizen groups, and interested and diverse groups."

San Juan County's Stewardship Area: The Downside of Going It Alone

San Juan County took a different approach than Port Orford in the way they formalized their stewardship area, and their experience offers a somewhat cautionary lesson about what happens when community-based initiatives fail to gain adequate influence through partnerships with agencies that can ensure needed compliance. Given the consensus-based nature of decision making in the San Juan MRC, efforts to develop marine protected areas with regulatory teeth were set aside in favor of less contentious approaches. The MRC was not interested in working with state agencies to regulate local activities, preferring to develop voluntary restricted use zones. Northwest Straits Commission director Ginny Broadhurst recalls,

> The San Juan MRC was really concerned with rockfish populations and they're so *not* enamored with regulatory agencies they just said, "We'll just create our own bottomfish reserves. We'll do it on a voluntary basis since we don't have any authority. We'll draw lines on a map and we'll ask people not to fish there." The Department of Fish and Wildlife wouldn't even publish that information. The San Juan MRC had to buy advertisement space in DFW's pamphlet that goes out to sport fishermen every year.

The San Juan MRC's independent go-it-alone approach, however, meant that any potential users of the stewardship area needed to understand and be committed to its objectives. Hence implementation of the marine stewardship area plan relies on engaging and educating community members. Its effectiveness is predicated on community concurrence and compliance. As San Juan MRC member Jonathan White explained, "It's all voluntary . . . our number one strategy is to develop a stewardship ethic in residents and visitors through outreach and education. . . . We are putting a lot of stake into that education and outreach. We have a subcommittee that's ongoing, we get funding every year for it . . . it is our number one priority. We are committed to that [strategy] as being our most effective measure." Education and outreach activities include signage, workshops and training, and broad distribution of stewardship guides, newsletters, and maps that promote the plan, explain best practices, and clearly identify different use zones in the stewardship area.

Unfortunately, compliance has been problematic. Some believe that identification of different use zones in the stewardship area may have actually encouraged activities it was meant to discourage. As Jonathan White explained,

> We established, back in 1996, voluntary bottomfish recovery zones, about eight of them in our county. We've been monitoring them ever since and here it is thirteen years later and we've discovered that they're not working . . . most likely due to a lack of compliance. . . . In some cases people are using the [zoning] maps to identify the best fishing areas. . . . We have done a lot of outreach and now we

are at the point where we are seeing that a regulatory measure may be necessary.

While greater regulation might have been necessary to protect San Juan fisheries, government authority is not always required to ensure compliance with needed restrictions. Indeed, many community-based initiatives around the world are effective at creating a shared sense of ownership with access rules, though often they focus on a defined fishery or area with a smaller number of participants who jointly create and self-enforce rules.[26] At times, bottom-up initiatives are more effective than top-down regulatory efforts at securing compliance because they are more likely to engage stakeholders and avoid reactive antigovernment behavior. Effective community-based initiatives evaluate what is needed in their situation and create strategy and partnerships to achieve it.

Conclusion

The previous chapters have described the unique characteristics and challenges associated with different types of marine ecosystem-based management initiatives. Community-based initiatives emerge in a unique and organic manner, arising from the concerns of local citizens and their desire to move from the status quo. However, "The status quo is a giant immovable object," observed POORT fisherman Aaron Longton, "You just chip away, chip away, and chip away at it." Since collaborative EBM is a significant shift away from traditional management, sustained effort is needed.

Community-based initiatives need to carefully bring their communities along, and that takes hard work, which often produces slow progress. As Longton put it, "We want to go there *now*. But it doesn't work that way when you're going bottom up; you've got to lobby and win and gain support all along the way." Both POORT and the San Juan County MRC demonstrate the wisdom of Longton's comment. The initiatives carefully developed their legitimacy and credibility in a way that sought to avoid making other community members or government agencies feel threatened, while still promoting significant change. However, sustaining community support can be an ongoing challenge.

Having individual champions in the community was critical to the progress of these efforts, but they also needed support from outside. Few people involved in community-based marine ecosystem-based management processes have ever done anything like it before. They usually need help getting organized, establishing a productive focus, and acquiring resources and direction. In its early stages, POORT received essential assistance from the David and Lucile Packard Foundation, Ecotrust, Environmental Defense Fund, the Ford Family Foundation, and Surfrider. Once they got their bearings, they eventually reached out to the state for assistance with studies. The San Juan County effort similarly capitalized on the resources and support of the Bullitt Foundation, the National Fish and Wildlife Foundation, The Nature Conservancy, Northwest Straits Initiative, Puget Sound Partnership, Surfrider, and others.

Knowing that other places were trying similar approaches was empowering. As Leesa Cobb commented, "We felt very alone; we live in a remote area of the coast, in a little town. We needed to know other people were doing this and to learn from them what will help make our project successful." POORT belonged to the Packard Foundation–funded West Coast Ecosystem-Based Management Network, which provided them with moral support, camaraderie, and good ideas. POORT currently belongs to the Community Fisheries Network, and the San Juan MRC has a close relationship with other MRCs under the Northwest Straits Initiative umbrella.

Strategic partnerships with other levels of government were critical. These relationships developed by finding synergies between a community's aspirations and capabilities and the resources and authorities of government agencies. They were most effective when they provided benefits to both sides. However, identifying and demonstrating these synergies often require patience and proof of what is possible. For example, a Northwest Straits commissioner commented on the gradual evolution that occurred before state agencies came to realize that MRCs were not a threat but an asset. Over time, the relationship has transformed their perspectives on each other while getting needed work done:

> At first I think they were threatened by what the MRCs were trying to do. . . . I think that many of the natural resource agencies have really shifted their view . . . realizing that it really is a source of funding and connecting to real people in northern Puget Sound that allows them to get a lot better information. This is especially true in tough economic times. If the MRCs can do a lot of work that otherwise couldn't be funded, that can't be viewed as anything but beneficial.

Chapter 7

Bricks:
Tangible Elements That Support & Guide
Marine Ecosystem-Based Management

While the preceding chapters have described the variations associated with different types of marine conservation initiatives, the next two chapters describe attributes that these initiatives share in common. The initiatives we examined arose independently in different regions of the world; they are embedded in different sociopolitical contexts and involve different individuals and organizations. Nonetheless, they all exhibit several essential characteristics. They all have organizational elements and process qualities that have enabled them to stay on track and make progress.

Some of these factors are tangible and can be easily replicated; others are intangible and are embedded in the motivations and attributes of the people involved. Both are critical to sustained and productive marine ecosystem-based management (MEBM). As already described, we refer to the tangible structures as the bricks and the intangible qualities as the mortar that holds the bricks together. This chapter describes the structural elements supporting MEBM—the bricks.

Constructing the Missing Table

Proximity matters. People cannot effectively tackle complex issues of shared concern when their paths seldom cross and when they lack a context within which to work together; they need a *table* to gather around. "The old patterns of intermittent and ad hoc activity . . . [were] inadequate to meet the needs of a growing region that places a high value on its natural environment," commented Jamie Alley about the gap that existed before the Puget Sound Georgia Basin International Task Force was formed. He continued:

> A mechanism for regular liaison was missing. . . . Contacts had been irregular, and considerable mistrust had built up. [Officials on both sides of the border were] unsure of the degree to which they were mandated or authorized to exchange information or to cooperate with a "foreign" government. . . . Where officials were working together, they did not have formal reporting mechanisms or means to resolve minor issues and disputes as they arose. Most important, consideration of issues failed to include an understanding of their broader regional context, and no sense of strategic priorities existed.[1]

David Keeley used the same terminology when describing the missing forum that triggered formation of the Gulf of Maine Council: "I was the director of the Maine coastal program at the time and had worked extensively with colleagues in other states. While each of us had interesting programs in place, we didn't really have any formal mechanism to talk about interstate things."[2]

A surprising number of participants spoke about the critically important "table" provided by their initiatives: they created a place where people could convene, and where conversations could begin taking place. As Glen Herbert of Canada's Eastern Scotian Shelf Integrated Management process put it, "It's important to set up these tables and places where people who normally wouldn't talk to each other have an opportunity to talk." His comments were echoed three thousand miles away and almost verbatim by Northwest Straits Initiative commissioner Terrie Klinger, who emphasized that "one of the real strengths of the Initiative is bringing all sorts of people into the same room to talk that otherwise would never sit around a table together." Fellow Northwest Straits participant Duane Fagergren concurred: "It is the way to involve the whole realm of people . . . it is the table that everybody can sit around, sometimes have a difference of opinion, but be respectful about how it gets done."

Each of the initiatives we examined constructed the missing table around which those concerned about their marine ecosystem could convene. Providing this simple but all important place was the first brick in their foundations, but it was not the only one. They recognized that a table without legitimacy, purpose, and structure would be an insufficient mechanism for interaction; a place without purpose in today's busy world will quickly gather dust.

Those who constructed these MEBM initiatives did so in an iterative fashion and built a system brick by brick that responded to several functional needs. Each initiative exhibits a governance infrastructure that delineates leadership and administrative roles and responsibilities. Each has a purpose and a scope that define its niche relative to other marine conservation activities in the region. Each contains organizational elements to ensure that work gets done and the initiative has impact. Their governance system includes mechanisms that link the initiatives to external organizations and communities; it also integrates science and ensures that resources are available.

The initiatives we examined were governed in a deliberate fashion; none was an ad hoc free-for-all. Each initiative, regardless of scale or scope, confronted the following questions in establishing a governance system that focused and supported its work:

- What is our niche?
- What is our unique purpose and reach?
- How should we organize to have impact?
- Who will make decisions for the group, in what manner, and based on what criteria?
- Who will manage the process?
- How will we relate to others with jurisdiction or interest in the ecosystem?
- What will be the roles and responsibilities of those involved?

Delineating an Initiative's Niche: Authorities, Purpose, and Scope

No MEBM initiative is established on a blank slate. All are formed within a context of preexisting policy, jurisdictional arrangements, ongoing uses, and management activity. Thus each initiative needed to carefully define its niche within an established institutional context. They needed to clarify their goals and objectives for their own members and for other agencies and governments. They needed to explicitly define what they aspired to achieve and how those goals related to other entities involved in marine conservation in the region.

The first step in doing so was to recognize the limits of their authority and bound their scope in a manner that complemented existing jurisdictions and authorities. The Gulf of Maine Council (GOMC) was explicit from the outset that "authority to act rests with individual jurisdictions and federal agencies." GOMC's influence was rooted in its "moral suasion, peer-

pressure, and working toward the common good."[3] Similarly, the Port Orford Ocean Resource Team (POORT) and the State of Oregon established
a formal memorandum of understanding that enabled their collaboration
but explicitly noted that their work together "neither changed the jurisdictional boundaries of the state, nor changed the federal legal regimes under
which the resources of the exclusive economic zone are managed."[4]

Most aspired to introduce an ecosystem-scale perspective on marine
resource management activity to enhance cross-jurisdictional and cross-
sector communication and coordination. Some, like the national marine
sanctuaries, had explicit authority to manage and regulate use and activity.
However, most did not possess formal authorities with which to mandate
participation or regulate the activity of others. Most could only provide
opportunities for interaction in a manner that respected existing authorities
and jurisdictions. As Glen Herbert of the Eastern Scotian Shelf Integrated
Management process explained, "[ESSIM is] based on coordination and
collaboration. There's nothing in the [Oceans Act] legislation that allows
us to force or coerce anyone to make any decisions."

Herman Verheij, of the Trilateral Wadden Sea Cooperation, similarly
emphasized that "every country has its own regime." The Cooperation
provides each country with expertise, strategies, and guidance that can be
exercised in accordance with what is appropriate given their own national
contexts. Jens Enemark, former secretary of the Common Wadden Sea Secretariat, noted that the Cooperation was "not perceived as being a legal
issue," but rather "a matter of how the countries could commonly establish
a framework" for the conservation and wise use of the Wadden Sea.

Tom Cowan, first director of the Northwest Straits Commission, underscored that the Northwest Straits Initiative "is just one tool" in a broader
institutional domain:

> The whole Northwest Straits Initiative . . . is just one tool; it's just one
> aspect of trying to recover Puget Sound. You have to have a strong
> regulatory role whether it's state, federal or county . . . and you have
> to have a funding role; it takes money to do this. . . . Another role is
> making sure that citizens are involved and that's where the Northwest
> Straits Initiative shines, but it's not the whole thing, that's for sure.
> It's just one leg of the stool, but boy those other legs are also very im-
> portant and necessary, and not necessarily a good fit for the Initiative.

Perhaps the greatest dilemma faced by most initiatives was determining their relationship to fisheries management. Fisheries are the one marine

resource for which there are long-standing governance regimes throughout the world. Most initiatives concluded that their added value was building bridges and filling gaps, not challenging existing institutions. Consequently, most left fisheries issues off the table. As GOMC councilor Lee Sochasky explained, "In the very beginning, they would hardly mention the word *fish*. Now we do but certainly steer clear of getting involved in planning for fisheries management. [It] is already being done by others—so the opportunity for the Council is to focus on areas where there isn't already good structure."

According to Phil Bass, the state policy director for the Gulf of Mexico Program, a similar assessment and conclusion was reached in the Gulf of Mexico Alliance:

> It was decided fairly early on that we were going to work to establish five issue areas with a state being the lead for each one and all states participating. There was discussion about what those issues were going to be. Probably the issue we had the lengthiest discussion about was whether there should be a fisheries and living marine resources component to this. We decided there was already collaboration on fisheries issues, and that those issues were sometimes very contentious, and we didn't want to be seen as trying to supersede any existing entity.

Having defined their niche, most initiatives explicitly captured their purpose and scope in formal mission and goal statements expressing their overarching philosophy and aspirations. These mission and goal statements vary; some are quite simple and straightforward in tone and language, such as that of the Port Orford Ocean Resource Team (box 7-1). Others, like the Channel Islands National Marine Sanctuary, more explicitly and comprehensively detail a range of specific goals (box 7-1). In either case, these mission and goal statements provide a standard against which initiatives develop strategies and assess progress.

The Governance Infrastructure of Marine Ecosystem-Based Management Initiatives

Each MEBM initiative we examined had a carefully constructed governance infrastructure. These structures were developed over time as initial discussions occurred among individuals, and, eventually, formal organizational

BOX 7-1. EXAMPLES OF MISSION AND GOAL STATEMENTS

Port Orford Ocean Resource Team Mission and Goals

The Port Orford Ocean Resource Team works to ensure the long-term sustainability of Port Orford's ocean resources and our community that depends on them by uniting science, education, local expertise, and conservation.

We are dedicated to maintaining access to natural resources by people who are fishing selectively, while promoting sustainable fisheries and protecting marine biological diversity. We operate on the triple bottom line: ecology, equity, and economics.

(Source: POORT, http://www.oceanresourceteam.org)

Narragansett Bay Estuary Program Mission Statement

To protect and preserve Narragansett Bay and its watershed through partnerships that conserve and restore natural resources, enhance water quality, and promote community involvement.

(Source: NBEP, http://www.nbep.org/about-theprogram.html)

Channel Islands National Marine Sanctuary Goals

1. Protect the natural habitats, ecological services, and biological communities of all living resources inhabiting the Channel Islands National Marine Sanctuary, and the sanctuary's cultural and archaeological resources, for future generations.
2. Enhance public awareness, understanding, and appreciation of the marine environment and the natural, historical, cultural, and archaeological resources of the Channel Islands National Marine Sanctuary.
3. Support, promote, and coordinate scientific research on, and long-term monitoring of, Channel Islands National Marine Sanctuary resources.
4. Where appropriate, restore and enhance natural habitats, populations, and ecological processes within the Channel Islands National Marine Sanctuary.
5. Provide comprehensive and coordinated conservation and management of the Channel Islands National Marine Sanctuary, as well as the activities affecting it, in a manner complementing existing regulatory authorities.
6. Create models of and incentives for ways to conserve and manage national marine sanctuaries, including the application of innovative management techniques.
7. Facilitate to the extent compatible with the primary objective of resource protection, public and private uses of sanctuary resources not prohibited pursuant to other authorities, and enhance such uses where they are wise and sustainable.

BOX 7-1. CONTINUED

8. Cooperate with national and international programs encouraging conservation of marine resources.
9. Develop and implement coordinated plans for the protection and management of the Channel Islands National Marine Sanctuary, with appropriate
   federal agencies, state and local governments, Native American tribes and
   organizations, international organizations, and other public and private
   interests concerned with continuing the sanctuary's health and resilience.

(Source: U.S. Department of Commerce, National Oceanic and Atmospheric Administration, *Channel Islands National Marine Sanctuary: Final Management Plan* [Santa Barbara,
CA: NOAA, 2009], 8–9.)

---

commitments were made. They all started with the notion that working
together in new ways might be a more promising path to addressing issues
of shared concern. They translated this idea into action by iteratively adding organization as their objectives, participants, roles, and responsibilities became clear. Eventually, each possessed an "organizational chart" that
identified core functions and relationships.

In general, the organizational structure of MEBM initiatives reflects six
core functions (table 7-1): providing leadership and establishing policy direction; managing the process; assessing issues, making recommendations
and undertaking projects; linking to external agencies, organizations, and
communities; integrating science; and generating resources. As the scope,
scale, and jurisdictional complexity of an initiative increased, the organizational structure encompassing these core functions expanded.

The organizational structure of the relatively small Port Orford Ocean
Resource Team (described in chap. 6) illustrates these functional elements
in a simple form (fig. 7-1). A board of directors—the Fishermen's Board—
provides policy direction and leadership to the initiative. It meets monthly
and consists of five commercial fishermen. An executive director admin-
isters the process and is supported by a staff consisting of an administrative assistant, several program coordinators, and periodic interns and
volunteers. In addition, a ten-member community advisory team provides
a link between POORT and the broader community. It also provides advice on issues and opportunities to the board of directors. Consultants
and nongovernmental organizations contribute science and help with
project implementation.

In contrast, the multistate and multiprovince Gulf of Maine Council

TABLE 7-I. Core functions and organizational forms common to marine ecosystem-based management initiatives

Core function	Organizational form
Providing leadership and establishing policy direction	Board of directors Intergovernmental councils
Managing the process	Executive director Secretariat Staff/coordinator
Assessing issues, recommending actions and undertaking projects	Issue teams Working groups and committees Partnerships Contractors
Linking to external agencies, organizations, and communities	Standing advisory councils Parallel governmental organizations
Integrating science	Science and technical committees Science coordinators and translators Research conferences and workshops Independent science panels and reviews
Generating resources	Member dues Independent foundations Strategic partnerships Volunteer programs

on the Marine Environment (GOMC, described in chap. 2 and illustrated in fig. 7-2) has a more complex organizational structure enabling it to span two countries, involve high-level policy makers, coordinate several agencies, and tackle more varied issues. While the core policy, administrative, and work group elements are present, each has been expanded and tailored in a manner that accommodates its broader scope and unique position straddling an international border.

Providing Leadership and Establishing Policy Direction

At the helm of each initiative are policy makers that provide leadership and policy direction. These range from POORT's Fishermen's Board, or the County Council in the case of the San Juan Initiative, to the governors of

FIGURE 7-1. Port Orford Ocean Resource Team, organizational structure. (Adapted from Port Orford Ocean Resource Team, http://www.oceanresource team.org/about/.)

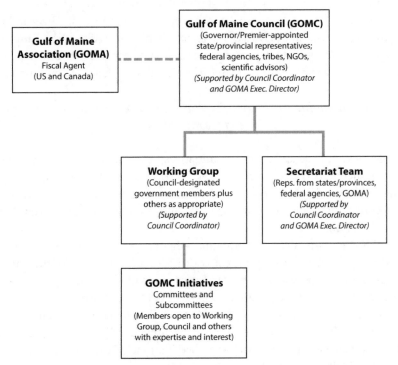

FIGURE 7-2. Gulf of Maine Council on the Marine Environment, organizational structure. (Adapted from Gulf of Maine Council, http://www.gulfofmaine.org/2/ wp-content/uploads/2015/12/GOMC-Reference-Guide-December-2015.pdf.)

the five Gulf States in the Gulf of Mexico Alliance. The Alliance Management Team is the vehicle through which the five governors stay apprised of the effort and provide it with high-level guidance. Each governor has appointed two designees—a regular representative and an alternate—to represent him or her at Alliance Management Team meetings. These gubernatorial representatives are heads of key environmental agencies, such as Florida's secretary of the Department of Environmental Protection, a commissioner from Texas's Commission on Environmental Quality, and Mississippi's director for the Department of Marine Resources.

The Narragansett Bay Estuary Program has a management committee that provides leadership and policy direction. Key environmental and natural resource management agencies in Massachusetts and Rhode Island are represented on this committee, along with individuals from local environmental organizations, academic institutions, and other stakeholder groups. The management committee meets quarterly to "establish program priorities and approve annual work plans that identify projects and funding for the coming year." The Narragansett Bay Estuary Program's executive committee consists of a subset of management committee members and is authorized to act on the Estuary Program's behalf. The Albemarle–Pamlico National Estuary Partnership has a policy board that serves a similar function to the Narragansett Bay Estuary Program's management committee.

Managing the Process: Executive Directors, Secretariats, and Coordinators

Regardless of scale and scope, all initiatives need a coordinator or facilitator. Someone needs to be responsible for overseeing the process, managing its day-to-day functioning and ensuring that progress is being made. Executive directors, secretariats, staff, and coordinators all served this core function.

Most initiatives have an individual who functions as an executive director and is explicitly responsible for coordinating the activities of the initiative. This point person is recognized as the individual to call, the one overseeing all aspects of the initiative. Leesa Cobb, POORT's executive director, fulfilled this function. Each National Estuary Program has a program director, such as Tom Borden with the Narragansett Bay Estuary Program and Bill Crowell with the Albemarle–Pamlico National Estuary Partnership.

The Gulf of Mexico Alliance has an executive director who oversees all aspects of the Alliance's work. This position was added in 2010 when the Alliance created a headquarters office to "keep the organization running smoothly and to maintain the requirements of a $501(c)(3)$ organization."[5] The new organizational structure is intended to lessen the vulnerability of the Alliance to ebbs in the time available for agency staff to volunteer in various Alliance teams, whether due to contracting budgets, changes in political priorities, or the unexpected demands of events like the Deepwater Horizon oil spill. All of the teams continue to meet, but some of their coordinating functions and day-to-day work is being done by paid staff. Phil Bass explained his support for this development:

> The driver for me has always been leadership. . . . [The chair of the Alliance Management Team] has put in countless hours on Alliance work. We simply can't expect him or others to continue to do that. We need an executive director to take the pressure off of handling the day-to-day work, by doing things like preparing the chair of the Alliance Management Team for meetings and conference calls.

With similar organizational management concerns in mind, GOMC established a secretariat that gave process leadership and management responsibility to each state and province on a rotating two-year cycle. The secretariat is responsible for convening Council and working group meetings and developing all meeting agendas and materials. It provides advice on GOMC management, program, policy, and finance issues. The secretariat structure ensures that the states and provinces share the administrative burden of the process.

GOMC also employs a coordinator to manage the day-to-day logistics of the GOMC process. Michelle Tremblay served as the GOMC coordinator for many years and described the "nutshell version" of her role in this way:

> My focus is on internal policy and governance; the day-to-day operations of the organization is primarily what I do. There has also been an administrative assistant who has provided very basic services like meeting notes and general administrative things. But as far as coordinating all of the internal activities of the Council, getting agendas ready for meetings, conference calls, coordinating the committee's activities, our awards program, and just general contact for the external part of the organization, that's me.
>
> When we were putting together our action plan, I'm the one who did the crosswalk or correlation of all of the plans in the Gulf or in the watershed that had been drafted, looking for confluences where those

organizations, those studies, those plans kind of intersected with our own and, in doing so, was able to help the council set priorities for the current action plan.

The GOMC coordinator has proven essential to ensuring organizational continuity during the initiative's secretariat transitions every two years.

The Gulf of Mexico Alliance has formalized an Alliance Coordination Team within its organizational structure. This team forms a communication bridge between members of its priority issue teams and Alliance policy makers. The Alliance Coordination Team includes four designated coordinators whose job is to attend Alliance Management Team and Priority Issue Team meetings in order to ensure that all teams are kept apprised of the issues, concerns, and activities of the others.

Getting Work Done: Assessing Issues, Recommending Actions, Undertaking Projects

The substantive work of the initiatives is undertaken by staff and ad hoc work groups in smaller community-based initiatives, and by formal working groups, issue teams, and committees in the more expansive initiatives. As described in chapter 3, six priority issue teams are the day-to-day workhorses of the Gulf of Mexico Alliance. Each priority issue team is focused on one of the six priority issues and each Gulf state has taken responsibility for the work of one team. One or more state officials facilitates each team; these individuals are usually senior program managers in a state's environmental, coastal, or fish and wildlife agencies. Similarly, the Gulf of Maine Council's Working Group assists the policy-level Council to develop and implement five-year action plans. This working group includes representatives of both state and provincial governments and U.S. and Canadian federal agencies, and relies on several committees and subcommittees (GOMC Initiatives) to undertake issue-specific tasks (see fig. 7-2).

In a similar manner, each national marine sanctuary's advisory council establishes working groups to address specific issues or topics best handled by a smaller group. For example, the Channel Islands National Marine Sanctuary Advisory Council is supported by numerous working groups, including the Research Activities Panel, the Conservation Working Group, the Sanctuary Education Team, the Commercial Fishing Working Group, the Recreational Fishing Working Group, and the Chumash Community Working Group. Each group is chaired by a sanctuary advisory council member but is composed of advisory council members and individuals from outside the council.[6] The chairperson of the working group is typically responsible for gathering noncouncil members who have expertise in the particular issue to serve on the working group. In this manner, a standing advisory council is able to extend the network of individuals and organizations that understand and contribute to the sanctuary's work.

Contractors are employed by some initiatives to implement program activities. Reflective of its fluctuating budget and transnational context, the Gulf of Maine Council hires contractors as needed and when funds are available.

Partnerships with agencies, nongovernmental organizations, universities, and businesses are another mechanism through which MEBM initiatives can undertake substantive work. The San Juan County Marine Stewardship Area was developed primarily in partnership with The Nature Conservancy, using and modifying their Conservation Action Plan process to fit the needs of the marine resources committee. POORT sought the assistance of nongovernmental organizations, foundations, and outside consultants for their science projects and planning efforts. Partnerships were essential to development of their stewardship area and POORT's efforts more broadly. The mapping of commercially and ecologically important fishing territories was led by Portland-based Ecotrust and helped identify potential sites for a marine research reserve and sustainability area that would meet POORT's goals of maintaining ecological and economic sustainability. Outreach and water quality monitoring efforts were provided by the Surfrider Foundation and helped the Port Orford community conceptualize and respect the "land–sea connection," a hallmark of ecosystem-based management.

The Albemarle–Pamlico National Estuary Partnership is similarly involved in a host of scientific partnerships. Staff members contribute to monitoring partnerships, such as FerryMon, in which local universities and federal agencies utilize the state ferry transportation system to monitor water quality.[7] Their Submerged Aquatic Vegetation Partnership involves various divisions of the North Carolina Department of Environment and Natural Resources, the Department of Transportation, the Wildlife Resources Commission, various universities, the North Carolina Coastal Federation, The Nature Conservancy, and a range of federal agencies.[8]

Linking to External Agencies, Organizations, and Communities

To acquire expertise, advice, resources, and support, MEBM initiatives need to be linked to other agencies, organizations, and communities, entities that in many cases have jurisdiction over elements of the marine eco-system. As described in the cases, valuable synergies between the initiatives and external organizations enabled work that bridged sectors and scales in a manner that benefited all involved.

All of the MEBM initiatives we examined had organizational struc-tures with established linkages with outside groups. These mechanisms took the form of standing advisory councils and community boards that enabled ongoing dialogue between the initiative and outside communities and organizations. They sometimes took the form of parallel organizations that were explicitly structured to serve as an interface with the initiative. By creating these formal structures, the initiatives embedded themselves in their broader institutional context.

STANDING ADVISORY COUNCILS

A common element in many MEBM governance structures was a stand-ing advisory council that enabled sustained dialogue between the initiative and interested stakeholders, community representatives, nongovernmental organizations, and other government agency representatives. For example, as described in chapter 4, formal sanctuary advisory councils have been established to provide a regular mechanism for sharing information and promoting dialogue among citizens, stakeholders, and government agen-cies with an interest in national marine sanctuaries. Voting advisory coun-cil members include representatives of nongovernmental interests, such as conservation, fishing and tourism, shipping, and local communities. Nonvoting members include the National Oceanic and Atmospheric Ad-ministration sanctuary superintendent and representatives of most of the federal and state agencies with interests and jurisdiction in the sanctuaries. As described in chapter 6, the community-based POORT had a community advisory board that served the same function.

Standing advisory councils are seldom a minor appendage to an MEBM process. Most play an integral role informing and influencing initiative de-cisions. Sean Morton, interim Florida Keys National Marine Sanctuary su-perintendent, took new initiatives before the sanctuary advisory council at a very early stage in their development. "We never start any process without probably a year of workup with the advisory council, to even frame how we're going to approach any new activity," he noted.

Those involved in the Trilateral Wadden Sea Cooperation also recog-nized a need to establish a formal mechanism for incorporating stakeholder perspectives and knowledge in their deliberations. They established a Wadden Sea Forum that began with forty-one members but grew to more than three hundred. Like the sanctuary advisory councils, participants in the Wadden Sea Forum represent local and regional governments, nature protection agencies, and agriculture, energy, fisheries, tourism, industry, and harbor interests. The Forum embodies several working groups that address issues such as fisheries, shipping, tourism, and energy. The working groups develop recommendations for consideration by the Wadden Sea Forum plenary, which are then forwarded to the formal Trilateral Cooperation.

PARALLEL ORGANIZATIONAL STRUCTURES

A unique element of the Gulf of Mexico Alliance's governance is its Federal Workgroup. While the Alliance is a multistate initiative with state-level leadership and objectives, federal agencies still have significant interest in helping the effort succeed while ensuring that national interests are considered. In a move that may create a good model for other regional ocean partnerships, the participating federal agencies convened a separate Federal Workgroup to coordinate their support for the Alliance. It is not a formal part of the Alliance's management structure but its representatives are highly involved in Alliance issue teams.

Similarly, the Northwest Straits Commission instituted its annual Marine Managers Workshops to provide a cross-jurisdictional forum for dialogue and coordination. Commissioner Duane Fagergren describes the value of regularly convening these marine managers to instill a sense of place and a broader ecosystem perspective:

> I think Ginny [Broadhurst] really moved us in a positive direction when she called the first Marine Managers Workshop. That brought the federal agencies, state agencies, tribal governments and funding institutions—existing resource managers—to the same table and . . . [she asked] "how might we use the combined regulatory or voluntary approaches to marine managed areas to our mutual benefit?" It brought the managers that were not even used to working together to think in a more holistic way.

Integrating Science

All of the MEBM initiatives we examined had to deal with a significant amount of scientific complexity and uncertainty. Each acknowledged the need for credible, well-informed, and adaptive decision making firmly grounded in the best available science. Each initiative integrated science into its governance structure in different ways, including creating scientific and technical advisory committees, hiring science coordinators and translators, incorporating independent review processes, providing seats for scientists in working groups and advisory bodies, sponsoring research conferences and workshops, and instituting scientific data systems and decision support tools.

STANDING SCIENTIFIC AND TECHNICAL COMMITTEES AND WORK GROUPS

Science and technical committees were a formal element of the governance structures of most MEBM initiatives. These committees served three critical purposes. First, they ensured that science was front and center in the initiatives' deliberations. Second, they provided a forum within which scientists working on different regions or topics could confer, share information, and harmonize data. Third, standing committees provided an opportunity for dialogue between scientists and managers to influence research directions to better inform management.

The Northwest Straits Initiative Science Team reviews proposals, provides advice on use of the Northwest Straits Commission's ecosystem fund, and ensures coordination with other science-based teams in Puget Sound. It has six members with different areas of expertise—salmon, wastewater, engineering, GIS, estuarine systems, and climate change. Their role is to:

- Advise commissioners on issues pertaining to science that is relevant to and consistent with the goals and objectives of the Northwest Straits Initiative
- Help guide deliberations of the Commission's Science and Technical Committee
- Interact with similar science advisory bodies in other regional initiatives and programs on issues of mutual interest

In 2014, the Narragansett Bay Estuary Program Management Committee formally established a science advisory committee with sixteen to twenty-one members representing "a broad range of committed research scientists, engineers, environmental managers, and other practitioners drawn from the relevant physical, chemical, geological, biological, social, and economic sciences."[9] The resolution establishing the committee clearly defined its purpose and role as "integration of science into the effective

BOX 7-2. NARRAGANSETT BAY ESTUARY PROGRAM, SCIENCE ADVISORY
COMMITTEE ROLES AND RESPONSIBILITIES

The Science Advisory Committee shall:

a. Provide a forum for the Narragansett Bay Estuary Program and its partners to examine, discuss, and exchange scientific findings and technical information to facilitate the integration of science into the effective management of Narragansett Bay Region and its watershed.

b. Provide for the exchange and synthesis of existing and emerging scientific issues.

c. Support the development of conceptual frameworks that integrate physical, chemical, biological, geological, ecological, economic, and policy dimensions of the watershed.

d. Provide a mechanism to integrate science with management decision making and strengthen the science focus of the Estuary Program.

e. Develop recommendations for research, monitoring, and assessment priorities.

f. Identify funding opportunities for these priorities.

g. Make recommendations to develop and prioritize the content of the Estuary Program's annual Work Plan.

h. Ensure the peer review of scientific and technical products generated by the Estuary Program.

i. Assist in the development of requests for proposals as needed.

j. Support selected report generation, aid the development of science conferences, and assist in the development or publishing of science proceedings.

(Source: Narragansett Bay Estuary Program, "Resolution 2014-01, Establishment of a Science Advisory Committee" (June 18, 2014), http://nbep.org/pdfs/Resolution%20 2014-01%20Science%20Advisory%20Committee.pdf.)

management of Narragansett Bay Region and its watershed" (box 7-2).

Scientific committees and work groups are designed to provide scientific advice to an initiative, conduct or oversee research on pressing questions, and/or guide assessment and monitoring. For example, the Gulf of Mexico Alliance's Ecosystems Integration and Assessment Team is responsible for developing a "natural resource data portal and information system" for the initiative. It was established with three long-term goals: "to develop regional data systems that contain environmental and economic data; establish strategic partnerships to fill environmental and ecological data gaps; and provide ecosystem decision-support tools to address priority issues within the Gulf."[10]

Similarly, the Trilateral Monitoring and Assessment Program and the

Trilateral Monitoring and Assessment Group are two core components of the Trilateral Wadden Sea Cooperation. They are responsible for ensuring that data collection and assessment are harmonized between the three countries at the level of the Wadden Sea ecosystem as a whole. Folkert de Jong explained the circumstances that existed before the Trilateral Cooperation was formed:

> There were obviously quite a lot of research programs going on in the three countries, but they had largely different intervals, different everything. And the Trilateral Monitoring and Assessment Program has made an effort and basically succeeded in harmonizing all of this. So that you get the total picture of what's going on, rather than three different pictures of what's going on.

The Trilateral Monitoring and Assessment Group meets regularly to monitor and assess the state of the Wadden Sea ecosystem. Their findings are compiled every three years in "Quality Status Reports" that inform governmental conferences. The data contributing to the reports are also stored in a public database managed by the Cooperation. When problems are identified, the Trilateral Monitoring and Assessment Group is able to establish ad hoc expert working groups to assess the issues.

SCIENCE COORDINATORS AND TRANSLATORS

Relevant science may exist but not always in a form that can be readily accessed by managers. Consequently, some of the larger MEBM initiatives employ staff responsible for coordinating science and translating existing science into accessible language and forms for use by managers. For example, GOMC formed a Gulf of Maine Science Translation Project to ensure science was effectively disseminated. Peter Taylor, the GOMC contractor who served as the initiative's science translator, explained:

> Talking with the managers and the scientists, there was a realization that there's quite a bit known about marine habitats in the Gulf of Maine that isn't necessarily within the realm of what the managers already know. We realized that something we could do was translate existing information about marine habitats in a way that was useful and accessible to the managers.

Taylor emphasized that his role "was not to try to advise on what to do about management issues, it was just to get the information to people who make the decisions."

Science coordinators also help initiatives develop and implement research strategies. The Narraganset Bay Estuary Program's chief scientist, Chris Deacutis, considered it his job "to go and get funding for the science." He spent a good deal of his time writing grant proposals to secure federal funds for projects that had been identified by the management committee or other partners in the Narragansett Bay monitoring efforts.

INDEPENDENT SCIENCE PANELS AND REVIEWS

Because credibility and confidence in science were deemed imperative, several initiatives relied on formal science panels and scientific review processes to independently assess and synthesize the science and identify issues or processes needing attention. For example, the U.S./Canada Environmental Cooperation Council described in chapter 2 established an independent Marine Science Panel consisting of recognized experts. The Panel provided twelve recommendations to the Environmental Cooperation Council, which then established the Puget Sound Georgia Basin International Task Force to act on the recommendations. As the Task Force began its work, the Marine Science Panel's synthesis of key issues provided an immediate focus for Task Force members and helped them to move beyond long-standing tensions. Tom Laurie, the Washington coordinator for the Environmental Cooperation Council described it this way:

> The science panel was so useful to say, look, the issue of shared water quality in the shared waters is not Victoria's sewage; it's toxics, it's interbasin water transfer, it's disappearance of subtidal lands, it's shoreline conversion. Once the science panel really identified what the issues were, it made it easier to get focused on what program delivery priorities ought to be.

Independent scientific review of assessments and research helps to enhance credibility and build confidence in initiative strategies. The Narragansett Bay Estuary Program funded over 110 scientific and policy-related research projects from 1985 to 1991. Their objective was to encourage scientists to advance understanding of environmental problems and trends in the Bay and its watersheds. Every study was subject to extensive peer review, and investigators were required to submit all original data to be permanently archived in the Narragansett Bay Data System. Similarly, the

San Juan Marine Resource Committee solicits independent scientific and technical reviews of their biodiversity viability and threat assessments.

SCIENTIFIC DATA SYSTEMS AND DECISION SUPPORT TOOLS

In many of the regions where initiatives were located, considerable research and monitoring had been occurring for extended periods of time. However, this research and monitoring seldom occurred in a coordinated and consistent fashion. Data were often dispersed in different locations, organized in different formats, and collected for different purposes. Most initiatives needed to pool and harmonize existing data and identify critical gaps. Hence the first task undertaken by most of the initiatives was creation of a common data system that pooled existing science and harmonized ongoing monitoring; this system established a shared information resource for the initiative and its member organizations.

As described in chapter 3, one of the major strategies in the first Governors' Action Plan in the Gulf of Mexico Alliance was to develop an "accurate and comprehensive inventory of Gulf coastal habitats." This task required pooling and harmonizing dispersed, often incompatible, data sets and standardizing collection of future data. Participants aimed to reduce duplication of effort and the inefficiencies and extra cost it produces, and to improve the quality of data available to the National Oceanic and Atmospheric Administration for building an effective Gulf Coastal Ocean Observing System.

The Gulf of Maine Council undertook a similar set of activities. Those involved recognized that they needed Gulf of Maine maps that did not exist at the time but that would facilitate their planning and decision making. They developed the Gulf of Maine Mapping Initiative that conducts comprehensive seafloor imaging, mapping, and biological and geological surveys. The Council also helped to establish the Gulf of Maine Ocean Observing System, which delivers open-source oceanographic data that are used by commercial mariners, coastal resource managers, scientists, educators, search-and-rescue teams, and public health officials. In partnership with the Gulf of Maine Council, the Gulf of Maine Ocean Observing System has also developed a web-based system that enables sharing, integration, and use of coastal habitat monitoring data.[11]

Generating Resources

It goes without saying that MEBM efforts need resources to function. Initiatives can only undertake what their resources allow. While some are fortunate to have dedicated budgets, most initiatives are opportunistic, seeking funding and resources from whatever source possible. Some initiatives have embedded mechanisms to generate resources into their organizational structure. For example, the Gulf of Maine Council has membership dues. Initiatives have incorporated parallel independent foundations, strategic partnerships, and volunteer programs to leverage available financial, information, and human resources to advance their work.

Initiative-specific foundations

A few initiatives established or capitalized upon parallel independent foundations with the explicit purpose of generating and managing funds to support initiative work. For example, the Northwest Straits Foundation is a nonprofit organization established to work with the Northwest Straits Initiative to leverage additional funding for its scientific, restoration, and education projects. The Foundation is a separate but complementary body to the Initiative, with its own development director. Establishing the Foundation was a way to insulate the Initiative from the ebb and flow of federal funding, as well as to take on regional projects without reducing support for individual marine resources committee activities supported by federal and state funds. The majority of Foundation funds are used to support regional, ecosystem-wide projects, with 10 percent going to marine resources committee projects.

Similarly, as described in chapter 2, the Gulf of Maine Council established paired financial management associations: the Association of Canadian Delegates to the Gulf of Maine Council and the Gulf of Maine Association. Both have charitable or nonprofit status in their respective countries and can receive grants and contributions to be spent on priorities identified by the Gulf of Maine Council. The Gulf of Maine Association is responsible for the Council's day-to-day contractual and fiscal operations; it includes Canadian representation on its board of directors. The Association of Canadian Delegates manages contracts from Canadian funding sources and is able to transfer funds to the Gulf of Maine Association.

Strategic partnerships

Strategic partnerships are integral to most initiatives. These partnerships both directly and indirectly provide resources that help advance initiative objectives. The Gulf of Mexico Alliance "relies heavily on nongovernmental partners, such as academic organizations, nonprofit organizations, and businesses." They describe it as follows:

> Whether piloting new programs, or implementing full-scale efforts, these partners provide the talent and resources to implement on-the-ground projects. These partners have aligned their goals to those of the Alliance in order to create tangible results, thereby realizing the potential for change associated with a grand-scale collaborative effort such as the Gulf of Mexico Alliance.[12]

Notably, the Gulf of Mexico Alliance has engaged its member agencies in the region to coordinate each of its priority issue teams: the Florida Department of Environmental Protection coordinates the Data and Monitoring Team; the State of Louisiana Coastal Protection and Restoration Authority coordinates the Habitat Resources Team; the Harte Research Institute coordinates the Wildlife and Fisheries Team; the Mississippi Department of Environmental Quality coordinates the Water Resources Team; the Mississippi Department of Marine Resources coordinates the Coastal Resilience Team; and the Dauphin Island Sea Lab coordinates the Education and Engagement Team. Each "sponsoring organization" provides "funding assistance to further the goals and objectives of their priority team."[13]

Volunteer programs

Volunteers are core to most initiatives and provide an essential resource to accomplish a variety of activities. For example, the Gulf of Maine Council's Ecosystem Indicator Partnership provides a regional-scale indicators and reporting system that reflects the overall health of the Gulf of Maine. Over one hundred volunteers representing interests and organizations from around the Gulf assist the Ecosystem Indicator Partnership in selecting and compiling information on specific indicators of ecosystem health.

The marine resources committees making up the Northwest Straits Initiative are wholly volunteer based and are the implementing arm of the Initiative. Local elected officials appoint these county-based volunteer committees to do the following:

> Address local threats to the marine environment, complementing the efforts of existing authorities. Each MRC has specific local preservation and protection actions that reflect local priorities in their areas yet contribute to broader marine conservation goals. Projects carried

out by MRCs include restoring nearshore, intertidal and estuarine habitats, mapping eelgrass beds, providing outreach and education to local communities, restoring native shellfish populations, installing rain gardens and many more.[14]

Codified Roles and Responsibilities

While an organization's infrastructure provides a forum for interaction, codified roles and responsibilities dictate how interaction is intended to occur and are equally important to governance. Most initiatives had explicit written instructions that enabled those involved to easily understand and navigate their roles. These tools included formal constitutions and charters, Intergovernmental Cooperative and/or Co-Management Agreements, Memoranda of Understanding, and explicit Protocols and Decision Criteria. These written documents served as navigational instruments that guided the participants' work together and kept them from foundering.

Constitutions and Charters

Formal constitutions or charters have been adopted by some initiatives to explicitly describe and bound their work. For example, in August 2012 the Gulf of Mexico Alliance adopted a sixteen-page constitution that detailed the purpose, structure, membership, and roles and responsibilities of those involved. The constitution's preamble explains the following:

> The States of the Gulf of Mexico, as further defined in Article II below, establish this Constitution of the Gulf of Mexico Alliance, the mission of which is to promote the protection, restoration, enhancement, understanding, awareness and wise use of the natural resources of the Gulf of Mexico through aligned and cooperative efforts involving research, planning, management, information and resource sharing, public education and informed support.
>
> The following Articles of this Constitution shall describe, define and delineate this organization by structure and function.[15]

Formal charters detail roles, objectives, and decision protocols that govern the national marine sanctuary advisory councils (described in chap. 4). Training sessions are held for new advisory council members to familiarize themselves with the provisions of their charter and the specific expectations for fulfilling their role in providing advice to the national marine sanctuary superintendent (box 7-3). Following a particularly contentious set of deliberations, the Channel Islands National Marine Sanctuary Advisory Council supplemented their charter with a detailed set of Decision-Making and Operational Protocols.[16] These protocols clarified eight specific dimensions of their decision-making process that had proven particularly challenging or ambiguous: use of a consensus approach; the role of *Robert's Rules of Order*; what to do in the case of minority views on sanctuary advisory council proposals; and the role of alternate members.

BOX 7-3. CHANNEL ISLANDS NATIONAL MARINE SANCTUARY ADVISORY COUNCIL, ROLES SECTION OF CHARTER

Roles

1. The Council, in accordance with the [National Marine Sanctuaries] Act, shall provide advice to the Sanctuary Superintendent regarding the management of the Channel Islands National Marine Sanctuary.

2. The Council shall act solely as an advisory body to the Sanctuary Superintendent. Nothing in this charter constitutes authority to perform operational or management functions, or to represent or make decisions on behalf of the Sanctuary, NOAA, or the Department of Commerce.

3. The Council shall draw on the expertise of its members and other sources in order to provide advice to the Sanctuary Superintendent.

4. The Council may serve as a forum for consultation and deliberation among its members and as a source of advice to the Sanctuary Superintendent. Such advice shall fairly represent the collective and individual views of the Council members.

5. Council members shall serve as liaisons between their constituents and/or communities and the Sanctuary, keeping Sanctuary staff informed of issues and concerns, as well as providing information to their respective communities on the Sanctuary's behalf.

6. The Council shall develop an annual work plan, in consultation with and approved by the Sanctuary Superintendent, to establish an agenda for specific issues and projects the Council intends to address.

(Source: Channel Islands National Marine Sanctuary, "Advisory Council Charter" (July 21, 2014), 3, http://channelislands.noaa.gov/sac/pdfs/sac_charter_072114.pdf.)

Intergovernmental Cooperative Agreements

Large-scale initiatives that cross multiple jurisdictions usually require an authorizing agreement that sanctions and directs the process. For example, the governors and premiers of Massachusetts, New Hampshire, Maine, New Brunswick, and Nova Scotia created the Agreement on Conservation of the Marine Environment of the Gulf of Maine between the Governments of the Bordering States and Provinces when they formally established the Gulf of Maine Council on the Marine Environment. This high-level intergovernmental agreement is not lengthy but nonetheless explains the composition, scope, and intent of their collaborative work and the broad principles that guide Gulf of Maine Council activity (box 7-4).

The agreement recognized that the "natural resources of the Gulf of Maine are interconnected and form part of an overall ecosystem that transcends political boundaries." It also established a shared duty to protect and conserve Gulf resources and a need for planning and management of human activity. Importantly, it commented, "that the most effective means of protecting, conserving, and managing the region's resources is through the cooperative pursuit of consistent policies, initiatives, and programs."[17] In addition, this agreement identified two specific tasks—development of an action plan and joint monitoring—that provided an immediate focus and created momentum for the process.

Co-management Agreements

When an initiative seeks to manage an ecosystem that transcends two or more jurisdictions, co-management agreements provide a tool for clarifying roles and responsibilities. In the Florida Keys, for example, an innovative co-management agreement was signed to navigate a complex set of agency jurisdictions that would otherwise frustrate management. With sixty-five percent of the Florida Keys National Marine Sanctuary located in state waters, a lot of coordination was needed with the State of Florida. In addition, the size of the marine sanctuary required resources to be leveraged across levels of government. A state-federal partnership was also necessary to allay political concerns of opponents of the sanctuary who feared loss of control over resources in the Florida Keys.

The 1997 Co-Trustees Agreement for Cooperative Management governs the formal partnership between the National Oceanic and Atmospheric Administration and the Florida Department of Environmental Protection. The purpose of the agreement was to

clarify the relative jurisdiction, authority, and conditions of Co-Trustee management of the Florida Keys National Marine Sanctuary. It clarifies the State's continuing authority and jurisdiction over submerged

---

BOX 7-4. AGREEMENT ON CONSERVATION OF THE MARINE ENVIRONMENT OF THE GULF OF MAINE BETWEEN THE GOVERNMENTS OF THE BORDERING STATES AND PROVINCES

1. The Parties agree to establish a Gulf of Maine Council on the Marine Environment to discuss and act upon environmental issues of common concern including but not limited to:
   • the protection and conservation of the ecological balance within the Gulf of Maine ecosystem;
   • the problem of marine debris and medical waste;
   • the relationship between land use and the marine environment;
   • the sustainable use of resources within the Gulf of Maine;
   • cooperative programs to better protect and conserve the Gulf's natural resources.
2. The Gulf of Maine Council on the Marine Environment will be composed of three representatives from each of the Gulf of Maine States and Provinces to be appointed by their respective Governors and Premiers within 60 days of the effective date of this Agreement.
3. The Gulf of Maine Council on the Marine Environment will produce its first annual report on environmental trends and conditions including specific recommendations on a Gulf of Maine Action Plan within 15 months of its appointment.
4. The Parties agree to minimize actions that would result in degradation of environmental quality or depletion of resources that individually or cumulatively could result in significant adverse impacts on resources leading to loss of sustainable use or environmental viability.
5. The Parties agree to design and develop a coordinated monitoring program to provide improved information for future decisions concerning the Gulf.
6. The Parties agree that the successful conservation of Gulf resources will require the development of additional agreements or protocols on specific issues or concerns that may be raised from time to time.

(Source: Gulf of Maine Council, http://www.gulfofmaine.org/2/wp-content/uploads/2014/09/GOMC-Agreement-1989.pdf)

---

lands and other State resources within the Sanctuary. It also sets forth provisions on how NOAA and the State will cooperate on specific matters such as regulatory amendments, permits, and other matters.[18]

The Co-Trustees Agreement specifies that the national marine sanctuary superintendent and the National Oceanic and Atmospheric Administration cannot unilaterally amend the management plan or change sanctuary regulations without review or approval by the State of Florida. The governor of Florida has the power to seek changes to the management plan, and can object to and invalidate portions of it. The agreement also specified that the management plan would apply in both state and federal waters. It provided for consistent and cooperative regulations regarding fisheries, submerged cultural resources, and enforcement within sanctuary boundaries.

This cooperative management agreement references several parallel agreements that establish procedures and mechanisms for addressing issues such as cultural resources, fisheries management, enforcement, civil claims, and emergency response. Additionally, it notes that nothing in the agreement "is intended to conflict with current State or Federal laws, policies, regulations, or directives." In other words, the agreement dictates the terms and procedures by which both state and federal entities uphold their own respective obligations and policies.

Memoranda of Understanding

Some agreements are captured in memoranda of understanding (MOUs), which establish a cooperative relationship among two or more entities and identify specific activities in which they intend to engage. MOUs vary considerably depending on who initiates them and for what purpose. Some are symbolic and simply express intent to work together. Others are prescriptive, indicating in some detail who is going to do what. MOUs identify compatible goals and interests of the signatories and describe the activities that will be undertaken to advance those shared interests. Port Orford's city administrator, Mike Murphy, underscored the importance of their MOU with the Port Orford Ocean Resource Team (POORT), and encourages other initiatives that are getting under way to

> write up a memorandum of understanding that lists out all the duties of each party very very carefully. People change, issues change, granting agencies change—you're going to be working with multiple funding streams, multiple partners and it's really easy for things to get screwed up. So, at the very beginning line it out very carefully. We did that upfront. If we did it again, we would probably be even more specific.

For community-based initiatives such as POORT, MOUs also provide an opportunity to formalize a relationship with an agency possessing the authority to implement actions that are beyond the scope of the community group. As described in chapter 6, POORT signed an MOU with the Oregon Department of Fish and Wildlife outlining the terms for their collaborative science and management activity. The detailed MOU has three central elements: it bounds the purpose of the collaboration between POORT and the Department of Fish and Wildlife; makes explicit the roles and responsibilities of the two entities in undertaking a cooperative fisheries pilot project (box 7-5); and clarifies how the data derived from their joint research activities will be managed to ensure confidentiality.

BOX 7-5. PORT ORFORD OCEAN RESOURCE TEAM AND OREGON DEPARTMENT OF FISH AND WILDLIFE, MEMORANDUM OF UNDERSTANDING

Section A. Cooperative Fisheries Research, Monitoring and Management

Through a pilot project approach, POORT and the Department will cooperate on fisheries research, monitoring and management within the marine component of the Stewardship Area. Pilot Project activities carried out by POORT and the Department will be informed by the mission, vision, and goals of the Port Orford Stewardship Area Plan, consistent with the Department's Nearshore Strategy Recommendations.

   The parties will:
1. Identify a Pilot Project area including resources of interest and linkages to federally managed species.
2. Identify and prioritize collaborative research and monitoring projects needed to support resource management goals, including aspects of fish management that can be effectively influenced by local area conditions, interests and fish status. Collaboration may include shared expertise for project design and execution, shared funding, and shared personnel and equipment for data collection, processing and analysis.
3. Identify research and monitoring necessary for environmental, social and economic data to support resource management relevant to the Pilot Project, and which will provide for local involvement.
4. Identify resource management tools and methods that could potentially be used to address issues.
5. Recommend actions to implement the Pilot Project.
6. POORT and the Department shall establish a set of performance standards for data quality assurance including review of statistical adequacy of sampling design, establishing procedures to minimize error during data collection, verification procedures for data entry and processing, and appropriate review of data analyses and project conclusions.

BOX 7-5. CONTINUED

7. Identify needed funding and funding sources to implement the Project.
8. Conduct an annual review of the Pilot Project, including review of research, monitoring, fishery access, collaborative projects, critical fisheries issues and fisheries management options, and then develop appropriate regulations for consideration by the Fish and Wildlife Commission, if required.
9. Act consistent with this MOU in any actions and recommendations in other bodies, including but not limited to the Pacific Fishery Management Council, subject to the Department's responsibilities to collaborate and coordinate with other interests.

   POORT may, if requested by the Department, assist by hosting the public process and/or providing white paper analyses of options to be evaluated by Department staff in a manner similar to the Scientific and Statistical Committee of the Pacific Fishery Management Council when it reviews information produced by the groundfish stock assessment teams and Groundfish Management Team.

(Source: Memorandum of Understanding between the Port Orford Ocean Resource Team and the Oregon Department of Fish and Wildlife, September 7, 2008, personal copy, original available from POORT.)

Guiding Principles and Protocols

Many MEBM initiatives frame a set of principles that are intended to bound and guide the process of interaction and provide specific decision-making criteria. Guiding principles are quite simple in some cases. For example, POORT adopted two overarching operating principles that embraced concepts of ecosystem-based management and community-based fisheries management for their work (box 7-6).

In contrast, some initiatives craft more comprehensive principles, and explicitly distinguish between the *process* within which they interact and the nature of the *outcomes* that they seek. The Pacific North Coast Integrated Management Area Initiative, for example, adopted a set of outcome principles that embraced sustainable development, integrated management, and precautionary approaches. They also detailed a comprehensive set of process principles that established expectations for a respectful, inclusive, and consensus-seeking process that was efficient, transparent, and adaptive (box 7-7). This group's principles are often referenced by other marine conservation initiatives worldwide.

BOX 7-6. PORT ORFORD OCEAN RESOURCE TEAM, GUIDING PRINCIPLES

1. Ecosystem Based Management is an integrated approach to management that considers the entire ecosystem, including humans. It is driven by the integration of all types of knowledge, information and people to minimize conflict and comprehensively manage coastal areas to overcome management problems of the past.
2. Community Based Fisheries Management is a system in which local fishermen and fishing communities participate in the responsibility for the stewardship and management of their local areas. This includes taking part in the decision-making process for all aspects of management, such as harvesting, access, compliance, research and marketing.

(Source: POORT, http://www.oceanresourceteam.org/about/operating-principles/.)

BOX 7-7. PACIFIC NORTH COAST INTEGRATED MANAGEMENT AREA
INITIATIVE, PROCESS PRINCIPLES

Sustainable development: Environmental, social and cultural values are considered with the aim of meeting the needs of the present without compromising the ability of future generations to meet their needs.

Integrated management: A cooperative process that brings together all partners in the planning and management of activities in estuarine, coastal and marine waters while seeking balanced consideration of the full range of biological, social and economic objectives and perspectives.

Precautionary approach: Erring on the side of caution.

Inclusiveness: A diversity of stakeholder interests will be included and engaged in a meaningful way in PNCIMA initiatives and stakeholder interests will be considered equally in all recommendations or decisions.

Authorities: Each party brings authorities and mandates to the PNCIMA initiative and will respect, and will together benefit from those authorities and mandates in the process.

First Nations: Federal and provincial governments have fiduciary relationships with aboriginal people. The PNCIMA initiative reflects a relationship between the federal and First Nations governments that is of a different character than that between governments and stakeholders.

Consensus: Participants in the PNCIMA planning process will seek to develop recommendations through consensus.

BOX 7-7. CONTINUED

Efficiency: Issues will be addressed in a timely manner.

Transparency: Recommendations will be made openly, with information and results shared with all participants.

Adaptability: The process is designed to permit and support evolution and will be monitored and evaluated to support shared learning and adaptation through adaptive management.

Knowledge-Based: Recommendations will be based on best available information and will include both science-based and traditional ecological/local ecological knowledge, information and data.

(Source: PNCIMA, http://www.pncima.org/site/what.html.)

Decision Criteria

Decisions made by the Northwest Straits Commission in supporting marine resources committee projects are informed by explicit "Benchmarks for Performance" that emphasize substantive action and encourage measurable results (box 7-8). As former Commission director Tom Cowan explained, "There needs to be an overarching goal that's defined and clear. A series of benchmarks to guide and help evaluate are really important." These benchmarks are intended to be realistic and achievable without additional regulatory authority, relying instead on existing authorities to execute recommendations. Each marine resources committee designs its own projects, within the framework of the benchmarks. To receive funding, projects proposed by marine resources committees must satisfy at least one of the benchmarks.

National marine sanctuary advisory councils have a detailed sixty-six–page "Implementation Handbook" that provides comprehensive policy and procedural guidance, including decision-making protocols and criteria.[19] Similarly, the Narragansett Bay Estuary Program Comprehensive Conservation and Management Plan lists twelve "implementation principles" that govern their decision-making process (box 7-9).

Conclusion

MEBM initiatives are able to function in a focused and deliberate manner when they have constructed a process containing the core elements—the

---

BOX 7-8. NORTHWEST STRAITS INITIATIVE, PERFORMANCE BENCHMARKS

1. **Broad participation.** Broad county participation in Marine Resources Committees (MRCs).
2. **Network of MPAs.** Achieve a scientifically based, regional system of Marine Protected Areas (MPAs).
3. **Protect nearshore habitat.** A net gain in highly ecologically productive nearshore, intertidal, and estuarine habitat in the Northwest Straits, and no significant loss of existing, high-value habitat; improve state, tribal, and local tools to map, assess, and protect nearshore habitat and prevent harm from upland activities.
4. **Reduction in shellfish closure.** Net reduction in shellfish harvest areas closed due to contamination.
5. **Bottomfish recovery.** Measurable increases in factors supporting recovery of bottomfish (such as rockfish)—including numbers of fish of broodstock size and age, average fish size, and abundance of prey species—as well as sufficient amounts and quality of protected habitat.
6. **Increase marine indicator species.** Increases in other key marine indicators species (including those identified in the 1997 West report on Puget Sound marine resources).
7. **Coordinate scientific data.** Coordination of scientific data (for example, through the Puget Sound Ambient Monitoring Program), including a scientific baseline, common protocols, unified GIS, and sharing of ecosystem assessments and research.
8. **Outreach and education.** Coordinate with the Puget Sound Action Team and other entities on an effective outreach and education effort with measurements of the numbers of people contacted as well as changes in behavior.

(Source: Northwest Straits Marine Conservation Initiative, "Five Year Evaluation Report" (April 6, 2004), http://www.nwstraits.org/media/1257/nwsc-2004-evaluationrpt.pdf.)

---

bricks—that respond to organizational imperatives: What is our niche and purpose? Who makes decisions and establishes policy? What codifies reach, roles, and responsibilities? How will decisions be informed and implemented? Who will manage the process, and how?

As we noted at the outset, there is no one right way to carry out MEBM, and each of the cases examined in this book responded to their organizational imperatives in ways that reflected their scale, scope, and context. Unique challenges like transboundary financial management were addressed through tailored organizational structures. Advisory committees and work groups ensured communication and coordination

---

BOX 7-9. NARRAGANSETT BAY ESTUARY PROGRAM, IMPLEMENTATION
PRINCIPLES

1. Better integrate water management planning including stormwater, waste-water treatment, water supply and septic systems to achieve efficiency and multiple benefits.
2. Develop interstate and regional mechanisms that facilitate adoption of a watershed approach for ecosystem issues.
3. Identify specific measurable environmental targets to address priority goals and objectives, and track progress toward them.
4. Collaborate broadly to identify priority bay and watershed science issues, needs and solutions and invest in scientific research that will support effective management of natural resources.
5. Evaluate and increase efficiency and effectiveness of existing management actions and agency coordination mechanisms in both states; allocate resources to proven best practices.
6. Increase investment in environmental protection and restoration for ecosystem health, regional prosperity and quality of life.
7. Monitor watersheds in a connected, coordinated and efficient way, supported by sufficient resources to collect, analyze and manage data.
8. Identify priority bay and watershed science issues, needs and solutions using a regional, collaborative approach.
9. Apply watershed based management principles at the bi-state level to address cumulative impacts of development and climate change impacts.
10. Communicate with people and policy makers in a way that enhances stewardship and creates action toward solutions for watershed problems.
11. Build capacity of municipalities to implement priority actions.
12. Build, support and coordinate partnerships between governmental and non-governmental organizations to implement priority actions.

(Source: NBEP, "2012 Workplan, CCMP Implementation," 8, http://www.nbep.org/work plans/NBEP-2012-2013Workplan.pdf.)

---

with external organizations, stakeholders, and community members. Science was integrated into their decision making through specific organizational mechanisms.

As we heard time and again in our conversations with people involved in these cases, MEBM initiatives are a lot of work: they take time and resources, and are almost always a backdrop to other aspects of people's jobs and lives. Hence those involved recognize that, if they are going to undertake this work, it needs to be done in a serious manner that ensures progress. Constructing the process with bricks such as those described in this chapter establishes a solid structure within which organized activities can occur. As explored in the next chapter, the manner in which work occurs, and whether or not progress is made, however, also depend on the mortar that holds the bricks together.

Chapter 8

Mortar:
Intangible Factors That Propel & Sustain
Marine Ecosystem-Based Management

When we began this study of marine ecosystem-based management (MEBM) initiatives, we knew that we needed to probe their structures, legal mandates, information sources, and funding. After all, we wanted to identify features that could be adopted by others trying to advance MEBM. But as much as we would probe these items in our conversations with participants, they would invariably emphasize the less tangible dimensions of their experiences. We came to appreciate that the structures and features represented by the "bricks" described in chapter 7 were only part of the story. What happens within those structures is entirely dependent on the people who are involved. The "mortar" that holds these processes together is a function of how those individuals are motivated to be involved, the relationships that they form, the personal skill sets they bring to the table, and their commitment to the process.

Here is an example. When reflecting on what really mattered to the San Juan Initiative, Lovell Pratt, a San Juan County Council member and Initiative participant, echoed the sentiments of many interviewees:

> It couldn't have happened without an effective facilitator, as was Amy Windrope. It couldn't have happened without community leaders being willing to engage with the process. It couldn't have happened without that grassroots engagement that it had, and I don't think it could have happened without the partners from state and federal agencies. That was really significant. Where you can get that collab-

orative and concerted buy-in on all of those different levels—that's really significant.[1]

Similarly, reflecting on his experience in the Gulf of Mexico Alliance, Larry McKinney noted the synergy between the process structure and the individual behaviors that gradually emerged within his issue team:

> You need a framework to build trust a little bit at a time, to create a foundation, and then there is a tipping point at which people begin to think, well maybe we can work together, and then they start thinking about *how* they can work together, not just that they have to do that. With GOMA, we reached that tipping point with the second action plan. . . . At our last All Hands Meeting in Alabama, which brought everyone together to launch the plan, I had fifty people in the room, and every time we said, "How about if we did this," someone would stand up and say, "I can help with that." We had more volunteers from agencies saying, "We can help on that" than I had ever seen in my life.

The level of engagement in these initiatives was particularly remarkable since these processes are often described as being side-of-the-desk or collateral duty; they were not part of the core responsibilities of the participants. Wilson Laney, cochair of the Albemarle–Pamlico National Estuary Partnership (APNEP) Science and Technical Advisory Committee, commented on the magnitude of this challenge: "It's a problem with any effort where you have professional folks being asked to do this as a collateral duty. Four meetings a year, and preparation for them, as well as involvement in issue paper preparation and review of draft indicator and monitoring proposals, and things like that. It's pretty demanding when you're doing it as a collateral duty." This reality begs the question, why do participants do it—and with enthusiasm and commitment? What was it about these processes that enabled them to overcome such significant challenges?

The structural bricks elements described in chapter 7 provide a foundation upon which MEBM activity can be undertaken. These structures and legal obligations are not sufficient, however, to energize and sustain the interaction needed for an initiative to have impact. Mortar is also needed. In our case studies, a sense of place and common purpose motivated engagement. Patience, civility, and collegiality rooted in personal and professional relationships set the stage for constructive engagement. The initiatives were constructed in a way that they were perceived to be compelling and worthwhile, and they were managed in a manner that instilled a sense of ownership. Above all, commitment and leadership by individuals and political actors got these processes going and sustained them through difficult times. These seemingly intangible factors make up the mortar that holds processes together and facilitates their progress even in the face of significant challenges.

People: Their Motivations and Relationships

Although MEBM initiatives take the visible form of organizational structures, laws, plans, and agency programs, fundamentally they are made up of individual human beings, and people largely do what they as individuals feel compelled to do. They behave in ways that reflect their interests, personalities, and relationships. Given that most of the initiatives we examined were effective to some degree, what accounted for the generally constructive and collaborative behavior of the individuals at the table?

Friendly, Adaptable "People Persons"

A standard refrain in any group process that goes well is, "It was the people who were involved." We heard this comment time and again in response to the question, "What mattered to your process?" "It comes down to personalities," commented Ellen McCarron, the Florida lead for Gulf of Mexico Alliance's Water Quality Priority Issue Team. "You need 'people persons' involved. With a few exceptions, the people selected by states have been people persons: they are easy to work with, can-do, positive, agreeable. They are great packages as state representatives. It's the people we have involved, the culture we are building, and the personal relationships. These are intangibles that are sometimes undervalued."

There is no denying the critical contributions of individuals who enjoy working with other people, are adaptable and flexible, and are willing to chip in to help with any task. Their interpersonal skills help create the conditions for trust and cooperation to flourish. Director Richard Ribb attributed the Narragansett Bay Estuary Program's ability to make progress to the people staffing the program: "Part of it is the kind of people that are attracted to this kind of work. [They are] Swiss Army Knife kind of people who can go from facilitating a meeting, to writing a technical report, to planning an outreach campaign. . . . There are a lot of really dedicated people who bring a lot of skill sets to it." Marine ecosystem-based management is hard work and often entails many meetings over an extended period of time. Friendly, adaptable, and skilled people persons are needed to keep the effort energized and on course.

Patience, Civility, and Respect

Scientific complexity and uncertainty, high stakes, and overlapping jurisdictions set the stage for protracted conflict over management of marine resources. Indeed, clashes between agency managers, scientists, fishermen, environmentalists, and others are the norm, and distrust can often be rampant. MEBM processes need to navigate these rough waters. Even people persons need to find their way through tense processes. Marine ecosystem-based management necessitates that people find ways to work together constructively, be willing to listen, and try to understand conflicting perspectives.

While conflict is often unavoidable in natural resource management, the MEBM initiatives we examined usually evidenced a markedly different dynamic. Those people involved demonstrated patience and were civil and respectful of one another; their behavior enabled dialogue to move beyond distrust toward more productive exchange. These attributes—patience, civility, and respect—are uncommon in today's world yet essential to sustained marine ecosystem-based management. They took root partly because of "personalities" but, moreover, because those involved recognized that they needed to work together. Duane Fagergren, a Northwest Straits Commission member, captured this point when he said, "We all come to the Northwest Straits Commission wearing a different hat as we come into the room, but we take our hats off at the door and we sit down and talk as equal members. There's never been an 'I'm more important than you.'. . . If anybody even implied that they would probably get booted."

Without question, it takes time to overcome old tensions and divisiveness and it takes a willingness to do so. Those involved evidenced a level of humility as they began their interactions, and, over time, this fostered a more open, patient, and respectful exchange. As the Eastern Scotian Shelf Integrated Management Initiative's Bruce Smith put it, "Fishermen and environmentalists have to learn to talk to each other, and relationship building takes time." Similarly, Herman Verheij, of the nongovernmental organization Seas at Risk, commented on how important it was for participants to recognize the legitimacy of each other's perspectives in the Wadden Sea process: "They're legitimate interests. Even if we don't like them, they're legitimate. My experience is that, as soon as you start talking to these people on the basis that 'Yes, I understand that you have a legitimate interest and maybe you'll understand that I have mine, and maybe we can understand each other," then you'll have the basis for successful cooperation." Danish farmer Kristen Fromjeser concurred, "We discuss our views and we respect one another; although we are not agreeing on everything, we have found a way to communicate with each other."

Patience was a theme highlighted by many of our interviewees. They acknowledged that it takes time to establish understanding, rapport, and new relationships across diverse people, communities, and organizations. Leesa Cobb of the Port Orford Ocean Resource Team underscored the importance of continually "touching base" at the community level to make sure "you're not getting ahead of the community. Going back, we realize 'wow, we're out in front of people'; going back, touching base is important. This has to be a community-driven project where there's buy-in to be successful and we want it to be driven by the community—so you have to be careful about how fast you move. Change happens really, really slowly so you have to go back and touch base."

Slow progress can be discouraging. Port Orford city administrator Mike Murphy encourages groups to be realistic as they move forward: "Figure out how much time it's going to take, then double it. Give it a good estimate, then double that amount of time, then work as fast as you can. Maybe you'll have enough time. It's really true. It takes a lot to reach people. It takes even longer if those people are opposed initially to get their minds changed, that takes awhile." As Florida Keys National Marine Sanctuary superintendent Sean Morton explained, "You need a lot more conversations with people, but that's how it works. . . . The more you demonstrate through your research, your monitoring, and your outreach that these things are working and having a benefit to all of the users, the blood pressure goes down, the temperature goes down. And the next time you do something, there's a little bit more trust."

The norms of patience, civility, and respect enabled constructive communication to occur even when those involved had sharp differences of opinion. Many of the successful MEBM initiatives have instilled a culture that encourages listening and learning, thereby building an understanding of the issues at hand and the varied ways in which those issues might be addressed. Those involved acknowledged that individually they did not have all the answers or expertise, and that they benefited from the collective set of ideas and perspectives.

This patient and respectful approach to their interactions proved reinforcing for many. Just as negative behaviors can undermine dialogue, positive behaviors can be contagious, and that was what many interviewees observed. "People feed on each other," commented Channel Islands Sanctuary

Advisory Council member Dick McKenna. "Everybody is involved. It's not just one or two people driving the issues as much as everyone having their two cents' worth."

Of course, these processes reside in a world that is not equally patient, civil, and respectful, and those involved recognized that they needed to help others to appreciate the need for patience. "Setting up partnerships takes time," noted APNEP director Bill Crowell. APNEP scientist Dean Carpenter similarly urges others just getting under way with an MEBM process to build "the understanding of upper management that you don't see a lot of products up front. There is a lot of [investment in] forming that foundation. So you have to resist the political pressures to go certain ways—and just plead for patience."

Personal and Professional Relationships

The collegiality observed in these initiatives was often rooted in personal and professional relationships. As an APNEP participant put it, "Business happens among friends."[2] Personal and professional relationships often helped in the early stages of an initiative, where communication could occur among colleagues or friends, which would diminish some of the fears associated with following a new path. Sometimes these relationships were preexisting; most often, they formed as people began working together with a shared purpose.

Many participants echoed this sentiment. Priscilla Brooks, a nongovernmental organization (NGO) representative from the state of Massachusetts, describes the dynamic of Gulf of Maine Council (GOMC) members: "There's a tremendous amount of collegiality in this group. People that have been in this business for a long time, who know each other, who like working together." GOMC councilor Lee Sochasky pointed to the importance of a certain "comfort level" operating across individuals:

A lot of the comfort level is with the individuals around the table. One of the great successes is building professional partnerships, both at the individual and agency level, so that these different entities feel comfortable working together even knowing that the big boss upstairs, the federal or state government, might want to set different priorities. They find ways to make things happen because they're all for achieving a common goal. So developing that comfort level and those partnerships both at the individual and agency level is what makes the thing work.

The central role of personal and professional relationships in enabling marine ecosystem-based management cannot be understated. Nor can such relationships be prescribed or externally imposed. They can only be fostered through opportunities and willing partners. While some describe "networks" in brick-like terms (i.e., physical connections between organizational structures), what we heard in our conversations with MEBM participants sounded a lot more like mortar. GOMC councilor Sochasky explained it as follows:

> Without the exchange, without these personal professional relationships that are developed, governments would continue to stay within their own silos and manage within their own jurisdictions, which generally do not fall along the ecosystem line. . . . Political systems and legislatures are focused on their own jurisdiction. It is only by building these bridges that you're able to work within the other person's system, and come to the table, and have many sides agree to make a small change in their normal way of doing business to better the ecosystem as a whole.

Not surprisingly, strong personal relationships played a central role in community-based processes, particularly in the early stages when the initiative was taking form. Without dedicated, locally based staff and leaders, it is doubtful that the Port Orford Ocean Research Team would have been established. Charlie Plybon of the Surfrider Foundation identified Leesa Cobb's grounding in the community as a critical factor to the team's taking off:

> You need people on the ground with experience in the community that have relationships or develop relationships over time. And I'm not talking about someone that hangs out for a couple years, and is gone. Someone that lives there, understanding community and needs, has their trust, and has knowledge, tireless drive and effort to be on it all the time. And that's Leesa Cobb. . . . It's one thing to have a single person there, but if all her partnerships, funding, and support were coming from an entity not present or recognizable, then the community may have lost trust.

It was the same story in San Juan County where a local port commissioner and county commissioner discussed the idea of creating a committee composed of a diverse group of citizens with the mission to address local marine conservation issues. As county commissioners, they personally knew many of the individuals who had been opposed to a national marine sanctuary proposal yet who also remained concerned about San Juan County's marine environment. Jim Slocomb described the formation of the marine resources committee (MRC): "It was an interesting and fairly high-powered group. It had the advantage of the fact that virtually everybody on the Committee personally knew the public officials. It's a small world up here. . . . It was a very close and chummy relationship."

While we were not surprised to observe the importance of personal relationships at the community-level, we were struck by the same emphasis offered about initiatives at larger scales, even at the transnational level. In response to our question, "What has kept people engaged over the years in this Gulf of Maine process that has no regulatory teeth and few dedicated funds?," David Keeley laughed and said, "Personal relationships are really important; that is the first thing that I would mention." He continued: "I was very involved running the Maine Coastal Programs. As a result of that I got to know my colleagues in all thirty-five coastal states around the country. We became friends. We saw each other three or four times a year. We talked a lot on the phone and emailed and exchanged materials and ideas, and, you know, to this day I've got colleagues around the country who know my family. You know, we go out at night and go drinking. We work long days in meetings, and it's really that glue that binds us—those personal relationships."

Three thousand miles away, reflecting on the Puget Sound Georgia Basin International Task Force, John Dohrmann offered the same observation: "The funny thing is that it does finally come down to the people and the relationships you build, and in some ways that's why—in spite of all the technology and stuff you can do by email—getting together and having a meeting and having a coffee break . . . we used to have the most amazing discussions."

Sense of Place and Purpose

While it is great that these processes engaged people and leveraged their relationships to support MEBM processes, *why were these individuals so dedicated?* What motivated them to behave in these constructive ways? We heard two core motivations in our conversations with participants: a shared concern for the place, and a sense of common purpose in addressing issues in that place.

Sense of Place and Shared Identity

Participants consistently spoke with pride about the resource they were managing, and that was true regardless of ecosystem scale or country context. GOMC councilor Priscilla Brooks identified "passion for the Gulf of Maine among the members of the Council" as its core sustaining force. "All the agencies, NGOs, business members share a passion for this resource, and an understanding of just how important it is on a global scale and how magnificent it is," she commented. This unifying sense of place contributed to a shared identity among participants that provided a focus and anchored their connection.

This passion about a shared sense of place was echoed in a toast offered by LaDon Swann, director of the Mississippi–Alabama Sea Grant Consortium, at the Gulf of Mexico Alliance's ten-year celebration in May 2014: "The Gulf of Mexico connects us culturally, spiritually, and economically. We are who we are because of it. Ten years ago, some of us may have known each other, but through networks like GOMA, we've had the good fortune to build and nurture some enduring professional and personal relationships. May our joys be as deep as the Gulf and our misfortunes as light as the foam!"[3]

Similar comments were expressed on the opposite side of the Atlantic by participants in the Trilateral Wadden Sea Cooperation. Henning Enemark, of the Danish Outdoor Council, described the strong bonds and shared identity among participants: "If you talk to the civil servants, they have this identity of being part of the Trilateral Cooperation. So when they exchange views with their colleagues in Germany and the Netherlands, I think it also influences the way of administering the areas. When you create these groups of civil servants, they feel attached to each other. If they want to have ambitious goals in one country, I think it also is contagious to the other countries."

Shared Sense of Purpose and Responsibility

A shared passion for place was reinforced by a strong sense of common purpose and collective responsibility to protect that place. As Ginny Broadhurst, director of the Northwest Straits Commission, explained: "There's a motto amongst the Commission and MRCs, specifically, 'Just Do It.' Don't sit around and wait for the agencies because you could be waiting your lifetime." Mel Cote described a similar motivation in the Gulf of Maine Council: "Most of it is due to the individuals and organizations that believe it's the right thing to do." Bill Ruckelshaus underscored the motivation for the

San Juan Initiative, a community-based partnership in Washington: "All of us share the amenities of Puget Sound. They will not be sustained unless all of us pull together in their preservation."[4]

A purpose shared in common by diverse interests is far more motivating than one imposed from above. Russell Galipeau, superintendent of the Channel Islands National Park, acknowledged the value of their collaboration: "There are a lot of benefits of being a partner. If all of you can agree what is the right direction, that's better than just one agency standing up on their bully pulpit expressing that 'we're doing it just because we have the authority.'"

The Trilateral Wadden Sea Cooperation has inspired a common sense of purpose among the three participating nations to understand, manage, and assess the Wadden Sea as one ecosystem. As Folkert de Jong, deputy secretary of the Common Wadden Sea Secretariat, explained:

> I think what is most important is this general approach to dealing with one ecosystem. And also, it has allowed the three countries to harmonize their conservation policies. We have succeeded in several respects: we have a joint assessment of the system, a joint monitoring program, joint objectives for conservation. It has been, I think, also a very positive feedback between the national management and the Trilateral Cooperation. Approaches have been different between the three countries [but] you do see that they are converging more and more.

Just because disparate groups are members of a common initiative does not mean that their conflicts go away. However, recognition of a shared purpose helps those involved to navigate their differences. As Channel Islands Sanctuary Advisory Council member and former chairperson Dianne Black explained: "At a base level, everybody is there for the same reason, and it's because they really care about the community and they really care about ocean resources. But I think how that manifests itself kind of depends on where people sit in the community. The fishing representatives certainly don't have the same view as the conservation representatives."

An Effective and Rewarding Process

Frustrating organizational processes are legion. The widely popular and long-running *Dilbert* cartoon series provides testament to that fact. People abhor meetings that have no purpose, are poorly managed, and have little positive effect. They stop attending or paying attention at such meetings. Follow-through with assigned tasks lags, and implementation of decisions proves problematic. What was it about these MEBM processes that enabled them to avoid these all-too-common dysfunctions?

Chapter 7 described the governance structures and associated bricks that organize MEBM initiatives. What happens within these structures, however, is a function of several intangible aspects of the process. All of these initiatives have an organizational structure that connects agencies and organizations. However, the existence of the structure alone is not enough. What matters is how well it functions. What happens within the process? How is it perceived? What does it encourage? How is it managed? What is its focus and dynamic?

The processes we examined exhibited four essential qualities that help explain why they were effective and that distinguish them from similarly structured initiatives that failed to gain traction. First, these processes made a difference; they were compelling and worthwhile to those involved; consequently, engagement was enthusiastic and sustained. Second, these processes instilled a sense of ownership among those involved, and that included ownership of the resource, the process, and the activities and projects promoted by the process. Third, effective processes were perceived as credible by those directly involved and those external to the process. This credibility was rooted in their transparency and inclusivity and by the way in which the interests and concerns of those involved were addressed in a fair manner. Finally, these processes were well managed so that they were focused and continued to make progress.

Compelling and Worthwhile

People are more inclined to engage in processes that provide value to them and that they deem worthwhile. This dynamic was readily apparent in the MEBM initiatives we examined. The significant value associated with participation in GOMC, for example, was underscored time and again by those involved. As Michelle Tremblay put it, "They made it valuable so that those participating can't imagine life without the Council. I hate to make it sound trite like that, but that's the idea." Her perspective was repeated in interviews with other participants. David Keeley emphasized the very pragmatic genesis of the GOMC: "When we created this thing, we saw it as a way to get stuff done." Councilor Lee Sochasky concurred: "It wasn't initiated by crisis. It was initiated by the intention to simply manage better in the future." The same perspective was provided by Priscilla Brooks, an NGO representative from the state of Massachusetts: "What has sustained it . . . is simple: it's very useful for management. There is information shared; you get to connect with your colleagues; there is the GulfWatch program that's generating a lot of data. They support things like the Gulf of Maine Mapping Initiative and data networks that provide useful tools for management."

What made a process compelling and worthwhile varied among the cases we examined. For some, it was the simple fact that the initiative enabled them to be much more effective at their jobs. For others, it was a visible problem that needed their engagement. The opportunity to think about and work on issues in a more integrated and comprehensive manner was compelling to others. And, for still others, it was evidence of impact: a sense that their work was recognized and valued by others, that it mattered more broadly.

These initiatives provide a unique opportunity for those involved to gain new knowledge and ideas. As Mel Cote put it, "A lot of it is just simply the opportunity to learn and network and share information so that we can all do our respective jobs better." Part of the effect comes from learning about others' approaches. Ted Diers, manager of New Hampshire's coastal program, comments about the value of the GOMC to his ability to take action:

> I tend to use it as a place where I can learn from other jurisdictions about the interesting things they have going on. If we're thinking about a submerged lands leasing program, for example, well we ought to look at the Maine program to understand a little bit about what they've gone through, and that's pretty easy because I now know those people and I sit down and talk to them all the time. I can get to the right person really quickly. It both informs where we are headed as well as gives us some rationale or backup on other things we want to do. We're not weird to do something in particular because the rest of the Gulf is doing the same thing.

GOMC councilor Lee Sochasky also suggests that the interaction can be transformative for the individuals and personally rewarding for them, which is why they endure seemingly endless meetings: "It's a real eye-opener. You see a different perspective. And that's useful at all the agency levels. Many of the provincial agencies, they've learned a lot from their state counterparts simply because states have more of a resource management focus and there's also federal funding tied to delivery on water quality and different issues. And there isn't a similar system on the Canadian side. They've learned a lot about what might be done."

The fact that their involvement mattered and that it was making a difference to sanctuary management has empowered and motivated Sanctuary Advisory Council (SAC) members. Moreover, the SAC's credibility was enhanced as those external to the process observed the group's advice being taken seriously by sanctuary managers. As Bruce Popham, the Florida Keys Sanctuary Advisory Council chairman, explained, "This is one of the beauties of the Advisory Council. You've got a very diverse group of very smart people who are actively engaged in the community who are actively involved in making recommendations to the staff on what direction we think they should go. And that's a powerful thing. And I would say probably from my experience the majority by far of the recommendations from the SAC (are) taken up by the management staff. And that's an incredible thing. That's what empowers those councils." This level of responsiveness makes it worthwhile for people to participate and demonstrates to others that the process is truly collaborative, not a rubber stamp for preordained agency decisions.

Visible accomplishments build an awareness of the possibilities inherent in an initiative that can snowball over time. "This helps bring people to the table," noted Richard Ribb, former director of the Narragansett Bay Estuary Program (NBEP) process, "and once they start seeing the benefits of working in these partnerships, it becomes a much bigger thing."

The community-based groups described in chapter 6 were in a position to provide essential resources, expertise, and support to local, regional, and state authorities without which action could not occur. These mutually beneficial partnerships enabled government programs needing public support to be implemented, local ordinances to be enacted, and pilot projects to be tested. Partnerships such as these are necessary for community-based initiatives that otherwise have few resources and limited influence.

Visible results also help motivate volunteers and breed enthusiasm for their continued engagement. Volunteers often need to see results of their labors to feel like they are making a difference. Several initiatives, including the GOMC, made sure to recognize and reward the contributions of those involved through award ceremonies and newsletter profiles; some even named programs or awards for notable individuals.

A sense of pride in their accomplishments has also proven motivating. Phil Bass, of the Gulf of Mexico Alliance, highlighted how key this dynamic has been: "We have given states an opportunity to be regional and national leaders. All of us tend to like that. Most scientists are introverts, and it's difficult for us to beat our own drum. But when you collectively, as a state, can be recognized either regionally or nationally as a leader on a particular issue, you take a lot of pride in that."

Folkert de Jong offered a similar observation from the other side of the Atlantic, suggesting that the Wadden Sea process has been compelling for those involved, partly because it provided a broader perspective and sense of hope: "The Trilateral Cooperation has been very inspiring in managing the Wadden Sea. It has been important for bringing in new elements, for example, this integrated approach; including water quality and integrating it with nature protection aspects. From a generic perspective, I think it has been very inspiring for the three countries." Many participants were inspired by the opportunity to view systems at a broader scale and in a more comprehensive and integrated manner; to know that their actions had an impact on bigger problems was particularly empowering.

Instills Ownership

Quite often, natural resource management initiatives are the product of top-down directives and mandates—government programs that are perceived to be *theirs* not *ours*. Hence they are often viewed with suspicion and distrust. When people own something—when it is *theirs*—they are far more inclined to take care of it than is the case when it is imposed upon them or belongs to someone else. That is just human nature. Hence ownership of the process and its activities was a critical part of the mortar holding MEBM initiatives together.

When participating agencies and organizations were provided the opportunity to work on issues of direct concern to them and in a manner over which they had some measure of control, a level of energy and enthusiasm was sustained; having ownership proved empowering. As Brian Keller, the Florida Keys Marine Sanctuary research director, commented, "It boils down to ownership, and the sense that the community has stewardship over its resources, and we federal managers are literally just there to help out. We often get ahead of ourselves and try to bring a top-down approach, and there has to be some of that. But to have a strong bottom-up approach that then unifies with the top-down (approach) to provide an overall approach to management is, I think, a big lesson from the Florida Keys."

The same dynamic was observed with the marine resource committees in the Northwest Straits Initiative. While the commission establishes overarching criteria for selecting projects to be funded, the individual MRCs develop their own proposals in a manner that satisfies local interests and commission-level objectives. As Tom Cowan, Northwest Straits Initiative founding director, explained, "They can choose which [project] is important. What is good about that is it really energizes these MRCs because they're empowered. They get to decide what is really important and they get tools to address those issues."

Community ownership has enabled the Northwest Straits Initiative to increase voluntary compliance with conservation goals and harness local energy to generate projects that benefit the ecosystem. As the Initiative's director, Ginny Broadhurst, explained, "I use the word 'citizen stewardship' to describe what goes on here. We provide a forum for tapping into that energy and understanding . . . in a way that you just can't get from agencies . . . and that's the success . . . projects like the Jefferson County 'no anchor, eel grass protection zone.' That's such a cool example of a project that would never have gotten done. An agency could never have gotten away with it . . . that would have been met with such outrage but because it was the local people's idea. . . . They got this buy-in that they would never have gotten otherwise."

Ownership was a key factor in establishing the Gulf of Mexico Alliance. The fact that the governors of the five Gulf States initiated it breathed new life into the long-standing Gulf of Mexico Program, a federal program that was "not invented here." Florida governor Jeb Bush believed that a new partnership led by the Gulf States had a good chance of elevating the Gulf in federal environmental funding priorities. He spoke directly to this possibility in his 2004 letter to fellow Gulf State governors Blanco, Barbour, Perry, and Riley: "If our state governments take the initiative, we can ensure the effort is steered primarily by the states bordering the Gulf—those most knowledgeable and affected by the conditions of the Gulf. I am hoping the federal government, seeing our partnership and commitment, will help us pursue our priorities."[5]

State-level ownership of the subsequent initiative facilitated leadership on key issues. As Phil Bass recalled, "Once the five issues were selected, the states decided which ones would be the lead [for each issue] very quickly during a conference call. It was not contentious at all. It probably took ten minutes to decide. Alabama was interested in education. Florida was interested in water quality. Mississippi, because of the river and hypoxia and agricultural issues, was interested in nutrients."

Credible, Fair, and Inclusive

These MEBM initiatives are not vigilante enterprises in which a self-selected group of people work outside "the system" to advance their own marine conservation objectives. Quite the opposite; those involved recognized that, to have impact, their efforts needed to be broadly credible and accountable to agencies and constituencies. As Glen Herbert of Canada's Eastern Scotian Shelf Integrated Management process commented, "You've got to instill capacity and facilitate the ability of the people who are at the table to share information and collect information with their constituent groups. If they're going to meetings, and they're going back to their small little group, but not spreading it out any further, then you're failing."

Credibility was rooted in transparency, the breadth of participation, and a concerted effort to be inclusive and address all perspectives on the issues at hand. In turn, for many MEBM initiatives, their perceived credibility, accountability, and fairness have contributed to their stature and impact. For example, chapter 6 described the extensive outreach efforts undertaken by the Port Orford Ocean Resource Team to ensure that community members were kept informed of the organization's activities and to ensure that organization was responsive to community concerns. Similarly, staff members cite APNEP's ability to bring different agencies and NGOs to the table as a facilitating factor. It helps "to be seen as an unbiased program that makes things happen in the community." Director Bill Crowell believes, "People do come to us with a need. They say, maybe APNEP can do this. We can work with APNEP to do that."

Being perceived as fair and inclusive enhanced the credibility of these processes. In the Channel Islands National Marine Sanctuary process, commercial urchin fisherman and Marine Reserves Working Group member Bruce Steele noted the importance of the perception of "burden sharing" among affected groups: "We tried to make it so it was as fair as possible. That's both a loaded word and also a difficult thing to do in government. To get fishermen's support or to keep them from totally going ballistic, we had to maintain the notion of fairness, such that no one fisherman bore the burden, no one fishery bore the burden. As much as possible, whether it was sport, commercial, north, south, big boat, small boat, one fishery to the next, everybody bore some equal burden for the closures. That, from my perspective, was a really incredibly important part."

A similar dynamic was observed in the Florida Keys where a concerted effort was made to acknowledge and address divergent perspectives in development of a no-take zone. The working group report emphasized, "We have tried to build trust and reach agreement. In the past, extreme positions are staked out, and are then compromised away for a final result. This time, effort was made to address all concerns to see if the group can come up with a decision they can all live with and support. The goal is to get away from strategic positioning with extreme options."[6] This inclusive, interest-based approach enabled establishment of a no-take zone that would protect a diverse range of habitats along with some of the healthiest coral in the Keys.

Focused and Well Managed

Simply convening people in a room will not magically create a constructive dialogue. Collaborative processes succeed when groups are provided a compelling task and facilitated in a way that effectively achieves that task. Most of the MEBM cases we examined were managed in a manner that was attentive to logistics and also encouraged listening, learning, and problem solving. Some of the most successful focused on meaningful, near-term tasks. In the Gulf of Maine, the region's governors and premiers encouraged the GOMC to develop joint action plans. As Keeley explained: "The initial agreement between the governors and premiers basically did two things: it created the Council and it called for the Council to create five-year plans." This structure and clear set of deliverables helped provide an immediate focus for the group.

Chris Deacutis, NBEP's science director, reflected on the process management skills provided by NBEP staff: "I think the value of the estuary program is that you build a team, with different people and jobs within that team. . . . What we do is break up tasks. Meg Kerr is the person who can really get people together. I get the scientists together and get them interested in the science. You need a diplomat to a certain extent, a person who can get people together and talk to the politicians and the powers that be."

Robert Warner, a Sanctuary Advisory Council member involved in the Channel Islands Marine Reserve Working Group, similarly pointed to the value of facilitators skilled at promoting dialogue: "People like Satie Airamé and some others really attempted to convey as much information as possible from the science to the stakeholders and also involved stakeholders in higher-level discussions about the whole issue. It was very important to the communication. The facilitators to a small extent and others to a larger extent were probably the most important. In the end, if a result occurs that someone doesn't like, they will immediately ascribe it to a lack of communication; that 'People didn't understand my point.' In truth, I think there was a lot of give and take, a lot of listening, and a lot of involvement."

State agency managers have provided leadership that has guided the Gulf of Mexico Alliance Priority Issue Teams. Each state assigned a senior state agency manager to pull together and lead a priority issue team with a range of experts from the other Gulf States and from academic and nonprofit organizations. These state leads worked hard and invested significant time to build agreements among their team members about what ought to be done on their state's issue. Since the priority issue teams involve resource managers and scientists, information collection has been effectively targeted on science that informs management. This is not always an easy process. Larry McKinney, a benthic ecologist and team leader for the Ecosystem Integration and Assessment Team, commented, "Managers of teams have to work steadily at integrating people. Scientists can be hard to work with, they can be in amongst the trees, and it can be hard to get them out to look at the forest. We need to explain to them, 'Sure, basic science is fine, but we really need to answer these management questions. What can you do to help us answer them?'"

The team leaders have also played a crucial role in creating the conditions for effective teamwork. They all hold senior posts in their agencies, a fact that gives them credibility with their peers. Perhaps more importantly, though, these individuals have brought facilitation skills to their roles. They have consciously taken on the responsibility of observing and improving the team process. "I try not to have any agendas myself," said McKinney, who leads the Ecosystem Integration and Assessment Team. "I have my own biases as a fisheries manager and a benthic ecologist, but I try to keep that out of the way. And sometimes I don't even participate in the discussion."

McKinney offered an example of how he helped his team improve its effectiveness. At one point, he realized that people interested in the information technology aspects of ecosystem assessment were dominating discussions; others were rapidly losing interest. Because he saw it as his responsibility to monitor the quality of the discussion and the level of engagement in the room, he was able to detect the problem and respond. He prompted a discussion about how to make the team work better for all members, and they collectively decided to form a subgroup for those especially interested in IT tools. He then redirected team meetings toward a broader set of questions about the best approaches for evaluating ecosystem conditions. Reflecting on this experience, he commented,

> It's a challenge every day; it's just the nature of the beast. You just have to put a framework in place that really fosters talk and allows people to say here's what I need and here's what I can do, and here's what we all need to do. There are conflicts in priorities all the time. To manage them, you need a critical mass of a mix of folks. It's an iterative process you go through every time: you allow everyone to lay out what they think is best, and your goal is to get these people

with different priorities to open up a little bit and recognize that there are other priorities, and begin to build some consensus. I don't know how you do it. You just do it.

Sustained Commitment and Leadership at All Levels

"Commitment is the biggest thing," commented Michelle Tremblay in response to our question about what has sustained the Gulf of Maine Council for more than 20 years. "People like David Keeley and the others that started it years ago, they really wanted to see it happen and they made it happen." Individual "champions" who heralded the processes and provided leadership, support, and encouragement were present in all of the cases we examined. Some of these champions were individual community members like Leesa Cobb in Port Orford. Others were agency managers like David Keeley. Sometimes political officials external to a process endorsed its efforts and funneled resources its way.

Getting a process going, and then keeping it going, requires the sustained commitment and leadership of people both within and beyond the process. As Phil Bass noted of GOMA, "It's amazing to me where we are now. . . . We've been blessed with lots of good people . . . that see the benefit of Alliance, and that have jumped in with both feet, and are just working their rear ends off." Without the personal conviction and commitment of individual champions, many MEBM processes would never get off the ground. Without sustained political and organizational commitment, many of these processes would languish. And, of course, there was the sustained commitment of individual participants who stuck with it despite challenges and setbacks. Commitment and leadership are essential mortar factors that played a huge role in sustaining the MEBM processes we examined, and when commitment faltered, their progress was undermined.

Ginny Broadhurst underscored the value of U.S. senator Patty Murray's (D-WA) sustained support for the Northwest Straits Initiative: "Senator Murray, she loves the project and feels an affinity for it and sees the value of it and hears from her constituents that it is worth funding, and that makes all the difference. . . . Having a champion definitely makes a difference, and having a champion that happens to be a fairly powerful senator doesn't hurt either. . . . She's been great to work with, her staff has been great to work with."

In the Gulf of Mexico case, Colleen Castille, the secretary of Florida's Department of Environmental Protection, and her lead for its marine protected areas program, Florida DEP staff member Kacky Andrews, began systematically building support for the idea of a multistate alliance. Margaret Davidson, director of the National Oceanic and Atmospheric Administration's Coastal Services Center, pointed to Andrews as an example of how influential a single motivated individual can be. "At the beginning, it was a house of cards," she recalled. "Kacky is the original Energizer Bunny. She had good access to Colleen, and she persuaded her that this would be a good thing and would make [Governor] Jeb [Bush] look like a stand-up guy."

The National Oceanic and Atmospheric Administration's National Marine Sanctuary Program director, Dan Basta, instilled a collaborative leadership style that was much more consensus seeking and less authoritative than is usually the norm in government. He established a sense of purpose and cross-sanctuary learning that empowered individual sanctuary managers. Ed Cassano, one of the Channel Islands' sanctuary superintendents, seized on the proposal for a network of marine reserves and the need for an advisory council as an opportunity to implement ecosystem-based management. Sean Hastings, the Channel Islands Sanctuary resource protection coordinator, pointed to the role played by Cassano: "A lot of credit needs to be given to the sanctuary manager at that point who came into a small program, recognized the potential, recognized the strengths of the statute and the need in the region for bringing parties together. It takes a visionary like that to see potential and to make things happen. In his three- or four-year tenure, he brought in the staff and the research vessel, created the SAC, and took on the reserve issue where it all came together."

Both the GOMC and the Puget Sound Georgia Basin efforts benefited from the presence and energy of dedicated individuals who championed transboundary work. Given the incentives that discourage collaborative work, it is hard to imagine these processes working effectively without these individuals and the relationships that they forged among partner groups. GOMC councilor Lee Sochasky remarks, "You can't make a difference in an ecosystem that is divided by jurisdictions until you can build bridges between those jurisdictions. And you don't build bridges at the legislative level, you build them quite often at the agency level with individuals. . . . When I want to seek to make change in management, it isn't entities that make decisions, it's individuals. And you have to find the right individual who will say, 'Yeah, we can make that happen.'" Chris Deacutis offered a similar observation from his experiences with NBEP: "What I see as valuable is when you get people that are really good and dedicated, and have the authority to use their head and say, 'This is something we should jump on.'"

Sustained political commitment was needed by most initiatives. For example, the Eastern Scotian Shelf Integrated Management Initiative's strong legislative foundation does not ensure that government officials will buy into its integrative process. Glen Herbert emphasizes the need to "get instruments of senior government buy-in and commitment early so that government departments can't just come and go, or send very junior officers who really have no authority." Since the Canadian Oceans Act does not allow existing jurisdictions to be overridden, it is very important "to have government at the table and to have them commit, and be held accountable to doing things."

On the other hand, initiatives lagged when political commitment was withdrawn, as was true with the impetus for completion of an integrated NBEP plan. Director Richard Ribb explained, "I think that if we had a governor that said this is a priority to me, and got involved and said, 'Let's figure out how to make this work,' I think that would have helped tremendously." Similarly, as described in chapter 2, waning political interest and commitment contributed to the demise of the Puget Sound Georgia Basin International Task Force.

Conclusion

We were not trying to be amusing by comparing the tangible and intangible factors that facilitate MEBM to bricks and mortar. In fact, we believe the analogy is quite fitting. As any good mason knows, the strength of a brick structure lies in both its bricks and its mortar. When the mortar decays, the structure crumbles regardless of how solid the bricks may seem, but too much mortar gluing together too little brick creates a very brittle structure.

In the MEBM realm, however, policy makers and scientists have paid more attention to building bricks at the expense of the less tangible but equally important mortar elements. At times we heard people say, "relationships, motivation, committed people, that's just common sense." Perhaps that is true, but given how limited investments in mortar can be, common sense might not be so common. It is also easy to dismiss mortar with the lament, "people and personalities—we can't do anything about that!" The cases we examined, however, suggest that nothing could be further from the truth.

Seizing upon the passion for place, and doing things to elevate a region's awareness, connection, and concern about an ecosystem, clearly makes a difference. Seeking out and motivating energetic and creative individuals and building on preexisting relationships and networks all facilitate MEBM. Making the process worthwhile and credible and imbuing tasks with purpose and impact help to motivate and sustain engagement. Ensuring that meetings and networks are well facilitated and effectively led can enable progress and reinforce the mortar elements. Strategies like these can help provide the intangible qualities necessary for effective MEBM, as the cases in this book vividly illustrate.

People do the work of MEBM, not organizational charts, directives, or formal agreements. MEBM takes time and considerable effort, and it is people who invest their time to do that work. Great ideas, great policies, great programs, and great laws—all of these things matter only if acted upon. Whether or not the initiatives we examined had a significant effect on the problems they were organized to address was entirely in the hands of individuals. It is important to tend to those individual motivations, behaviors, and relationships. Mortar matters.

Chapter 9

Implications for Policy and Practice

We began our research on worldwide cases of marine ecosystem-based management (MEBM) assuming that we would find exemplars that could be used to create a model process, but those exemplars proved elusive. There is no single way to advance MEBM; rather, there are multiple ways to incorporate an MEBM perspective into management. We observed many places where people were trying to advance ecosystem considerations in decision making, following different paths, responding to different issues, and employing different strategies. All were steadfast in their insistence that they were still trying to figure it out. Yet their efforts reveal valuable insights about the critical factors that enable and sustain an MEBM process.

This chapter summarizes our overall conclusions and describes the implications of the lessons learned from the MEBM case studies. How can managers and practitioners design and manage processes that maximize the potential of an ecosystem-based management (EBM) approach? How might foundations and policy makers help them to succeed?

Overall Observations

Although various pathways can lead to an EBM approach, at the highest level, we would advise the following: consider the specific context of the place; build linkages that connect parts of the system to each other and the place to its neighbors; support people and motivate their commitment; and invest in science, an important but not sufficient element in achieving the goals of an EBM approach. Each of these observations is developed below, followed by specific recommendations for achieving them.

Context Matters: Common Principles but Varied Pathways

There is no single approach to advancing EBM considerations in marine conservation. This is not a one-size-fits-all domain. From the two dozen cases we examined in detail, it was evident that all were applying MEBM principles as best they could with the resources and opportunities at hand. The manner in which they did so varied depending on their objectives, history, issues, and parties involved. An EBM process needs to be embedded within this context, not viewed as a substitute or replacement for it.

Context includes a set of geographic and ecological characteristics, such as physiographic boundaries and levels of water quality, that create totally different problems and conditions for influencing potential solutions. It includes a set of issues—fisheries, offshore oil and gas development, shipping, marine mammals, and the like—that vary considerably by location. It includes communities and their culture, identity, and economic health. Context also includes capacity—available information, expertise, financial resources, and social capital—and motivation—a sense of threat, a perception of possible shared benefits, and a willingness to work collaboratively or engage in conflict. A place like Port Orford, Oregon, is vastly different from the Gulf of Maine, the Albemarle–Pamlico Sound, or the Wadden Sea. An MEBM approach must be sensitive to these differences and mobilize the unique but different assets available in these situations. The approach must also engage scientists, stakeholders, and decision makers in a shared process of learning about the context and its implications for the way forward.

Context also includes preexisting governmental jurisdictions, authorities, agencies, laws, and policies. An MEBM initiative does not supplant these institutional realities; instead, it must identify its own legitimate niche within this institutional context and adopt a complementary role. In most initiatives, the locus of authority for action resided with the member organizations, not the initiative itself. For example, the Gulf of Maine Council carefully defined its role as an organization that enabled its members to further the Gulf of Maine's ecosystem objectives within their own agency or ministry's policies, programs, and procedures. GOMC also influenced the decisions of others within this institutional context through strategic grant making that enabled ecosystem-sensitive programs and activities undertaken by nonmember organizations and communities.

Another important reality is that social, political, and ecological contexts are dynamic. Struggles one day may be surmounted the next; smooth sailing one day may encounter rough seas the next. Success may be swamped by those changes. In many of our cases, for example, programs and strategies were influenced by significant changes from inside or outside the process. For example, a proposal to consider a national marine sanctuary off Oregon's Port Orford coastline introduced tensions in the community that affected support for Port Orford Ocean Resource Team (POORT) due to its perceived role in advancing the idea. Changes in personnel and political leadership, seen vividly in Puget Sound Georgia Basin, but experienced to some extent in almost all of the cases, affected the functioning and potential of their initiatives. This does not mean that these approaches are doomed by exogenous change; rather, effective processes are attentive to changes, plan responses, and manage through the inevitable transitions in people, politics, and capabilities.

Some analysts and policy makers have advanced single tools as their policy approach, including marine spatial planning and zoning. The problem with prescribed tools is that all problems start to look the same. If my only tool is a hammer, then all problems start to look like nails. Many of these tools have great value and potential, depending on the context. An EBM *approach*, however, is just that: it is a way to start dissecting and acting on a situation. In doing so, participants might decide that the situation could benefit from use of a specific tool, or they may conclude that the tool is infeasible or counterproductive. The end goal is not to put a tool in place but to improve the ecological and social conditions in the place. Effective programs are usually derived from the combination of several strategies, adaptively managed.

Other analysts have attempted to define an idealized EBM process, generally by creating flow diagrams and process models, which when built out look a lot like diagrams of the New York or Paris subway systems. We have participated in these conversations, and they are useful and thought provoking. But they tend to die of their own weight, and by anticipating too many possibilities and incorporating too many feedback loops, they overwhelm practitioners who are just trying to do a good job on the ground.

Context does matter, but there are helpful formulations and sets of principles and ideas to have in mind when implementing an EBM approach. A rich literature captures many of these.[1] We have pointed them out through the preceding chapters, and some are amplified in the following discussion.

Linkages Matter: Connecting Pieces and Bridging Scales

EBM is a management approach that seeks to overcome fragmentation by finding ways to link different areas of information, values/uses/demands, areas of authority and jurisdiction, chunks of geography, and periods of time—the present, the past, and the future. It aspires to put pieces of the puzzle together so that scientists, managers, and stakeholders can realize more holistic and reasoned decisions. Indeed, the term *ecosystem* describes a real tangible place that can be outlined on a map, but it is also a metaphor for perceiving a place and its component parts and processes as an integrated system.

Taken as such, it is important to define boundaries in order to start understanding and acting on a system, and an EBM approach encourages decision making that considers boundaries that make sense ecologically—watersheds, physiographic regions, airsheds, problem-sheds, and the like. But even in the case of watershed management where gravity and the flow of water are good indicators of what's in and what's out, many important factors flow across boundary lines, including human demands, pollutants transported by air, and legal authorities. As a result, EBM needs to focus on effectively establishing linkages that include these interconnections and feedbacks.

Much debate in the EBM field has focused on the issue of appropriate scale—defining large landscapes or large seascapes, or watershed hierarchies, or mapping terrestrial ecosystems and drawing management boundaries around them. When adding humans to the picture, the question of scale includes considerations of a shared sense of place or identity. These are important questions and warrant attention by managers, and the thought process of imagining the system of interests is an important element of EBM. But our assessment of numerous EBM experiments leads us to the conclusion that the question of appropriate scale might be a red herring.

In fact, the initiatives we examined were at widely different scales. However, they all linked to different scales. The large transboundary Gulf of Maine Council influenced state- and province-level focus and activities through the members on the Council and its working groups. Similarly, GOMC influenced small-scale activities through a small grants program that supported the work of nongovernmental organizations, communities, and others, which, in turn, was mutually beneficial to the broader ecosystem and GOMC goals.

Linkages across scale were motivated by different needs. For example, POORT, as described in chapter 6, has no legal authority; it cannot force anybody to do anything. Consequently, it has numerous relationships with other organizations, agencies, and the Town of Port Orford that enable POORT to have impact despite a lack of authority. Through its linkage with the State of Oregon, it was able to get the Redfish Rocks Marine Reserve established and enforced by the state; what the state got was POORT's legwork in identifying and assessing the resource area, and a supportive community, leading to its first reserve without the conflict and opposition it was encountering in most other areas. Port Orford got state sanctioning, enforcement, and resources with which to promote and encourage sustainability of the area and enable scientific research focused on the local ecosystem to inform their own fishing activities and regulatory agency decisions.

In most cases, these up and down linkages were mutually beneficial; they provided something of value to each involved party. That is, they satisfied the interests of all parties and thus produced mutual gains, the win-win outcomes that are the holy grail of interest-based negotiation.[2] For example, smaller-scale groups can provide larger-scale initiatives with rich understanding about the feasibility of effective on-the-ground action; pilots or experiments at smaller scales, which can then serve as models that others can emulate; and visible support for larger-scale policy actions of real and symbolic value to higher-level policy makers. In turn, larger-scale initiatives can provide smaller-scale efforts with legitimacy, resources, incentives, and influence.

The exchanges that take place through these linkages are complementary and meet various needs, such as for resources or for political support. For example, the Northwest Straits Commission receives significant federal and state funding to support EBM-related efforts in the Straits. The Commission can establish and promote a vision for the Straits and coordinate efforts to pursue that vision, but it has no regulatory authority; it cannot tell anyone to do anything or stop anyone from doing anything. What they accomplish is largely a function of what the county marine resources committees (MRCs) are willing and able to accomplish.

From the linkage, the Northwest Straits Commission gets voluntary action at the local level, support for its broader goals and vision, and place-based projects that have cumulative benefits to the Straits ecosystem. In exchange, the MRCs secure resources for projects on places they care about; assistance in getting organized and developing proposals; guidance on what projects are worthwhile; and a forum in which to communicate with and learn from the other MRCs.

Building and utilizing linkages enables groups to make progress in a manner that is not possible through individual action, since unique advantages and opportunities are associated with each level of social and ecological organization. It may behoove the MEBM field to focus less on an optimal scale for operations and more on supporting a diverse set of initiatives with a mix of scales and authorities. Doing so creates a more robust and resilient overall system than would a single model applied at a single scale, not a surprising concept to those of us in the world of conservation.

People Matter: Sustained Individual Commitment Is the Lifeblood of Marine Ecosystem-Based Management

One of the clear messages from the EBM cases we examined is that EBM science and policy do not solve problems; people solve problems. Laws, directives, procedures, and scientific information may provide guidance and incentives, but in the end, action only occurs if individuals decide to take it. Without committed and entrepreneurial individuals, well-intended laws and policies will founder, and new science will sit on shelves.

We discussed the importance of people and relationships in chapter 8, but we want to reiterate this basic message. Although on one level it seems obvious, agencies and policy makers often neglect routine maintenance on their most important assets, people. In turn, analysts often focus on new policies or structures because a recommendation of investing in people seems a little nonanalytic. Yet individuals who had the capacity and motivation to do what was needed and who were able to sustain their energy and commitment were among the most catalytic forces in our EBM cases.

To enable and encourage individual action one must first select skilled and motivated people to participate in EBM initiatives, not just people who can be spared to go to meetings. Second, those selected must be provided with the needed skills in negotiation, communication, and management, and an understanding of ecosystem science. Third, they must be given the room to engage productively across boundaries so they are able to commit their organizations to action. Fourth, they must feel valued and that their work is important. Fifth, they need help as they manage through transitions. Discussion later in the chapter provides some specific suggestions along these lines.

Science Matters, but Not Just in the Way You Might Think

Scientific research and scientists were important in all of the MEBM cases we studied. Initiatives contracted for scientific assessments, monitoring of status and trends, and research on key uncertainties. Science was looked to as a means of developing an understanding of complex marine systems, and planning in many of these places was grounded in a scientific understanding of the issues requiring management. In some, such as the Narragansett Bay Estuary Program and the California marine protected areas, citizen science was used to collect information while simultaneously building public support for the initiatives.

But science was also important as a way to legitimize the efforts and as a relatively comfortable and logical place to start. Scientists and managers operating in dispersed organizations often shared paradigms and language; that shared culture enabled them to jointly focus on a task or set of priorities. "Doing science" was also less threatening than making choices, so scientists and managers often built relationships sitting around the table of science, before they were served the less palatable main courses of management problems (joined by their rowdier policy-making relatives).

In some cases, such as the work done by the Mid-Atlantic Regional Ocean Council, web-accessible databases were constructed to pool data. Those databases and the geographic information systems developed in parallel were helpful tools that enabled access while also allowing technical people and stakeholders to visualize the situation. In the California marine protected areas designation process, MarineMap, a GIS system developed at the University of California, Santa Barbara, allowed groups of stakeholders to define alternative networks of marine protected areas. The program's user-friendliness was as important as having twenty more layers of data.

At the same time, these MEBM efforts make it clear that there will never be enough science to resolve key uncertainties facing managers, and that complex models and complicated science may obstruct the learning needed to enable managers and policy makers to act. In the California marine protected area process, for example, science advisory teams were used to inform stakeholders and policy makers. Their most effective action resulted from development of some rough rules of thumb for size and spacing of marine protected areas within a network; their least effective mode of action consisted of complex bioeconomic models. In the same process, only a handful of scientists had the communication skills to speak effectively to a lay or policy audience. The MarineMap tool used in part of the process had its impact not only by enabling stakeholders to understand various habitat configurations but by shifting dynamics among users. Like a video game, it became a puzzle to solve, rather than a set of conflicts across a meeting table.

At bottom, science is important for the understanding it can bring, but in our cases its larger effect might have arisen from the fact that it provided a starting point for dialogue, and helped legitimize the efforts. Rarely was the science complete enough to provide answers. Marine scientists at times believe that we just need more science in order to do effective EBM. But waiting for science was not always a good EBM strategy because the core issues on the table had as much to do with value choices as scientific conditions, and they beg attention now. For those underwriting or guiding initiatives, the message seems to be that, although science investments are productive, they should not get in the way of all the other useful activities of EBM.

Marine versus Terrestrial: It May Matter More for Policy than for Practice

Some think marine EBM differs greatly from land-based EBM, but in practice, many of the challenges and success factors are the same.[3] Scientific complexity and uncertainty, jurisdictional complexity, competing interests and lack of a shared vision, ineffective plans, and limited resources are evident at many ecosystem-scale conservation efforts—on land and in the water. At the same time, success is more likely if several factors are present in either domain. These include brick-like factors, such as preexisting government programs or structures, authority derived from formal or informal sources, and the availability of scientific information and financial resources. They also include mortar-like factors, such as a sense of place or common purpose, evidence of political will or organizational commitment, and well-managed collaborative processes.

At a policy level, however, the experience with land-based EBM provides a cautionary tale. As noted in chapter 1, land management agencies embraced ecosystem management in the early- to mid-1990s as a way out of a crisis caused by a set of stalemated endangered species and public lands conflicts, a mechanism for accommodating new landscape-scale science, and a signal of policy change by the Clinton administration. The term *ecosystem management* was spotlighted, considerable investment was made in the science base and in collaborative place-based processes, and policy shifts (e.g., changes to the national forest planning process) were proposed and some were adopted. Ecosystem-level plans were developed, including the Sierra Nevada Framework and the Pacific Northwest Forest Plan.[4]

Significant changes occurred in many places: broader stakeholder engagement led to the realignment of constituent interests and empowered noncommodity interests; greater scientific understanding enabled more attention to issues of ecosystem integrity and sustainability; management strategies incorporated a larger landscape view and an understanding of ecological processes such as fire and hydrologic regimes; adaptive management concepts were explored; agencies tried to link management more strongly to science; and a broader set of strategies was utilized, including market-based mechanisms and negotiated solutions such as habitat-conservation plans. In many places, a long-standing atmosphere of conflict was attenuated, and in some, ecosystem improvements were achieved.

However, advancement of ecosystem management as a spotlighted concept (as opposed to a norm of practice) was stymied by the shift from the Clinton to the Bush administration, because ecosystem management was viewed as a Clinton policy. It also became evident that it was extraordinarily difficult to be successful at achieving an ecosystem management ideal, and a set of funders oriented to short-term outcomes found it difficult to recognize incremental steps as sufficient. Today, ecosystem management is less of a term of art and call to action than it was fifteen years ago. At the same time, many practitioners recognize its logic and routinely incorporate ecosystem considerations in planning and management.

Marine resource managers and policy makers face a situation that has important similarities, while other aspects are considerably different. Crisis-induced change at the national policy level (due to fisheries declines and the embrace of MEBM by the two ocean commissions and the Obama administration) and the adoption of state-level ocean protection laws are clearly reminiscent of the early "spotlight" days when ecosystem management was viewed as novel. In addition, "granddaddy" processes in both the land and marine domains have grappled with resource problems in a somewhat integrated, regional way for years—almost half of the MEBM cases we studied were fifteen to twenty-five years old—and as noted earlier, many day-to-day challenges of management practice are remarkably similar in both land-based and marine EBM.

There may well be more room for innovation in marine systems. In the terrestrial realm, fifty years of management conflict, a strong sense of property rights and entitlement, and a robust set of competing constituencies produced a long-standing set of conflicts that constrained opportunities for creative problem solving. Ecosystem management became management of this conflict as much as management of the land, and while it has achieved small-scale success, it has been extraordinarily challenging to move forward in many places.

In contrast, in the marine realm, rights are not as well defined; the systems themselves may be less intrinsically fragmented and more likely to be controlled by government; economic interests may be more threatened by declines in fisheries and hence willing to experiment with change; and community-based fishing interests may be less organized as single industries. MEBM initiatives outside the United States evidence a wider array of forms than those seen in land-based ecosystem management efforts, and agencies involved in MEBM initiatives within the United States may have greater political space to experiment. The National Oceanic and Atmospheric Administration and the Environmental Protection Agency may be able to follow emerging management concepts, whereas the U.S. Forest Service and its sister agencies were more directly dominated by political overseers.

At the same time, as with land-based ecosystem management, the practice of MEBM can be undermined by the need for short-term success and our propensity to jump from one novel, spotlighted term to another. That may be occurring as foundations shift their philanthropy from investing in MEBM and policy makers shift language to terms such as marine spatial planning. While there has been significantly less research aimed at understanding the process of MEBM than the process of land-based EBM, in all likelihood, many of the same bottom-line lessons remain. Investments in science need to be matched by investments in strategic and inclusive processes of management. Measures of success need to be defined in process and social and ecological terms, and all parties need to recognize that progress will be incremental and difficult. Climate and other global-scale changes underscore the imperative for EBM approaches but make those efforts more challenging. New legal and institutional structures can help, and indeed some of the shifts in state law may well provide new frameworks for marine management. But the overarching message from the land-based ecosystem management experience is that for MEBM to succeed, strategic and adaptive processes that build knowledge, relationships, and shared understanding must be sustained.

Advice for Practitioners and Agencies

How do these observations and lessons from the cases translate into action for agencies and professionals within them? Here are a few suggestions.

Build the "Missing Table"

A forum for interaction created at an appropriate scale and matched to the ecosystem or problem is one place to start. Where issues are pressing and people are motivated, simply creating and stocking "the table" will create opportunities for progress. Structures can be informal or formal, depending on the context. But it is critical to have a place for key parties in an ecosystem to engage, build relationships, learn together, and start to take action. In most cases, these can be created under existing authority, and their structure can evolve as needed over time. Many tools are available for codifying structure, as detailed in chapter 7. It is usually important to consider how an effort gains legitimacy or authority, recognizing that influence comes from both formal powers and informal persuasive capacity. It is almost always necessary to have a contact point and a coordinator. Nevertheless, it is not necessary to make a structure overly complicated. Start small, and adapt over time.

Often there are nascent committees or structures that could be used as a basis for ecosystem-scale interaction, but only if they are provided with a real mission supported by leadership and have a core of resources to incentivize engagement, facilitate coordination, and enable the group to gain on-the-ground traction. Clarity about the responsibilities and objectives of the forum is important, as are roles associated with it. It is also important to ensure effective facilitation and a regular and predictable place to work.

Consider the System: Build Linkages

As already discussed, EBM requires linkages at appropriate scales in order to overcome fragmentation. Hence practitioners should assess the needs and opportunities for linkages and work to create them. Needs assessment should incorporate a systems perspective, whereby the problems or issues facing the system should be unpacked and considered in terms of the appropriate scale and need for linkage.

Often this analytic process requires some level of scientific research and dialogue so that participants better understand their systems, including what is not known. It is often necessary to simplify the system in order to get work done, and that may mean setting boundaries on the issues or strategies considered, such as was done by the Gulf of Maine Council and the Eastern Scotian Shelf Integrated Management Initiative when they decided to stay away from issues related to fishing. On one hand, it seemed odd not to include a key resource and stressor, but the proponents recognized that historical conflicts and the existing regulatory system for fisheries management might doom progress on any other issues. The solution is to create linkages to parallel processes that deal with these off-the-table issues. For example, the Gulf of Mexico Alliance did not select Gulf fisheries as one of its five priority issues because fisheries management was the responsibility of the Gulf of Mexico Fisheries Management Council. To ensure communication and coordination between the two bodies, the Fisheries Management Council officially joined the Gulf of Mexico Alliance in 2011 and is an active participant in the Alliance ecosystems team. In turn, an ecosystems team member attends regular Fisheries Management Council meetings.

In considering appropriate scale, remember that place and relationships matter; they can require an effort small enough in scale to create a sense of place and build relationships. In order to consider larger ecosystem boundaries, a tenet of EBM, groups may need to create linked structures. In assessing linkages, think about potential partners. Ask the question, Who could benefit from our activity and assistance, while we benefit from them in some manner?

All of the linkages we observed evidenced interdependency. Altruism is not the underlying motivator; these linkages are two-way streets ensuring needs are met on both sides of the bridge. The San Juan Initiative, a partnership with Washington State's Puget Sound Partnership, for example, provided resources at the local level to pilot a voluntary, incentive-based program for private property owners to curb erosion and protect sensitive shoreline ecosystems. The success of the state salmon recovery program hinged on local-level action, but the Puget Sound Partnership had no authority at the county level with which to regulate development. San Juan County wanted to continue advancing marine ecosystem management principles but had insufficient resources. This cross-scale linkage enabled both to achieve objectives that would not have been met had they acted independently.

Instill Ownership and Compelling Purpose

Since mortar is necessary to ensure effective EBM, our basic message to agencies is to invest in mortar. That is, create the conditions under which people are motivated to engage and take action. Ensure that the group has a compelling purpose, one that is seen as worthwhile to the participants and their home organizations, either because it creates products that meet their individual interests or solves problems that are viewed as shared. Process alone is not enough. It needs to create something of value for the participants, and that can range from relationships, information, or ideas to shared authority and action.

Planning for and highlighting small wins can be motivating. Some may call these baby steps. They can be low-hanging fruit—tasks that are more easily accomplished—or simply larger tasks broken into smaller pieces. Demonstration or pilot projects develop capacity and build motivation.

According to POORT's Leesa Cobb, the group "didn't have a big win at the beginning and that was hard. . . . We need more wins to keep people engaged, there's no question."[5] On the other hand, Port Orford's mayor, Jim Auborn, noted that "inspiration coming from positive results" kept him going.

A related piece of advice is "Plan, but also do." It is a curse of the fact-based, rational, reductionist people who tend to get involved in EBM that the initial response to a situation is to unpack it, analyze its problems, and plan strategies for dealing with them. In many cases, planning is also a required task associated with existing government programs. The National Estuary Program and the National Marine Sanctuary Program each have requirements for constructing and updating plans, with different degrees to which their plans bind their management. In some of the other MEBM initiatives we studied, planning became an important first step, which focused attention and provided a framework for ongoing action by member organizations. For example, when the Gulf of Mexico Alliance was created, the governors set out a very short one-year time frame for producing an action plan, which helped to focus and limit the group's initial efforts. In the Gulf of Maine, the requirement to create five-year plans provided an immediate task for the group and began the effort of stitching together the jurisdictions' existing management plans to find synergies and create a common agenda.

However, in some cases we studied, people were trapped in rounds of planning, making participants feel a lot like Bill Murray in *Groundhog Day*. Sometimes, constructing a plan feels doable, whereas on-the-ground action may be harder. One response is to develop framework plans, then allow for a lot of flexibility and testing at specific places or for dealing with specific issues. And while planning, at least take initial steps to create better linkages and engage in enough small-scale action to test hypotheses and generate momentum.

A sense of ownership is also motivating. Ownership involves participants having a sense of control over the direction of the effort and real impact on the decisions it makes. Ownership creates a feeling of participant responsibility for the group's actions, lauded for its successes and accountable for its failures. This type of ownership at times may feel threatening to host organizations, including supervisors of the individuals participating in the collaborative initiatives, but it is important that they support their employees' engagement. Organizational managers often feel that their role is to dictate direction and their employees' role is to follow. But this outdated image of management seldom fosters the shared sense of influence and input on key decisions that motivates people.

Be Patient and Incentivize Patience

MEBM takes time. Those expecting quick action and results will likely be frustrated. This reality inevitably challenges the support needed for progress. Many of the problems in marine and coastal areas are a result of actions taken (or not taken) over decades of time, and the nature of the species and ecosystem processes is such that improvements or restoration may take similar periods of time.

Many of the key players in the MEBM initiatives we studied commented that there are no quick fixes. For example, POORT's director Leesa Cobb noted, "Change happens really, really slowly." As a result, it is important for groups not to get discouraged, and to allow for more time than they might anticipate for a change to occur. According to Port Orford's city administrator, Mike Murphy, interested groups should "figure out how much time it's going to take, then double it. Give it a good estimate, then double that amount of time, then work as fast as you can. Maybe you'll have enough time. It takes a lot to reach people. It takes even longer if those people are opposed initially to get their minds changed; that takes awhile." Certainly in established resource-dependent communities, resistance may be a sustained undercurrent, in part because of a fierce sense of independence or skepticism of the government and collective action.

Clearly one task for an EBM effort is to diagnose sources of concern and resistance and plan for ways to influence those perceptions. Besides this, there are several implications of the length of these processes. On one hand, it is reasonable to set expectations appropriately and tell participants that patience is a prerequisite and that perseverance is needed to demonstrate results. But that is not a particularly compelling message. Hence other strategies for dealing with the challenge include setting realistic deadlines and demonstrating progress against them, breaking tasks into small doable pieces, investing thoughtfully in sustaining the motivation of key people, including small wins as discussed earlier, and managing the inevitable transitions in people that occur during long processes.

Adaptive management is another way to deal with the long time frames of EBM, but as an academic concept it often feels overwhelming to EBM groups. It is important for them to learn from their efforts, which requires them to define clear objectives, think about what success looks like, and collect information periodically to see how they are doing. Setting up deadlines and reporting mechanisms to prompt reevaluation and strategic thinking is also valuable. Several of our cases enlisted the help of external evaluators to help them assess progress and refine strategies and organizational structures. But it is not necessary to do full-blown adaptive management, which involves hypothesis testing and deliberate experiments (though where there is capacity and will, some small experiments are a good idea). The most successful initiatives we studied had a thoughtful, reflective, and flexible mind-set about what they were doing, and they were not dogmatic about which version of adaptive management they were carrying out.

Invest in People and Manage Personnel Transitions

If people are the lifeblood of EBM initiatives, and relationships are the critical mortar, then it is clearly important to invest in people. Some of the motivational issues have already been discussed; capacity is also important. Providing training in mutual gains negotiation and collaborative process facilitation is one way to add to the perspectives and skill-set that can make collaboration work. Offering training in GIS, monitoring techniques, and similar tools to the EBM group is a way to enhance understanding while building relationships on uncontroversial tasks.

Investing in collaborative learning—tours, field trips, cooperative research projects—can develop both individual and collective capacity. Giving participants some slack to enable them to fully engage in these efforts can help avoid the "side-of-the-desk" problem, whereby the EBM effort gets no attention from some participants because their home organization sees EBM as marginal to their job.

Since EBM takes time, it is almost certain that transitions will occur in people and policies, and we saw numerous situations where initiatives lost steam when key people retired or were transferred to other places or tasks. One simple response is to manage the transitions to ensure overlap between old and new representatives; new members can then get up to speed, and the initiatives have continuous capacity without big ups and downs. Organizational leaders should be regularly briefed on the workings of the EBM effort and understand its value, which will also help if they are responsible for naming new representatives and equipping them with the ability to succeed.

Advice for Funders

Foundations, large nongovernmental organizations, and international institutions play a significant role in catalyzing and sustaining MEBM efforts. It was not hard to see the fingerprints of the Packard Foundation, the World Wildlife Fund, and the United Nations Environment and Development Programmes on numerous cases worldwide. In some places, they were a presence because of critical conservation challenges running up against a government with no resources or one that was corrupt or lacked the political will to act on the problems. In others, they were the purveyors of innovation providing slack resources to get people's attention and incentivize change. Assuming no notable institutional shifts, foundations and international institutions have a major role to play in future marine conservation efforts.

Facilitate Sustained Connections

MEBM efforts cut across the funding and regulatory lines of government and integrate disparate but interdependent efforts in an area. Due to turf, traditional patterns of independent activity, and few unused resources, organizations and agencies that should be talking to each other are often not communicating. Problems fester because only parts of them are worked on; resources are squandered because of duplication; and learning is limited because knowledge is not shared. In fact, we have been amazed by how little is known between organizations and EBM initiatives about what others are doing, or about opportunities on which they might be capitalizing.

Funders have the resources and mission to understand the bigger picture. By providing seed funding and the promise of future funding, they can create an incentive for people to come together and share. When foundations call a meeting, people respond. For example, the proponents of marine EBM were greatly benefited by the activities of the David and Lucile Packard Foundation and the Gordon and Betty Moore Foundation at encouraging disparate researchers to come together, and creating vehicles for researchers and practitioners to interact. We similarly benefited from the efforts of the William and Flora Hewlett Foundation to catalyze cross-investigator discussions in the area of conflict management. But when these investments stopped, the relationships between researchers and practitioners withered. All were motivated to maintain engagement, but they lacked the inducement and opportunity to find the ways and the time to do so.

Build Capacity, Catalyze Action

One reality in almost all of the places we studied—independent of country or region—was that the leaders and participants of the EBM efforts felt constrained by limited resources, including funding, staff, expertise, and tools. This was true of both the member organizations and the collaborative EBM groups. When faced with constrained resources, organizations retrench to what they know and do the minimum needed to satisfy statutory or other requirements. Slack resources—funding that is not committed to core activities—has a strange power to motivate people and enable them to act, far beyond the magnitude of funding. Demonstration grants, contributions by outside investors, and legislative earmarks were all sources of slack resources in the cases we studied. They enabled and incentivized action, and we would encourage the philanthropic community and international institutions to continue or expand their role as a source of nonroutine funding for ecosystem-scale work.

The needs go beyond money, however. Information, expertise, and skills are limited, particularly when you get beyond the basics of fisheries science and management. Experience with collaborative process, understanding of innovative tools (e.g., payments for ecosystem services and other market-based strategies), skills at effectively engaging public audiences, and understanding what level of political outreach is possible—these are all in short supply.

In some places, foundations have created learning networks that promote peer-to-peer sharing of ideas. The West Coast EBM network funded by the Packard Foundation is an example. Foundations have also funded shared, accessible databases, which are valuable as sources of information and also as ways to envision a common geography. While research partnerships are needed, they are more likely to be funded by government and scientific organizations; practitioner partnerships are less prevalent. Funding learning networks can help create synergies while also sharing hope, a force that has at times been less available. Hope and insight can also come from continued efforts to document and analyze success stories of MEBM, not unlike the project we were fortunate to have funded. As MEBM becomes less novel, documenting how groups sustain momentum and achieve success is critical.

Underwrite Research and Development

Government and universities have declined in their ability and willingness to provide a source of new ideas and road-tested strategies. Government faces self-imposed funding constraints and limited vision; universities have created a research environment that creates disincentives for researchers to study and actively engage in real-world situations. In some places, private capital is investing in market-based strategies that can promote marine conservation, including fisheries and invasive species management. But those are likely to be the exception, not the rule.

A critical role for foundations and multinational institutions is to underwrite the research and development needed to imagine and test new EBM strategies. They have the ability to generate ideas, while also advancing the application of these approaches in specific places. The Packard Foundation started doing this in the mid-2000s, and they were a catalyst for activity in places such as the Western Pacific, the Gulf of California, and the central California coast. But their investments were largely in EBM science and were not matched by parallel and sustained investments in EBM management and outreach. Thus, at the end of a five-year grant-making cycle, a frustratingly limited amount of change had occurred on the ground.

Be Thoughtful about Metrics

While foundations are justifiably focused on investments that produce measurable results, quantifiable effects on ecosystem health or integrity are probably among the most difficult to identify and document causality for, particularly in the five- to ten-year time horizon of a grant program. This mismatch of short-term reporting and long-term results does not mean the investments are not worthwhile; it just means that patience and surrogate measures are warranted.

The general life cycle of an EBM initiative runs from getting started, building effective working relationships, collecting information and planning, and undertaking pilot programs, to institutionalizing and adapting it to results.[6] In tracking outcomes, there is a rough stepwise pattern of progress moving from process to social to ecological improvements. Our advice to foundations is to work with grantees on understanding this life cycle, mapping it as a logic model, and creating performance metrics that relate to the different stages, then to create monitoring mechanisms for collecting information that operationalizes those metrics. In most cases, this means that EBM efforts would be validated on measures of intermediate outcomes, while encouraging groups to think strategically about their logic model and collect information that over time will show effects on target populations, ecosystem processes, or stressors.

From interviewing individuals in charge of a variety of MEBM initiatives, many of whom regularly sought foundation funding, it seemed clear that, although the groups valued the thinking involved in constructing logic models and imagining what success would look like, rigidly imposed quantitative constructs did undercut the ability of some to be opportunistic and adaptive. These groups generally operate in a context that involves much change; they need to be responsive in an informed and deliberate manner. Foundation staff with which we discussed this dynamic indicated that they are normally open to honest conversations with grantees about emergent opportunities and responses, but off-the-record conversations with MEBM grantees suggest that the dynamics around metrics has been a problematic aspect of their relationship with funders. Both sides need to find ways to navigate these tensions.

Invest for the Long Term

Finally, since MEBM is a long-term process of social and ecological change, foundations either need to be in it for the long term or be focused on stepwise tasks that build capacity or motivation or demonstrate progress. If the latter, it makes sense to pay attention to transitional support and capacity building that will enable an initiative to secure continued funding.

In some places, endowment funding would be helpful to create a base of activities aimed at improving ecosystem health through MEBM activities. Initiatives like the Gulf of Mexico Alliance, which received base funding from the BP oil spill restoration effort, have not only been able to do more, but the need to spend the annual yield on research and restoration in a deliberate and transparent way has created an incentive for scientists, managers, and policy makers in the area to discuss and decide on priorities, which is a healthy thing to do.

Advice for Policy Makers

Policy and politics tended to have a bimodal effect on the MEBM initiatives we examined. For some, they motivated and incentivized action; for others, they got in the way. Some went through cycles of both. Our overall message to policy makers is to find ways to put wind in the sails of well-intentioned efforts, not anchors in their wake. Enable, don't constrain.

Varying Policy Responses Needed in Different Places

Since one size of MEBM does not fit all, it follows that, on the policy level, a multipronged approach is needed. In some places, new legal authority or an incentivizing mandate is needed; in others, creation of new forums and small grant programs that enable action may be appropriate; in still others, the need is to cut out problematic policies that limit interagency communication and coordination; and, in many, continued investments in existing programs and structures are required given the time frame of effective EBM.

Based on our case studies, it is clear that authority can come in different forms. While legal mandates and organizational structures are often important building blocks of MEBM, they sometimes create the semblance of MEBM without the energy and drive needed to sustain progress. In some places, granting "authority" by backing up EBM efforts with political will and leadership support may be enough to initiate and sustain efforts.

Build on Existing Laws and Institutions

Existing government programs have been a nexus for EBM. National estuary programs, national marine sanctuaries, and national estuarine research reserves, among others, have created "tables" and core operating resources that have resulted in significant progress in numerous places. They have often catalyzed action, in many cases, without any regulatory authority.

National governments play an important role in programs functioning at the ecosystem scale, particularly with marine systems, and that should be sustained. Governmental entities can promote integration across political boundaries, support partnerships in a watershed, and negotiate effective relationships across international boundaries. As the Narragansett Bay Estuary Program director, Richard Ribb, recalled about the program, "It's a mistake to fund a watershed effort and walk away, which was the original intent of the NEP process. . . . You [need] a big picture national policy instead of expecting the states to just continue on with this."

We believe that investing in and supporting many of these existing structures are valuable from an EBM perspective. That means not bleeding them dry through budget reductions, and not undercutting their potential to make a difference by creating overlapping structures. Their planning and reporting requirements might need to be updated; for example, to ensure that they have identified short- and long-term metrics and can compile publicly accessible reports that indicate progress. It is also key to maintain their capacity and interest in engaging multiple stakeholder groups and the public. Well-supported demonstration grants and pilot programs as well as ongoing research and ecosystem-scale accessible databases can create incentives for engagement of nongovernmental groups and agencies from other levels of government.

Don't Keep Reinventing the Wheel

It is a fact of political life that new administrations will want to create *their* program, to make *their* mark. At times it is helpful to breathe new life, bring new resources, and pay more attention to initiatives, such as these EBM efforts. But leaders need to recognize the costs of organizational transitions and transformations. In a number of our case studies, participants lamented that their work was disrupted by "new initiatives" that were largely repackaged old ideas. People were assigned to attend meetings of the new efforts and had to cut back their involvement with existing initiatives. In the Puget Sound Georgia Basin and Gulf of Maine Council cases, shifts in governors and national policies resulted in new structures that overlapped existing ones. Participants commented that they brought "too much of a good thing," and took the wind out of the sails of the established efforts.

Truly new efforts that leverage significant new resources or opportunities or engage needed parties may be a good idea, as was the case with the Gulf of Mexico Alliance being created to expand beyond the existing federal Gulf of Mexico Program. But often, an infusion of new resources and attention to the established initiatives would have a greater effect. One of the lessons from the terrestrial ecosystem management experience was the cost of relabeling and repackaging for political purposes, and we would advise political leaders to exercise caution if they truly care about progress on the ground.

Leadership Support Is Critical; Allow and Celebrate Innovation

We may be living in a time when it is difficult to secure the political will for positive action, such as creating EBM opportunities. Yet, in places requiring new statutes, significant resources, or high-level political legitimacy, it is critical that political leaders muster the will to act. For example, political leadership was critical to the designation of most marine sanctuaries. The Florida Keys case involved the administrations of presidents Jimmy Carter and George H.W. Bush and other federal officials who saw it through.

Visionaries helped legitimize and promote the effort, including, for example, Dante Fascell, the Democratic congressman from Miami who sponsored the legislation. Fascell, a longtime fisherman in the Keys and Miami, saw firsthand the decline in fish stocks and water quality. He recognized the need for a multifaceted approach, backed by public support. As Fascell commented during testimony before the U.S. House of Representatives, "If we are going to save this reef, and if it is going to provide both ecology and economically, it is going to take the combined efforts of all the agencies at all levels of government, including the people. Nothing is going to work unless the people support it."[7]

State-level political leadership was also critical. While fifty-five percent of the ballots in a nonbinding referendum in Monroe County in 1996 were opposed to the sanctuary, Florida governor Lawton Chiles and his cabinet decided the management plan was in the state's best interests. Meeting in January 1997, Chiles and his cabinet unanimously voted in favor of the marine sanctuary management plan.[8]

EBM efforts may require different things from political leaders. At times, political leadership means staying out of the way of a group that is making progress. Sometimes a below-the-radar approach to these problems is productive because it engenders less opposition and noise. At other times, leadership comes in the form of the bully pulpit, where high-level officials shine a spotlight on an innovative effort. In an era where concepts of shared leadership are the norm, providing support for agency managers and encouraging leadership from nongovernmental champions may also result from the actions of political leaders. None of the advances in the Florida Keys and Channel Islands National Marine Sanctuary cases (chap. 4) would have been possible without the vision, patience, and open-mindedness of numerous individuals who supported creation of the sanctuaries, and championed them as opposition coalesced.

Sustained Leadership Is Essential; Manage Transitions

Four-year election cycles do not match the time scale of EBM, and sustained support is essential through political and policy transitions. This support involves commitment from both elected and appointed officials. Absent it, the initiatives have problems. As EPA staff member Margherita Pryor, a participant in the Narragansett Bay Estuary Program, explained, "We have to recognize that these things take off or not due to a variety of local influences. If you have a strong persistent advocate, you will see a different trajectory. You had to be nominated by a governor to be part of the NEP. The earlier programs didn't have that. The ones that came in with a governor's package, with grassroots support, were very successful because they start out that way."

As political administrations change, their appointees to EBM committees change; these transitions can challenge the efforts. For example, Steve Wolfe, coordinator of the Gulf of Mexico Alliance's Water Quality Priority Issue Team, commented, "When it started there was a lot of enthusiasm right up to the governor's offices. . . . But there is constant turnover of the state people who are involved in the Alliance. When we get a new governor, with new staff, it's hard. How do you get them fully vested in? They often downgrade their state's participation, and this makes it a lot harder to maintain as tight a connection to the state governments."

One way to inoculate EBM efforts against shifting electoral tides is to develop ongoing nongovernmental leadership in groups like sanctuary advisory councils and other stakeholder- or science-based groups. For example, George Barley, a wealthy business executive and conservationist, became the first chairman of the Florida Keys Sanctuary Advisory Council. Barley was instrumental in influencing the management plan to make it more palatable to residents. Commenting on the urgency of getting the plan enacted, Barley said, "Florida will grow by 20 percent over the next 10 years, and everybody who moves down here buys a boat. If we don't protect this resource, I promise you, it'll be gone. We're going to love it to death."[9]

Another response is for MEBM initiatives to engage in ongoing outreach to political officials and their staffs so that they understand the value of the efforts. Reasonable strategies include getting them involved in media events related to the initiatives and letting them claim some credit for positive results. Thinking about who political officials care about—their constituencies, opinion leaders, and friends—and doing outreach to those individuals is another common approach. In essence, EBM involves building a coalition of participants and supporters, and that coalition includes scientists, interest groups, agency managers and leaders, and elected officials. Their ongoing engagement and support are critical to long-term success.

Moving the Dials to Advance Ecosystem-Based Management in Specific Places

Many ask the bottom-line question, do EBM approaches make a difference? Do they result in improved functioning of ecosystem processes? Do they help to stabilize losses of key ecosystem parts? Do they create the conditions under which these outcomes occur?

There are no simple answers to these questions. In many of the cases, small changes are evident in population or ecosystem status. In others, even long-standing efforts, it may be too soon to tell given the complexity and long time lags in the systems, or other changes that might undercut success. In many places, for example, climate change is causing shifts that far exceed the capacity of local groups to do anything about them.

When asked directly about measures of success, most individuals involved in these initiatives pointed to both small scale ecological changes and intermediate outcomes that they fervently believed would lead to environmental improvements down the line: people working together who did not before; lower levels of conflict in communities; greater coordination among agencies; more and better organized scientific information; greater reporting of current conditions; a stronger sense of place and belief by key individuals in a need to act; and stronger perceived links between environmental improvements and economic conditions in communities. They felt that improvements in the social processes within communities would lead to improvements in social conditions, which will help realize environmental changes. Our earlier research on land-based EBM sites supports this chain of thinking.[10]

Another way to answer the impact question involves an honest reflection on the underlying baseline: Is EBM better than what comparison? Doing nothing? Probably so. How about an idealized notion that if we just mandate change, it will happen? Decades of research into implementation and program performance suggests that this rarely occurs, and the weak performance of many regulatory programs when faced with problematic attitudes and limited capacity bears this out.[11] For those who believe that we just need to mandate solutions, the considerable history of underachievement of objectives in areas like federal endangered species protection and marine protected area designation in California, both of which mandated protective action, might give them pause. The California marine protected area process produced results, but it was only after the failure of the "normal" system, and through an extraordinary investment of outside philanthropic dollars into a long and complex process. Real life is more complicated than some lawyers or scientists may think.

Few of the initiatives profiled in this book have made progress on all EBM elements. While some criticize initiatives for not showing dramatic progress on ecological and biological parameters, or for not adhering to an idealized concept of EBM, our perspective is that EBM is a process that improves the conditions of ecosystems and the services they provide, but it does so by expanding understanding, building relationships, and improving decision making, all of which require sustained effort. EBM should be viewed as a process of adjusting a set of continuous dials, not turning on–off switches. It is more like a mixing board in a sound studio, where hundreds of sliders and dials are adjusted in order to weave elements into a balanced musical track. Moving the dials in light of the unique context of a specific place moves a place toward an MEBM approach.

Indeed, success in MEBM comes not from "creating balance," "achieving collaboration," or "managing with complexity," but in taking steps to do more of these than was evident in the past. In our cases, most are striving to expand beyond a single-species or single-issue perspective. In doing so, they are working to understand and manage complex marine ecosystems and the conflicting needs of user groups. Over time, these adjustments result in changes in ecological conditions. It is important to know what the music should sound like and how far the mix is from that sound; that is, to define metrics associated with desired ecological conditions and to monitor whether strategies are moving you in the right direction. Ultimately, however, it is the mix of strategies that can be adjusted and there is no perfect mix.

Ultimately, an MEBM perspective is an opportunity. It enables attention to broader, cross-sector, cross-jurisdictional issues while also attending to narrower sector-specific or jurisdictional obligations. If managed well, it provides a space to think big while encouraging groups or organizations to act individually at appropriate scales. It is not immune to political interventions or problematic self-interested behavior, and it certainly is not easy. But can it make a difference? Yes, we think so. From our perspective having examined many initiatives, EBM is a valuable bridging process, one that connects and provides opportunities for learning and action that often would not occur otherwise.

To use a different metaphor, these initiatives are not like trains on a track leaving one station and heading in a straight-and-narrow path to the next. They are better likened to boats on the sea, adapting to fickle winds, shifting currents, and inevitable storms. While the desired destination is known, adaptation, innovation, problem solving, and navigation are required to keep moving in the desired direction.[12] And even if they never quite get there, the journey itself provides value and measurable improvements. Importantly, in a world torn asunder by conflict and dissension, the cooperative and innovative approaches embraced by people in the places profiled in this book, if nothing else, at least provide hope that people with divergent perspectives, differing knowledge, and varying capabilities and constraints can find ways to set preconceptions aside and focus on issues and places of shared concern. They can build bridges to advance marine conservation.

NOTES

Preface

1. Julia M. Wondolleck, *Public Lands Conflict and Resolution: Managing National Forest Disputes* (New York: Plenum Publishers, 1988); James E. Crowfoot and Julia M. Wondolleck, *Environmental Disputes: Community Involvement in Conflict Resolution* (Washington, DC: Island Press, 1990).
2. Steven L. Yaffee, *Prohibitive Policy: Implementing the Federal Endangered Species Act* (Cambridge, MA: MIT Press, 1982); Steven L. Yaffee, *The Wisdom of the Spotted Owl: Policy Lessons for a New Century* (Washington, DC: Island Press, 1994).
3. Steven L. Yaffee et al., *Ecosystem Management in the United States: An Assessment of Current Experience* (Washington, DC: Island Press, 1996); Julia M. Wondolleck and Steven L. Yaffee, *Making Collaboration Work: Lessons from Innovation in Natural Resource Management* (Washington, DC: Island Press, 2000); www.snre.umich.edu/ecomgt/collaboration.htm.
4. This is also a conclusion that Morgan Gopnik reached after studying ecosystem management on public lands and in the context of marine spatial planning. See Morgan Gopnik, *From the Forest to the Sea: Public Land Management and Marine Spatial Planning* (London: Earthscan/Routledge, 2015).

Chapter 1

1. Unless otherwise indicated, this quotation and all subsequent quotations in the chapter are taken from telephone interviews conducted with the named respondent by the authors or their research assistants, January 2009 to December 2010.
2. Quoted in World Wildlife Fund, "Florida Residents Give Thumbs Up as Largest No-Fish Zone in the US Gets the Nod," April 25, 2001, accessed March 26, 2016, http://wwf.panda.org/wwf_news/?2243/Florida-residents-give-the -thumbs-up-as-largest-no-fish-zone-in-the-US-gets-the-nod.
3. See, e.g., Tundi Agardy et al., *Taking Steps toward Marine and Coastal Ecosystem-Based Management—an Introductory Guide* (Nairobi, Kenya: United Nations Environment Programme, 2011); Katie K. Arkema, Sarah C. Abramson, and Bryan M. Dewsbury, "Marine Ecosystem-Based Management: From Characterization to Implementation," *Frontiers in Ecology and the Environment* 4 (2006): 525–32; Richard Curtin and Raul Prellezo, "Under-

standing Marine Ecosystem Based Management: A Literature Review," *Marine Policy* 34 (2010): 821–30; Verna G. DeLauer et al., "The Complexity of the Practice of Ecosystem-Based Management," *Integral Review* 10 (2014): 4–28; Sue Kidd, Andy Plater, and Chris Frid, eds., *The Ecosystem Approach to Marine Planning and Management* (London: Earthscan, 2011); Sarah E. Lester et al., "Science in Support of Ecosystem-Based Management for the US West Coast and Beyond," *Biological Conservation* 143 (2010): 576–87; James Lindholm and Robert Pavia, eds, "Examples of Ecosystem-Based Management in National Marine Sanctuaries: Moving from Theory to Practice," Marine Sanctuaries Conservation Series ONMS-10-02 (Silver Spring MD: US Department of Commerce, NOAA, 2010); Karen L. McLeod and Heather M. Leslie, *Ecosystem-Based Management for the Oceans* (Washington, DC: Island Press, 2009); Mary Ruckelshaus et al., "Marine Ecosystem-Based Management in Practice: Scientific and Governance Challenges," *BioScience* 58 (2008): 53–63.

4. N. L. Christensen et al., "The Report of the Ecological Society of America Committee on the Scientific Basis for Ecosystem Management," *Ecological Applications* 6 (1996): 665–91; R. Edward Grumbine, "What Is Ecosystem Management?" *Conservation Biology* 8 (1994): 27–38.

5. See, e.g., Peter A. Larkin, "Concepts and Issues in Marine Ecosystem Management," *Reviews in Fish Biology and Fisheries* 6 (1996): 139–64; National Oceanic and Atmospheric Administration, *New Priorities for the 21st Century: National Marine Fisheries Service Strategic Plan, Updated for FY 2005–FY 2010* (Washington, DC: U.S. Department of Commerce, 2004.)

6. Pew Oceans Commission, *America's Living Oceans: Charting a Course for Sea Change* (Arlington VA: Pew Oceans Commission, 2003); U.S. Commission on Ocean Policy, *An Ocean Blueprint for the 21st Century* (Washington, DC: U.S. Commission on Ocean Policy, 2004).

7. Exec. Order No. 13547. Stewardship of the Ocean, Our Coasts, and the Great Lakes. 3 *C.F.R.* 13547 (2010).

8. California Ocean Protection Act, 26.5 *California Public Resources Code* 35500–35650 (2004); Massachusetts Oceans Act, 114 *Massachusetts General Laws* 35HH (2008).

9. Canada's Oceans Act, S.C. 1996, c. 31.

10. See, e.g., Steven A. Murawski, "Ten Myths Concerning Ecosystem Approaches to Marine Resource Management," *Marine Policy* 31 (2007): 681–90; Heather Tallis et al., "The Many Faces of Ecosystem-Based Management: Making the Process Work Today in Real Places," *Marine Policy* 34 (2010): 340–48; Steven L. Yaffee, "Three Faces of Ecosystem Management," *Conservation Biology* 13 (1999): 713–25.

11. Karen L. McLeod et al., "Scientific Consensus Statement on Marine Ecosystem-Based Management," signed by 217 academic scientists and policy experts with relevant expertise and published by the Communication Partnership for

Science and the Sea (2005), http://compassonline.org/science/EBM_CMSP/ EBMconsensus.

12. See, e.g., Charles Ehler and Fanny Douvere, *Marine Spatial Planning: A Step-by-Step Approach toward Ecosystem-Based Management*, Intergovernmental Oceanographic Commission and Man and the Biosphere Programme, IOC Manual and Guides No. 53, ICAM Dossier No. 6 (Paris: UNESCO. 2009); and Tundi Agardy, *Ocean Zoning: Making Marine Management More Effective* (London: Earthscan, 2010).

13. Other researchers have used a cross-case analysis approach to study MEBM. See, e.g., Agardy et al., *Taking Steps toward Marine and Coastal Ecosystem-Based Management—an Introductory Guide*; Peter J. S. Jones, *Governing Marine Protected Areas: Resilience through Diversity* (London: Earthscan/Routledge, 2014); and McLeod and Leslie, *Ecosystem-Based Management for the Oceans*.

14. Julia Wondolleck and Steven Yaffee, "Marine Ecosystem-Based Management in Practice" (Ann Arbor: University of Michigan, 2012), http://www.snre .umich.edu/ecomgt/mebm.

15. Wondolleck and Yaffee, "Marine Ecosystem-Based Management in Practice."

Chapter 2

1. Gulf of Maine Council on the Marine Environment, "The Gulf of Maine in Context: State of the Gulf of Maine Report" (June 2010), 3, accessed March 28, 2016, http://www.gulfofmaine.org/state-of-the-gulf/docs/the-gulf -of-maine-in-context.pdf.

2. Maine Audubon, "Conserving Maine's Significant Wildlife Habitat Shore-birds," (Spring 2009), accessed March 26, 2016, http://maineaudubon.org/ wp-content/uploads/2012/08/MEAud-Conserving-Wildlife-Shorebirds.pdf.

3. Lawrence P. Hildebrand, Victoria Pebbles, and David A. Fraser, "Coopera-tive Ecosystem Management across the Canada–U.S. Border: Approaches and Experiences of Transboundary Programs in the Gulf of Maine, Great Lakes and Georgia Basin–Puget Sound," *Ocean and Coastal Management* 45 (2002): 421–57.

4. Gulf of Maine Council on the Marine Environment, "Agreement on Conser-vation of the Marine Environment of the Gulf of Maine between the Govern-ments of the Bordering States and Provinces," (1989), 19, accessed March 26, 2016, http://www.gulfofmaine.org/2/wp-content/uploads/2015/12/GOMC -Reference-Guide-December 2015.pdf.

5. The SeaDoc Society, "Salish Sea Facts," accessed March 28, 2016, http://www .seadocsociety.org/Salish-Sea-Facts/.

6. Stefan Freelan, "Map of the Salish Sea and Surrounding Basin," accessed March 26, 2016, http://staff.wwu.edu/stefan/salish_sea.shtml.

7. U.S. Environmental Protection Agency and Environment Canada, "Joint Statement of Cooperation on the Georgia Basin and Puget Sound Ecosys-tem 2008–2010 Action Plan," (November 2008), accessed March 28, 2016,

https://www.epa.gov/sites/production/files/2015-09/documents/salish_sea _soc_action_plan_2008-2010.pdf.

8. U.S. Environmental Protection Agency and Environment Canada, "Joint Statement of Cooperation on the Georgia Basin and Puget Sound Ecosystem 2008-2010 Action Plan."

9. Nicholas Brown and Joseph Gaydos, "Species of Concern within the Georgia Basin Puget Sound Marine Ecosystem: Changes from 2002 to 2006," *Proceedings of the 2007 Georgia Basin Puget Sound Research Conference*, accessed March 28, 2016, http://staff.wwu.edu/stefan/SalishSea/SpeciesOfConcern_brown -gaydos_07.pdf.

10. David Fraser et al., "Collaborative Science, Policy Development and Program Implementation in the Transboundary Georgia Basin/Puget Sound Ecosystem," *Environmental Monitoring and Assessment* 113 (2006): 49–69.

11. Jamie Alley, "The British Columbia–Washington Environmental Cooperation Council: An Evolving Model of Canada–United States Interjurisdictional Cooperation," in *Environmental Management on North America's Borders*, ed. Richard Kiy and John Wirth (College Station: Texas A&M University Press, 1998), 55; Environmental Cooperation Council, "2003 Annual Report," April 7, 2004, accessed March 26, 2016, http://www.env.gov.bc.ca/spd/ecc/docs/ annual_reports/ecc03.pdf.

12. Unless otherwise indicated, this quotation and all subsequent quotations in the chapter are taken from telephone interviews conducted with the named respondent by the authors or their research assistants, January 2009 to December 2010.

13. Gulf of Maine Council, "Mission and Principles," accessed March 28, 2016, http://www.gulfofmaine.org/2/mission-and-principles/.

14. Alley, "The British Columbia–Washington Environmental Cooperation Council," 54.

15. Alley, "The British Columbia–Washington Environmental Cooperation Council," 54.

16. Alley, "The British Columbia–Washington Environmental Cooperation Council," 56.

17. Alley, "The British Columbia-Washington Environmental Cooperation Council," 58–59.

18. Alley, "The British Columbia–Washington Environmental Cooperation Council," 59.

19. Alley, "The British Columbia–Washington Environmental Cooperation Council," 63.

20. After five years of hearings and consultation, the International Joint Commission released its judgment in 1984 to designate the specific boundary, commonly referred to as the Hague Line after the Netherlands venue where it was developed. The line extends out to the 200 nautical mile EEZ limit and awards the United States the majority of Georges Bank, designating only the east-

ernmost portion of the bank to Canada. Lawrence J. Prelli and Mimi Larsen-Becker, "Learning from the Limits of an Adjudicatory Strategy for Resolving United States–Canada Fisheries Conflicts: Lesson from the Gulf of Maine," *Natural Resources Journal* 41 (2001): 445–85.

21. GoMOOS was handed off to the Gulf of Maine Research Institute in 2009 and is now part of the Northeastern Regional Association of Coastal Ocean Observing Systems (NERACOOS). NERACOOS, "Welcome GoMOOS users!," accessed March 28, 2016, http://www.neracoos.org/gomoos _retired.

22. Alley, "The British Columbia–Washington Environmental Cooperation Council," 58.

23. Gulf of Maine Council, "Gulfwatch Contaminant Monitoring Program," accessed March 26, 2016, http://www.gulfofmaine.org/2/gulfwatch-home page/.

24. Transboundary Georgia Basin–Puget Sound Environmental Indicators Working Group, "Ecosystem Indicators Report" (Spring 2002), accessed March 26, 2016, http://www.env.gov.bc.ca/spd/docs/gbpsei.pdf.

25. Transboundary Georgia Basin–Puget Sound Environmental Indicators Working Group, "Ecosystem Indicators Report."

26. U.S. Environmental Protection Agency, "Health of the Salish Sea Ecosystem Report," accessed March 26, 2016, https://www.epa.gov/salish-sea.

27. Naureen Rana, "The Puget Sound–Georgia Basin International Task Force," in *Transboundary Collaboration in Ecosystem Management: Integrating Lessons from Experience*, ed. Elizabeth Harris, Chase Huntley, William Mangle, and Naureen Rana (Ann Arbor: University of Michigan, 2001), accessed March 27, 2016, http://www.snre.umich.edu/ecomgt//pubs/transboundary/TB_Col lab_Full_Report.pdf.

28. Gulf of Maine Council, "Opportunities," accessed March 28, 2016, http:// www.gulfofmaine.org/2/opportunities/.

29. Georgia Basin/Puget Sound International Task Force, "ECC Update," (April 2003), accessed March 26, 2016, http://www.env.gov.bc.ca/spd/ecc/ docs/2003April/Gb_PS_ITF_Update.pdf.

30. Georgia Basin/Puget Sound International Task Force, "ECC Update," (February 2004), accessed March 26, 2016, http://www.env.gov.bc.ca/spd/ecc/ docs/2004Feb/Gb_PS_ITF_Action.PDF.

31. Georgia Basin/Puget Sound International Task Force, "ECC Update," (February 2004).

32. Georgia Basin/Puget Sound International Task Force, "ECC Update," (February 2004).

33. BC/WA Environmental Cooperation Council, "Record of Discussion for ECC Meeting," (October 28, 2005), accessed March 28, 2016, http://www.env.gov .bc.ca/spd/ecc/docs/2005Oct/record_of_discussion_05oct28.pdf.

34. BC/WA Environmental Cooperation Council, "DRAFT Record of Discussion for ECC Meeting," (November 29, 2006), accessed March 28, 2016, http://www.env.gov.bc.ca/spd/ecc/docs/2006Nov/record_of_discussion.pdf.

35. Washington/British Columbia Coastal and Ocean Task Force, "Terms of Reference" (June 2007), accessed March 28, 2016, http://www.ecy.wa.gov/climate change/docs/gov_20070608_BCMOUappendices.pdf.

36. British Columbia/Washington Coastal and Ocean Task Force, Three Year Draft Work Plan (April 2008), accessed March 26, 2016, http://www.env.gov.bc.ca/spd/ecc/docs/2008April/COTF_workplan.pdf.

37. Gulf of Maine Council, "Gulf of Maine Restoration and Conservation Initiative," 3, accessed March 26, 2016, http://www.gulfofmaine.org/gomrc/Brief ingPaper093009.pdf.

38. National Ocean Council, Executive Office of the President, "National Ocean Policy Implementation Plan" (April 2013), accessed, March 26, 2016, http://www.whitehouse.gov/sites/default/files/national_ocean_policy_implementa tion_plan.pdf.

39. Gulf of Maine Association, "Gulf of Maine Association," accessed April 14, 2016, http://www.gulfofmaine.org/2/gulf-of-maine-association-homepage/.

Chapter 3

1. National Ocean Service, NOAA, "Gulf of Mexico at a Glance" (Washington, DC: U.S. Department of Commerce, 2008), accessed August 24, 2016, http://gulfofmexicoalliance.org/pdfs/gulf_glance_1008.pdf.

2. Gulf of Mexico Foundation, "Gulf of Mexico Facts," accessed March 16, 2016, http://www.gulfmex.org/about-the-gulf/gulf-of-mexico-facts.

3. Bryan Walsh, "The Gulf's Growing 'Dead Zone,'" Time, June 17, 2008.

4. Ian R. MacDonald, John Amos, Timothy Crone, and Steve Wereley, "The Measure of a Disaster," New York Times, May 22, 2010, A17.

5. Governor Jeb Bush, Letter to Governor Haley Barbour (April 26, 2004), personal copy.

6. "Testimony of Bryon Griffith, Director, Gulf of Mexico Program before the Senate Committee on Environment and Public Works" (November 9, 2009), accessed August 27, 2016, https://www.epw.senate.gov/public/_cache/files/9a43bfb3-0cde-4b24-8a46-ef028e38e288/bryongriffith11909leghear inggulfofmexicotestimonyfinal.pdf.

7. These accomplishments were outlined in Governor Jeb Bush, Letter to Governor Haley Barbour (April 26, 2004), personal copy.

8. Unless otherwise indicated, this quotation and all subsequent quotations in the chapter are taken from telephone interviews conducted with the named respondent by the authors or their research assistants, January 2009 to December 2010.

9. Governor Jeb Bush, Letter to Governor Haley Barbour (April 26, 2004), personal copy.

10. U.S. Commission on Ocean Policy, *An Ocean Blueprint for the 21st Century* (Washington, DC: U.S. Commission on Ocean Policy, 2004).

11. "U.S. Ocean Action Plan: The Bush Administration's Response to the U.S. Commission on Ocean Policy," 2004, 5, accessed August 27, 2016, https://data.nodc.noaa.gov/coris/library/NOAA/other/us_ocean_action_plan_2004.pdf.

12. 148 Cong. Rec. S9834 (Oct. 2, 2002) (testimony of Sen. Landrieu).

13. Gulf of Mexico Alliance, "Governors' Action Plan for Healthy and Resilient Coasts: March 2006-March 2009," accessed March 16, 2016, http://www.gulfofmexicoalliance.org/pdfs/gap_final2.pdf.

14. Currently, the GOMA Priority Issue Teams focus on Coastal Resilience, Data and Monitoring, Education and Engagement, Habitat Resources, Water Resources, and Wildlife and Fisheries. Three cross-Priority Issue Team regional initiatives were added in 2014: Comprehensive Conservation, Restoration and Resilience Planning, Ecosystem Services, and Marine Debris. Accessed March 16, 2016, http://www.gulfofmexicoalliance.org/our-priorities.

15. Gulf of Mexico Alliance, "Governors' Action Plan III for Healthy and Resilient Coasts: 2016–2021," 40, accessed August 28, 2016, http://www.gulfofmexicoalliance.org/documents/APIII.pdf.

16. Gulf of Mexico Alliance, "Business Advisory Council," accessed August 24, 2016, http://www.gulfofmexicoalliance.org/partnerships/pdfs/GOMA%20BAC%20Function%20and%20Format.pdf, 2.

17. Gulf of Mexico Alliance, "2015 Annual Report," accessed August 24, 2016, http://gulfofmexicoalliance.org/documents/goma-misc/2015/2015-annual-report.pdf, 1.

18. Laura Bowie, "10 Years of Building Partnerships for a Healthier Gulf," *Gulf of Mexico Alliance Newsletter* (June 12, 2014), accessed March 16, 2016, http://www.gulfofmexicoalliance.org/2014/06/10-years-of-building-partnerships-for-a-healthier-gulf.

Chapter 4

1. Daniel Suman, Manoj Shivlani, and J. Walter Milon, "Perceptions and Attitudes Regarding Marine Reserves: A Comparison of Stakeholder Groups in the Florida Keys National Marine Sanctuary," *Ocean & Coastal Management* 42 (1999): 1019–40.

2. U.S. Department of Commerce, National Oceanic and Atmospheric Administration, National Marine Sanctuary Program, *Channel Islands National Marine Sanctuary Management Plan* (Silver Spring, MD: NOAA, 2009), 19–28.

3. Leslie Abramson et al., "Reducing the Threat of Ship Strikes on Large Cetaceans in the Santa Barbara Channel Region and Channel Islands National Marine Sanctuary: Recommendations and Case Studies," Marine Sanctuaries Conservation Services ONMS-11-01 (Silver Spring, MD: U.S. Department of Commerce, NOAA, 2011).

4. U.S. Department of Commerce, *Channel Islands National Marine Sanctuary Management Plan* 5–6.

5. Unless otherwise indicated, this quotation and all subsequent quotations in the chapter are taken from telephone interviews conducted with the named respondent by the authors or their research assistants, January 2009 to December 2010.

6. U.S. Department of Commerce, National Oceanic and Atmospheric Administration, *Florida Keys National Marine Sanctuary Revised Management Plan* (Key West, FL: NOAA, 2007), 13–16.

7. Chuck Adams, "Economic Activities Associated with the Commercial Fishing Industry in Monroe County, Florida," Florida Sea Grant Program Report 92-006 (Gainesville, FL: University of Florida, 1992), accessed August 25, 2016, http://nsgl.gso.uri.edu/flsgp/flsgpt92006.pdf.

8. William O. Antozzi, "The Developing Live Spiny Lobster Industry," NOAA Technical Memorandum NMFS-SEFSC-395 (Springfield, VA: National Technical Information Service, 1996), 1.

9. U.S. Department of Commerce, *Florida Keys National Marine Sanctuary Revised Management Plan*, 5.

10. U.S. Department of Commerce, *Florida Keys National Marine Sanctuary Revised Management Plan*, 17.

11. U.S. Department of Commerce, National Oceanic and Atmospheric Administration, Sanctuaries and Reserves Division, *Florida Keys National Marine Sanctuary, Final Management Plan/Environmental Impact Statement, Volume 1* (Silver Spring, MD: NOAA, 1996), 2.

12. John C. Ogden et al., "A Long-Term Interdisciplinary Study of the Florida Keys Seascape," *Bulletin of Marine Science* 54 (1994): 1059–1071.

13. Brian D. Keller and Billy D. Causey, "Linkages between the Florida Keys National Marine Sanctuary and the South Florida Ecosystem Restoration Initiative," *Ocean and Coastal Management* 48 (2005): 869–900.

14. "A Third Freighter Runs Aground Off Keys," *New York Times*, November 12, 1989, accessed August 25, 2016, http://www.nytimes.com/1989/11/12/us/a-third-freighter-runs-aground-off-keys.html.

15. U.S. Department of Commerce, *Florida Keys National Marine Sanctuary, Final Management Plan/Environmental Impact Statement, Volume 1*, 2.

16. U.S. National Oceanic and Atmospheric Administration, National Marine Sanctuaries, "Galapagos of North America: Channel Islands National Marine Sanctuary," *Sanctuary Watch* (Fall 2012), 6.

17. Quoted in U.S. National Oceanic and Atmospheric Administration, "Galapagos of North America: Channel Islands National Marine Sanctuary," 6.

18. Quoted in U.S. National Oceanic and Atmospheric Administration, "Galapagos of North America: Channel Islands National Marine Sanctuary," 6.

19. Testimony of Dante Fascell before the U.S. House Committee on Merchant Marine and Fisheries, May 10, 1990, reprinted in Hearing on HR 3719, To

Establish the Florida Keys National Marine Sanctuary, Serial No. 101-94 (Washington, DC: Government Printing Office, 1990), 6.

20. K. Sleasman, "Coordination between Monroe County and the Florida Keys National Marine Sanctuary," *Ocean and Coastal Management* 52 (2009): 69–75.

21. U.S. Department of Commerce, *Channel Islands National Marine Sanctuary Management Plan*, 42.

22. U.S. Department of Commerce, *Channel Islands National Marine Sanctuary Management Plan*, 49.

23. U.S. Department of Commerce, *Channel Islands National Marine Sanctuary Management Plan*, 48.

24. U.S. Department of the Interior, National Park Service, *Channel Islands National Park, Final General Management Plan* (Santa Barbara, CA: NPS, April 2015), 22.

25. "Co-Trustees Agreement for Cooperative Management," May 19, 1997, accessed March 26, 2016, http://floridakeys.noaa.gov/mgmtplans/man_co trust.pdf.

26. Keller and Causey, "Linkages between the Florida Keys National Marine Sanctuary and the South Florida Ecosystem Restoration Initiative."

27. Keller and Causey, "Linkages between the Florida Keys National Marine Sanctuary and the South Florida Ecosystem Restoration Initiative."

28. The Fish and Wildlife Conservation Commission is well known to anybody on the water; it is the issuing agency for more than two hundred licenses, permits, and certifications for a wide range of activities regarding fish, wildlife, or boating.

29. Testimony of Doug Jones before the U.S. House Committee on Merchant Marine and Fisheries, May 10, 1990, reprinted in Hearing on HR 3719, To Establish the Florida Keys National Marine Sanctuary, Serial No. 101-94 (Washington, DC: Government Printing Office, 1990), 17.

30. U.S. National Park Service, "The Birth of Biscayne National Park," accessed March 26, 2016, http://www.nps.gov/bisc/historyculture/the-birth-of-bis cayne-national-park.htm.

31. National Academy of Public Administration, Center for the Economy and the Environment, *Protecting Our National Marine Sanctuaries* (Washington, DC: NAPA, 2000), 22.

32. Quoted in William Booth, "'Zoning' the Sea: New Plan for Florida Keys Arouses Storm," *Washington Post*, October 17, 1993, accessed August 24, 2016, www.washingtonpost.com/archive/politics/1993/10/17/zoning-the-sea -new-plan-for-florida-keys-arouses-storm/ee55f0a0-ad00-413d-842d-ccb33f 6befb1.

33. Channel Islands National Marine Sanctuary, Sanctuary Advisory Council, "Decision-Making and Operational Protocols," November 18, 2005, accessed March 26, 2016, http://channelislands.noaa.gov/sac/pdfs/rev_prot.pdf.

34. Channel Islands National Marine Sanctuary, "Working Groups and Subcommittees," accessed March 26, 2016, http://channelislands.noaa.gov/sac/working_groups.html.

35. U.S. Department of Commerce, *Florida Keys National Marine Sanctuary, Final Management Plan/Environmental Impact Statement, Volume 1*, 6.

36. National Academy of Public Administration, *Protecting Our National Marine Sanctuaries*, 22.

37. Partnership for Interdisciplinary Studies of Coastal Oceans, accessed March 26, 2016, www.piscoweb.org.

38. Gary E. Davis, "Science and Society: Marine Reserve Design for the California Channel Islands," *Conservation Biology* 19 (2005): 1745–51.

39. California Department of Fish and Game, "Appendix 3. History of the Channel Islands Marine Reserves Working Group Process," *Final Environmental Document, Marine Protected Areas in NOAA's Channel Islands National Marine Sanctuary* (October 2002), A3-2, accessed March 27, 2016, https://nrm.dfg.ca.gov/FileHandler.ashx?DocumentID=30729&inline.

40. California Department of Fish and Game, "Appendix 3. History of the Channel Islands Marine Reserves Working Group Process," A3-2.

41. The design criteria included considerations of "biogeographic representation, individual reserve size, human threats and natural catastrophes, habitat representation, vulnerable habitats and species, monitoring sites, and connectivity." Davis, "Science and Society: Marine Reserve Design for the California Channel Islands."

42. Davis, "Science and Society: Marine Reserve Design for the California Channel Islands."

43. California Department of Fish and Game. Master Plan for Marine Protected Areas, "Appendix H. Summary of Recent and Ongoing Processes Related to the MLPA Initiative" (January 2008), H-5, accessed March 26, 2016, http://www.dfg.ca.gov/mlpa/pdfs/revisedmp0108h.pdf.

44. Satie Airamé et al., "Applying Ecological Criteria to Marine Reserve Design: A Case Study from the California Channel Islands," *Ecological Applications* 13 (2003): 170–84.

45. John C. Jostes and Michael Eng, "Facilitators' Report Regarding the Channel Islands National Marine Sanctuary Marine Reserves Working Group," Interactive Planning and Management and U.S. Institute for Environmental Conflict Resolution, May 23, 2001, 13-14, accessed March 24, 2016, http://media.law.stanford.edu/organizations/programs-and-centers/enrlp/doc/slspublic/channelislandstn-exprt2.pdf.

46. Lydia K. Bergen and Mark H. Carr, "Establishing Marine Reserves: How Can Science Best Inform Policy?" *Environment* 45 (2003): 8–19.

47. California Department of Fish and Game, "Appendix 3. History of the Channel Islands Marine Reserves Working Group Process," A3-14.

48. California Department of Fish and Game, "Appendix 3. History of the Channel Islands Marine Reserves Working Group Process," A3-14.

49. National Oceanic and Atmospheric Administration, "Marine Zones Now in Federal Waters of NOAA's Channel Islands National Marine Sanctuary" (August 9, 2007), accessed March 27, 2016, http://www.publicaffairs.noaa.gov/releases2007/aug07/noaa07-r429.html.

50. Quoted in Joshua Kweller, "Channel Islands National Marine Sanctuary Advisory Council," in Kathy Chen et al., eds., *Sanctuary Advisory Councils: A Study in Collaborative Resource Management* (Ann Arbor: University of Michigan, 2006), accessed March 27, 2016, https://deepblue.lib.umich.edu/handle/2027.42/101680.

51. U.S. Department of Commerce, *Florida Keys National Marine Sanctuary, Final Management Plan/Environmental Impact Statement, Volume 1*, 5.

52. James Murley and F. Stevens Redburn, *Ready to Perform? Planning and Management at the National Sanctuary Program* (Washington, DC: National Academy of Public Administration, October 2006), 21.

53. Suman et al., "Perceptions and Attitudes Regarding Marine Reserves," 1031.

54. U.S. Department of Commerce, National Oceanic and Atmospheric Administration, Sanctuaries and Reserves Division, *Florida Keys National Marine Sanctuary, Final Management Plan/Environmental Impact Statement, Volume 2* (Silver Spring, MD: NOAA, 1996), 134.

55. Tortugas 2000 Working Group, "Meeting Minutes of April 1998," unpublished.

56. Tortugas 2000 Working Group, "Meeting Minutes of June 1998," unpublished.

57. Tortugas 2000 Working Group, "Meeting Minutes of May 1999," unpublished.

58. Quoted in World Wildlife Fund, "Florida Residents Give Thumbs Up as Largest No-Fish Zone in the US Gets the Nod," April 25, 2001, accessed March 26, 2016, http://wwf.panda.org/wwf_news/?2243/Florida-residents-give-the-thumbs-up-as-largest-no-fish-zone-in-the-US-gets-the-nod.

Chapter 5

1. U.S. Environmental Protection Agency, "Community-Based Watershed Management: Lessons from the National Estuary Program" (February 2005), accessed March 30, 2016, https://www.epa.gov/sites/production/files/2015-09/documents/2007_04_09_estuaries_nepprimeruments_srnepprimer.pdf.

2. For example, President Ronald Reagan issued an executive order in 1981 that terminated six federally authorized river basin commissions, including the Pacific Northwest, Great Lakes, and New England River Basin Commissions. Exec. Order No. 12,319 (Sept. 9, 1981), 46 Fed. Reg. 45,591, 3 C.F.R. (1981) Comp, 175.

3. Jennifer Steel, ed., "Albemarle–Pamlico National Estuarine System: Analysis of the Status and Trends" (April 1991), Report No. 90-01, vii, accessed March 30, 2016, http://www.apnep.org/c/document_library/get_file?uuid=36817de5 -6891-4563-896f-f5235d3d8dd4&groupId=61563.

4. National Audubon Society, "Important Bird Areas: North Carolina," accessed March 30, 2016, http://netapp.audubon.org/iba/Reports.

5. APNEP, "Fast Facts," accessed March 30, 2016, http://portal.ncdenr.org/web/ apnep/fastfacts#26.

6. Steel, "Albemarle–Pamlico National Estuarine System: Analysis of the Status and Trends."

7. North Carolina Coastal Resources Commission Science Panel, "North Carolina Sea Level Rise Assessment Report: 2015 Update to the 2010 Report" (March 31, 2015), 25, accessed March 30, 2016, https://ncdenr.s3.amazonaws .com/s3fs-public/Coastal%20Management/documents/PDF/Science%20 Panel/2015%20NC%20SLR%20Assessment-FINAL%20REPORT%20 Jan%2028%202016.pdf.

8. APNEP, "About the Partnership," accessed March 30, 2016, http://portal.ncd enr.org/web/apnep/about?p_p_id=15&p_p_lifecycle=1&p_p_state=normal.

9. NBEP, "Currents of Change: Environmental Status & Trends of the Narragansett Bay Region, Final Technical Report" (August 2009), accessed March 30, 2016, http://www.nbep.org/statusandtrends/CoC-finaltech-3aug09.pdf.

10. Narragansett Bay National Estuarine Research Reserve, "An Ecological Profile of the Narragansett Bay National Estuarine Research Reserve," Kenneth B. Raposa and Malia L. Schwartz, eds. (2009), accessed March 30, 2016, http:// www.nbnerr.org/profile.htm.

11. Frank Carini, "Narragansett Bay Watershed Feels the Heat," *ecoRI News* (May 14, 2014), accessed March 30, 2016, http://www.ecori.org/natural -resources/2014/5/14/narragansett-bay-watershed-feels-the-heat.html.

12. NBEP, "Currents of Change: Environmental Status & Trends of the Narragansett Bay Region."

13. Narragansett Bay National Estuarine Research Reserve, "An Ecological Profile of the Narragansett Bay National Estuarine Research Reserve."

14. David M. Bearden, *National Estuary Program: A Collaborative Approach to Protecting Coastal Water Quality*, CRS Report 97-644 ENR (Washington, DC: Congressional Research Service, Library of Congress, 2001), accessed August 25, 2016, http://digital.library.unt.edu/ark:/67531/metacrs1411/m1/1/high _res_d/97-644enr_2001Jan12.pdf.

15. NBEP, "About NBEP," accessed March 28, 2016, http://www.nbep.org/about -theprogram.html.

16. U.S. Environmental Protection Agency, "Comprehensive Conservation and Management Plans," accessed March 30, 2016, https://www.epa.gov/nep/ information-about-local-estuary-programs#tab-2.

17. Steel, "Albemarle–Pamlico National Estuarine System: Analysis of the Status and Trends."

18. APNEP, "Comprehensive Conservation and Management Plan: Albemarle–Pamlico Estuarine Study" (November 1994), 22, accessed March 30, 2016, http://portal.ncdenr.org/c/document_library/get_file?uuid=40eead85-a903 -4cac-b7aa-a249a94be3b3&groupId=61563.

19. APNEP, "Comprehensive Conservation and Management Plan," 1994, 86.

20. Katrina Smith Korfmacher, "Invisible Successes, Visible Failures: Paradoxes of Ecosystem Management in the Albemarle–Pamlico Estuarine Study," *Coastal Management* 26 (1998): 191–211.

21. Unless otherwise indicated, this quotation and all subsequent quotations in the chapter are taken from telephone interviews conducted with the named respondent by the authors or their research assistants, January 2009 to December 2010.

22. Rhode Island Department of Administration, "Comprehensive Conservation and Management Plan for Narragansett Bay," accessed March 30, 2016, http://www.planning.ri.gov/documents/guide_plan/ccmp715.pdf.

23. Rhode Island Department of Administration, "Comprehensive Conservation and Management Plan for Narragansett Bay."

24. APNEP, "CCMP 2012–2022: Collaborative Actions for Protecting the Albemarle–Pamlico Ecosystem," (March 14, 2012), accessed March 30, 2016, http://portal.ncdenr.org/c/document_library/get_file?uuid=e6600731-daed -4c5f-9136-253f23c9bbcf&groupId=61563.

25. Governor Beverly Eaves Perdue, "Albemarle–Pamlico National Estuary Partnership," State of North Carolina Executive Order #133, November 5, 2012.

26. APNEP, "CCMP 2012–2022," 1.

27. NBEP, "CCMP Update 2012: Revision to the Narragansett Bay Comprehensive Conservation and Management Plan" (December 2012), accessed March 28, 2016, http://www.nbep.org/ccmp-guidance.html.

28. NBEP, "CCMP Update 2012," 6.

29. Paul Cough, Director, EPA Oceans and Coastal Protection Division, letter to Richard Ribb, Director, Narragansett Bay Estuary Program, n.d.

30. NEPs across the nation have been found to facilitate networks and partnerships that are more extensive than in estuaries without NEPs, in that they span more levels of government, integrate more experts into policy discussions, and nurture stronger interpersonal ties between stakeholders, and thus lay the foundation for cooperative governance. See Mark Schneider et al., "Building Consensual Institutions: Networks and the National Estuary Program." *American Journal of Political Science* 47 (2003): 143–58.

31. "Narragansett Bay Water Quality Improving Thanks to Less Sewage Treatment Plan Discharges," *ecoRI News*, August 20, 2015, accessed August 25, 2016, http://www.ecori.org/narragansett-bay/2015/8/20/narragansett-bay-water -quality-better-thanks-to-less-sewage-plant-discharges.

32. APNEP, "APNEP Partners," accessed March 28, 2016, http://www.apnep.org/web/apnep/partners.

33. APNEP, "Albemarle–Pamlico Conservation and Communities Collaborative," accessed March 28, 2016, http://portal.ncdenr.org/web/apnep/ap3c.

34. U.S. Environmental Protection Agency, "Climate Ready Estuaries 2009 Progress Report," accessed March 30, 2016, 10, https://www.epa.gov/sites/production/files/2014-04/documents/cre_progress_report_v20_singlepages_draft.pdf.

35. Korfmacher, "Invisible Successes, Visible Failures."

36. Richard Salit, "Environmental Journal: Narragansett Bay Estuary Program Gets a Top-to-Bottom Makeover," *Providence Journal*, December 29, 2013, accessed August 25, 2016, http://www.providencejournal.com/article/2013 1228/NEWS/312289995.

37. New England Interstate Water Pollution Control Commission, "Change in Direction: A Talk with the Narragansett Bay Estuary Program's New Leader," *iWR e-news* (February 2014), accessed March 28, 2016, http://neiwpcc.org/e-news/iWR/2014-02/changeindirection.asp.

38. NBEP, "Currents of Change: Environmental Status & Trends of the Narragansett Bay Region."

39. NBEP, "Currents of Change: Environmental Status & Trends of the Narragansett Bay Region."

40. APNEP, "APNEP's History," accessed March 30, 2016, http://portal.ncdenr.org/web/apnep/about.

41. APNEP, "Science and Technical Advisory Committee (STAC) Action Plan For the Period November 2012 through June 2014," accessed March 30, 2016, http://portal.ncdenr.org/c/document_library/get_file?uuid=d78f3655-f7da-48f7-82c5-600bfc94b9fa&groupId=61563.

42. APNEP, "Monitor," accessed March 28, 2016, http://www.apnep.org/web/apnep/monitor.

43. "Ferry-Based Monitoring of Surface Water Quality in North Carolina," accessed March 28, 2016, http://www.unc.edu/ims/paerllab/research/ferrymon/images/index.html.

44. Korfmacher, "Invisible Successes, Visible Failures."

45. Steven L. Yaffee, "Why Environmental Policy Nightmares Recur," *Conservation Biology* 11 (1997): 328–37.

46. Steven L. Yaffee, "Cooperation: A Strategy for Achieving Stewardship Across Boundaries," in Richard L. Knight and Peter Landes, eds., *Stewardship Across Boundaries* (Washington, DC: Island Press, 1998), 299–324.

47. NBEP, "Bay Journal," accessed March 30, 2016, http://www.nbep.org/bay journal-currentissue.html.

48. In Korfmacher's review of the APES phase of APNEP's history, public participation was judged as a mixed success. Korfmacher, "Invisible Successes, Visible Failures."

49. Korfmacher, "Invisible Successes, Visible Failures."

50. Korfmacher, "Invisible Successes, Visible Failures."

51. Korfmacher, "Invisible Successes, Visible Failures."

52. Korfmacher, "Invisible Successes, Visible Failures."

53. Rhode Island Bays Rivers and Watersheds Coordination Team, "Systems Level Planning," accessed March 28, 2016, http://www.coordinationteam.ri.gov/slplanning.htm.

54. Korfmacher, "Invisible Successes, Visible Failures."

55. Cough, letter to Ribb, n.d.

56. Cindy Cook, Adamant Accord, Inc., "Facilitator's Assessment: Narragansett Bay Estuary Program" (November 2012), accessed March 30, 2016, http://docsfiles.com/pdf_cindy_cook_adamant_accord.html.

57. Salit, "Narragansett Bay Estuary Program Gets a Top-to-Bottom Makeover."

58. Salit, "Narragansett Bay Estuary Program Gets a Top-to-Bottom Makeover."

Chapter 6

1. Pacific Marine Conservation Council and Golden Marine Consulting, "Integrating Stewardship, Access, Monitoring and Research: Port Orford Community Stewardship Area" (2008), prepared for POORT, accessed August 1, 2010, http://www.oceanresourceteam.org/docs/StewardshipPlan.pdf.

2. Unless otherwise indicated, this quotation and all subsequent quotations in the chapter are taken from telephone interviews conducted with the named respondent by the authors or their research assistants, January 2009 to December 2010.

3. POORT, "Mission Statement," accessed March 30, 2016, http://www.oceanresourceteam.org.

4. San Juan County Marine Resources Committee, "Welcome to the San Juan County MSA," accessed March 30, 2016, http://www.sjcmrc.org/Marine-Stewardship-Area/MSA-Overview.aspx.

5. Dan Seimann, "Northwest Straits Marine Conservation Initiative: Five-Year Evaluation Report: submitted by the Northwest Straits Evaluation Panel" (April 6, 2004), 2, accessed March 30, 2016, http://nwstraits.org/media/1257/nwsc-2004-evaluationrpt.pdf.

6. Seimann, "Northwest Straits Marine Conservation Initiative: Five-Year Evaluation Report," 2.

7. Seimann, "Northwest Straits Marine Conservation Initiative: Five-Year Evaluation Report," 2.

8. San Juan Nature Institute and Marine Resources Committee, "Caring for Our Natural Resources: A Way of Life in the San Juans" (2008), personal copy. Original is available from the MRC.

9. San Juan County Marine Resources Committee, "2010 Annual report," accessed March 30, 2016, http://www.sjcmrc.org/uploads/pdf/AnnualReports/2010AnnualReport.pdf.

10. POORT, "Community Advisory Team," accessed August 27, 2016, http://www.oceanresourceteam.org/about/advisors.

11. Port Orford City Council, "Resolution 2006-41," June 29, 2006.

12. POORT, "Land-Sea Connection Workshop," accessed March 30, 2016, http://www.oceanresourceteam.org/initiatives/land-sea-connection/.

13. San Juan County Marine Resources Committee, "Who We Are," accessed March 30, 2016, http://www.sjcmrc.org.

14. POORT, "Successes," accessed March 30, 2016, http://www.oceanresourceteam.org/initiatives/successes/.

15. POORT, "Ecosystem Based Management," accessed March 30, 2016, http://www.oceanresourceteam.org/about/operating-principles/ebm/.

16. Surfrider Foundation, "Mission," accessed March 30, 2016, http://www.surfrider.org/mission.

17. POORT, "Port Orford Community Stewardship Area," accessed March 30, 2016, http://www.oceanresourceteam.org/initiatives/posa/.

18. Reprinted in "Memorandum of Understanding between Port Orford Ocean Resource Team and the Oregon Department of Fish and Wildlife" (September 17, 2008).

19. San Juan County Marine Resources Committee, "The San Juan County Marine Stewardship Area," accessed March 30, 2015, http://www.sjcmrc.org/Marine-Stewardship-Area.aspx.

20. Kirsten Evans and Jody Kennedy, "San Juan County Marine Stewardship Area Plan, Prepared by the San Juan County Marine Resources Committee" (July 2, 2007), 5, accessed March 30, 2016, http://www.sjcmrc.org/uploads/pdf/MSA%20plan%2002-Jul-2007%20Final.pdf.

21. Evans and Kennedy, "San Juan County Marine Stewardship Area Plan," 27.

22. Oregon Ocean Policy Advisory Council, "Oregon Marine Reserve Policy Recommendations," (2008), accessed March 30, 2016, http://www.oregon.gov/LCD/OPAC/docs/resources/opac_mar_res_pol_rec_final.pdf.

23. POORT, "Redfish Rocks Marine Reserve & Marine Protected Area," accessed March 30, 2016, http://www.oceanresourceteam.org/initiatives/successes/marine-reserve/.

24. 75th Oregon Legislative Assembly, "House Bill 3013: An Act Relating to Ocean Resources; and Declaring an Emergency" (2009), accessed March 30, 2016, http://www.oregon.gov/LCD/OPAC/docs/hb_3013.pdf.

25. POORT, "Stormwater Ordinance," accessed March 30, 2016, http://www.oceanresourceteam.org/initiatives/successes/stormwater-ordinance/.

26. See, e.g., Elinor Ostrom, *Governing the Commons: The Evolution of Institutions for Collective Action* (Cambridge UK: Cambridge University Press, 1990); Thomas Princen, "Monhegan Lobstering: Self-Management Meets Co-Management," in *The Logic of Sufficiency* (Cambridge MA: MIT Press, 2005), 223–90.

Chapter 7

1. Jamie Alley, "The British Columbia–Washington Environmental Cooperation Council: An Evolving Model of Canada–United States Interjurisdictional Cooperation," in *Environmental Management on North America's Borders*, ed. Richard Kiy and John Wirth (College Station: Texas A&M University Press, 1998), 56.

2. Unless otherwise indicated, this quotation and all subsequent quotations in the chapter are taken from telephone interviews conducted with the named respondent by the authors or their research assistants, January 2009 to December 2010.

3. Gulf of Maine Council, "Meeting Briefing Packet" (September 26, 2008), 17, accessed March 28, 2016, http://www.gulfofmaine.org/council/internal/docs/ gomc_wg_october_2008.pdf.

4. State of Oregon, "1994 Territorial Sea Plan Appendix G: Principal Policies of the Oregon Ocean Plan," accessed March 28, 2016, http://www.oregon.gov/ LCD/OCMP/docs/Ocean/otsp_app-g.pdf.

5. Gulf of Mexico Alliance, "Alliance Management," accessed March 28, 2016, http://www.gulfofmexicoalliance.org/about-us/organization/alliance-manage ment-team/.

6. Channel Islands National Marine Sanctuary, "Working Group & Subcommittees," accessed March 28, 2016, http://channelislands.noaa.gov/sac/working _groups.html.

7. "Ferry-Based Monitoring of Surface Water Quality in North Carolina," accessed March 28, 2016, http://www.unc.edu/ims/paerllab/research/ferry mon/images/index.html.

8. Albemarle–Pamlico National Estuary Program, "SAV Monitoring," accessed March 28, 2016, http://www.apnep.org/web/apnep/sav-monitoring.

9. Narragansett Bay Estuary Program, "Resolution 2014-01, Establishment of a Science Advisory Committee" (June 18, 2014), accessed March 28, 2016, http://nbep.org/pdfs/Resolution%202014-01%20Science%20Advisory%20 Committee.pdf.

10. Gulf of Mexico Alliance, "Ecosystems Integration & Assessment: Priorities for Managing Ecosystem Data," accessed August 27, 2016, http://www.gulf ofmexicoalliance.org/our-priorities/former-our-priorities/ecosystems-integra tion-assessment.

11. See chapter 2, note 21, for updated status of the Gulf of Maine Ocean Observing System.

12. Gulf of Mexico Alliance, "Power of Partnerships: Other Partners," accessed August 27, 2016, http://www.gulfofmexicoalliance.org/about-us/alliance -partnerships/other-partners.

13. Gulf of Mexico Alliance, "Power of Partnerships: Other Partners," accessed August 27, 2016, http://www.gulfofmexicoalliance.org/about-us/alliance -partnerships/other-partners.

14. Northwest Straits Commission, "Marine Resources Committees," accessed March 28, 2016, http://www.nwstraits.org/get-involved/mrcs/.

15. Gulf of Mexico Alliance, "Constitution," August 2012, accessed August 27, 2016, http://www.gulfofmexicoalliance.org/pdfs/Alliance%20Constitution% 20August%202012_final.pdf.

16. Channel Islands National Marine Sanctuary, Sanctuary Advisory Council, "Decision-Making and Operational Protocols" (November, 19, 2005), accessed March 28, 2016, http://channelislands.noaa.gov/sac/pdfs/rev_prot .pdf.

17. Gulf of Maine Council, "Agreement on Conservation of the Marine Environment of the Gulf of Maine between the Governments of the Bordering States and Provinces," accessed August 27, 2016, http://www.gulfofmaine.org/2/ wp-content/uploads/2014/09/GOMC-Agreement-1989.pdf.

18. "Co-Trustees Agreement for Cooperative Management," accessed August 27, 2016, http://floridakeys.noaa.gov/mgmtplans/man_cotrust.pdf.

19. U.S. Department of Commerce, National Oceanic and Atmospheric Administration, "National Marine Sanctuary Program, Sanctuary Advisory Council Implementation Handbook" (May 2003), accessed March 28, 2016, http:// sanctuaries.noaa.gov/library/national/sachandbook_new.pdf.

Chapter 8

1. Unless otherwise indicated, this quotation and all subsequent quotations in the chapter are taken from telephone interviews conducted with the named respondent by the authors or their research assistants, January 2009 to December 2010.

2. Katrina Smith Korfmacher, "Invisible Successes, Visible Failures: Paradoxes of Ecosystem Management in the Albemarle–Pamlico Estuarine Study," *Coastal Management* 26 (1998): 191–212.

3. Laura Bowie, "10 Years of Building Partnerships for a Healthier Gulf," *Gulf of Mexico Alliance Newsletter* (June 10, 2014), accessed March 10, 2016, http:// www.gulfofmexicoalliance.org/2014/06/10-years-of-building-partnerships -for-a-healthier-gulf.

4. San Juan Initiative, "Protecting Our Place for Nature and People" (December 2008), 5, accessed March 10, 2016, http://sanjuanco.com/cdp/docs/CAO/ SJI_Final_Report.pdf.

5. Governor Jeb Bush, "Letter to Governor Haley Barbour" (April 26, 2004), personal copy.

6. Tortugas 2000 Working Group, "Meeting Minutes" (May 1999), personal copy. See also Joanne M. Delaney, "Community Capacity Building in the Designation of the Tortugas Ecological Reserve," *Gulf and Caribbean Research* 14 (2003): 163–69; Benjamin Cowie-Haskell and Joanne M. Delaney, "Integrating Science into the Design of the Tortugas Ecological Reserve," *Marine Technology Society Journal* 37 (2003): 68–79.

Chapter 9

1. See citations in chapter 1, note 2.
2. Roger Fisher, William Ury, and Bruce Patton, *Getting to YES: Negotiating Agreement without Giving In*, 2nd ed. (New York: Penguin Books, 1991); Lawrence Susskind, Sarah McKearnan, and Jennifer Thomas-Larmer, *The Consensus Building Handbook: A Comprehensive Guide to Reaching Agreement* (Thousand Oaks, CA: Sage Publications, 1999.)
3. Morgan Gopnik, *From the Forest to the Sea: Public Land Management and Marine Spatial Planning* (New York: Routledge, 2014).
4. USDA-Forest Service, "Sierra Nevada Forest Plan Implementation," accessed March 30, 2016, http://www.fs.usda.gov/detail/r5/landmanagement/planning/?cid=stelprdb5349922; USDA-Forest Service, "Northwest Forest Plan," accessed March 30, 2016, http://www.fs.usda.gov/detail/r6/landman agement/planning/?cid=fsbdev2_026990.
5. Unless otherwise indicated, this quotation and all subsequent quotations in the chapter are taken from telephone interviews conducted with the named respondent by the authors or their research assistants, January 2009 to December 2010.
6. Steven L. Yaffee, "Collaborative Strategies for Managing Animal Migrations: Insights from the History of Ecosystem-Based Management," *Environmental Law* 41 (2011): 655–79.
7. Testimony of Dante Fascell before the U.S. House Committee on Merchant Marine and Fisheries, May 10, 1990, reprinted in Hearing on HR 3719, To Establish the Florida Keys National Marine Sanctuary, Serial No. 101-94 (Washington: Government Printing Office, 1990), p. 6.
8. David Olinger, "Preserving the Keys: A Sanctuary within the Sea," *St. Petersburg Times*, January 29, 1997.
9. Quoted in William Booth, "'Zoning' the Sea: New Plan for Florida Keys Arouses Storm," *The Washington Post*, October 17, 1993, accessed August 24, 2016, www.washingtonpost.com/archive/politics/1993/10/17/zoning-the -sea-new-plan-for-florida-keys-arouses-storm/ee55f0a0-ad00-413d-842d -ccb33f6befb1.
10. Yaffee, "Collaborative Strategies for Managing Animal Migrations."
11. See, e.g., Dale Goble, Michael J. Scott, and Frank W. Davis, eds., *The Endangered Species Act at Thirty: Renewing the Conservation Commitment* (Washington, DC: Island Press, 2006); C. M. Weible, "Caught in a Maelstrom: Implementing California Marine Protected Areas," *Coastal Management* 36 (2008): 350–73; Steven L. Yaffee, *Prohibitive Policy: Implementing the Endangered Species Act* (Cambridge, MA: MIT Press, 1982).
12. Our prescription here is similar to Kai Lee's compass and gyroscope analogy. See Kai N. Lee, *Compass and Gyroscope: Integrating Science and Politics for the Environment* (Washington, DC: Island Press, 1993).

Julia M. Wondolleck is Associate Professor of Natural Resources at the University of Michigan. She is an expert in the theories and application of dispute resolution and collaborative planning processes, and is the author or co-author of three books: *Public Lands Conflict and Resolution: Managing National Forest Disputes* (Plenum, 1988), *Environmental Disputes: Community Involvement in Conflict Resolution* (Island Press, 1990), and *Making Collaboration Work: Lessons from Innovation in Natural Resource Management* (Island Press, 2000). Raised in the San Francisco Bay Area, she spent her youth sailing on the Bay and hiking in the Sierra. As a result, her research interests span both terrestrial and marine realms, most recently examining collaborative science in the NOAA National Estuarine Research Reserve System, contributions of Sanctuary Advisory Councils in the NOAA National Marine Sanctuary Program, and community engagement strategies for the NOAA Marine Protected Areas Center. She has an undergraduate degree in economics and environmental studies from the University of California, Davis, and a Master's and Ph.D. in environmental policy and planning from the Massachusetts Institute of Technology.

Steven L. Yaffee is Professor of Natural Resources and Environmental Policy at the University of Michigan. He has worked for more than forty years on federal endangered species, public lands and ecosystem management policy and is the author or co-author of four books: *Prohibitive Policy: Implementing the Federal Endangered Species Act* (MIT Press, 1982); *The Wisdom of the Spotted Owl: Policy Lessons for a New Century* (Island Press, 1994); *Ecosystem Management in the United States: An Assessment of Current Experience* (Island Press, 1996); and *Making Collaboration Work* (Island Press, 2000). A native of Washington D.C., he spent his youth hearing stories about public policy and politics while experiencing firsthand the loss of native habitat associated with urban sprawl; ultimately, that led to an interest in improving the process of decision making so that more environmentally sound decisions can be made. He has facilitated numerous collaborative processes across North America, and assisted a set of philanthropic foundations with ways to develop evaluation metrics for their conservation programs. He is currently working on a new book detailing the history and lessons of the California Marine Life Protection

Act marine protected areas designation process. Dr. Yaffee received his Ph.D. in environmental policy and planning from the Massachusetts Institute of Technology. His undergraduate and master's degrees are in natural resource management and policy from the University of Michigan. He has been a faculty member at the Kennedy School of Government at Harvard University, and a researcher at the Oak Ridge National Laboratory and the World Wildlife Fund.

Island Press | Board of Directors